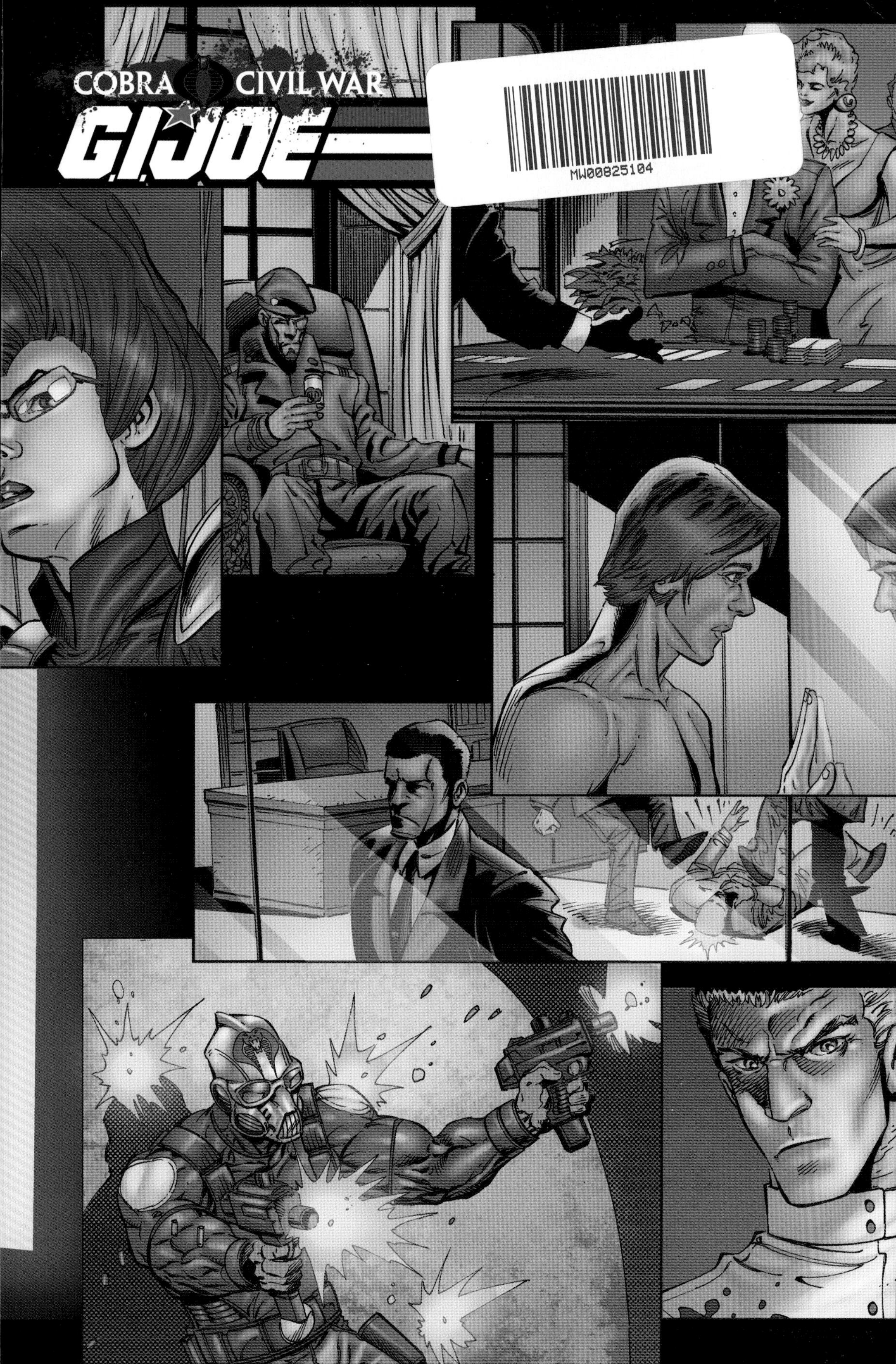
COBRA CIVIL WAR
G.I. JOE

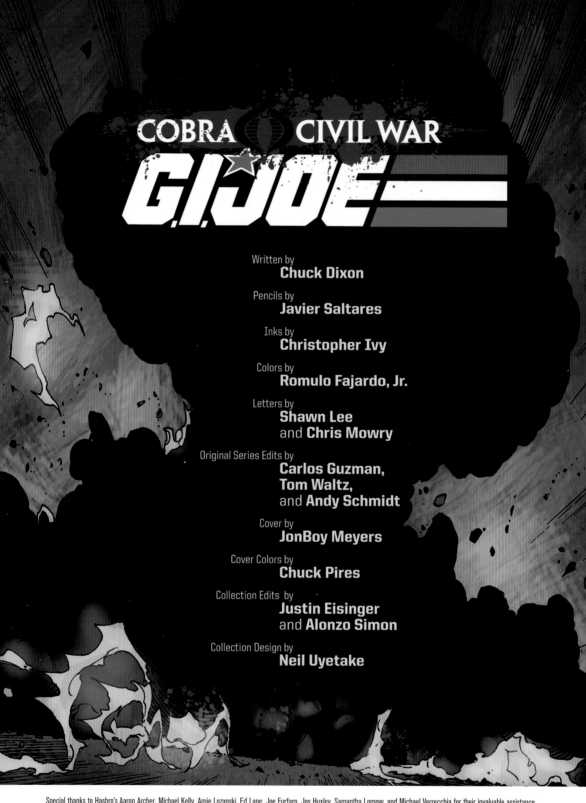

COBRA CIVIL WAR
G.I. JOE

Written by
Chuck Dixon

Pencils by
Javier Saltares

Inks by
Christopher Ivy

Colors by
Romulo Fajardo, Jr.

Letters by
Shawn Lee
and **Chris Mowry**

Original Series Edits by
Carlos Guzman,
Tom Waltz,
and **Andy Schmidt**

Cover by
JonBoy Meyers

Cover Colors by
Chuck Pires

Collection Edits by
Justin Eisinger
and **Alonzo Simon**

Collection Design by
Neil Uyetake

Special thanks to Hasbro's Aaron Archer, Michael Kelly, Amie Lozanski, Ed Lane, Joe Furfaro, Jos Huxley, Samantha Lomow, and Michael Verrecchia for their invaluable assistance.

ISBN: 978-1-61377-023-8

14 13 12 11   1 2 3 4

Ted Adams, CEO & Publisher
Greg Goldstein, Chief Operating Officer
Robbie Robbins, EVP/Sr. Graphic Artist
Chris Ryall, Chief Creative Officer/Editor-in-Chief
Matthew Ruzicka, CPA, Chief Financial Officer
Alan Payne, VP of Sales

Become our fan on Facebook **facebook.com/idwpublishing**
Follow us on Twitter **@idwpublishing**
Check us out on YouTube **youtube.com/idwpublishing**
www.IDWPUBLISHING.com

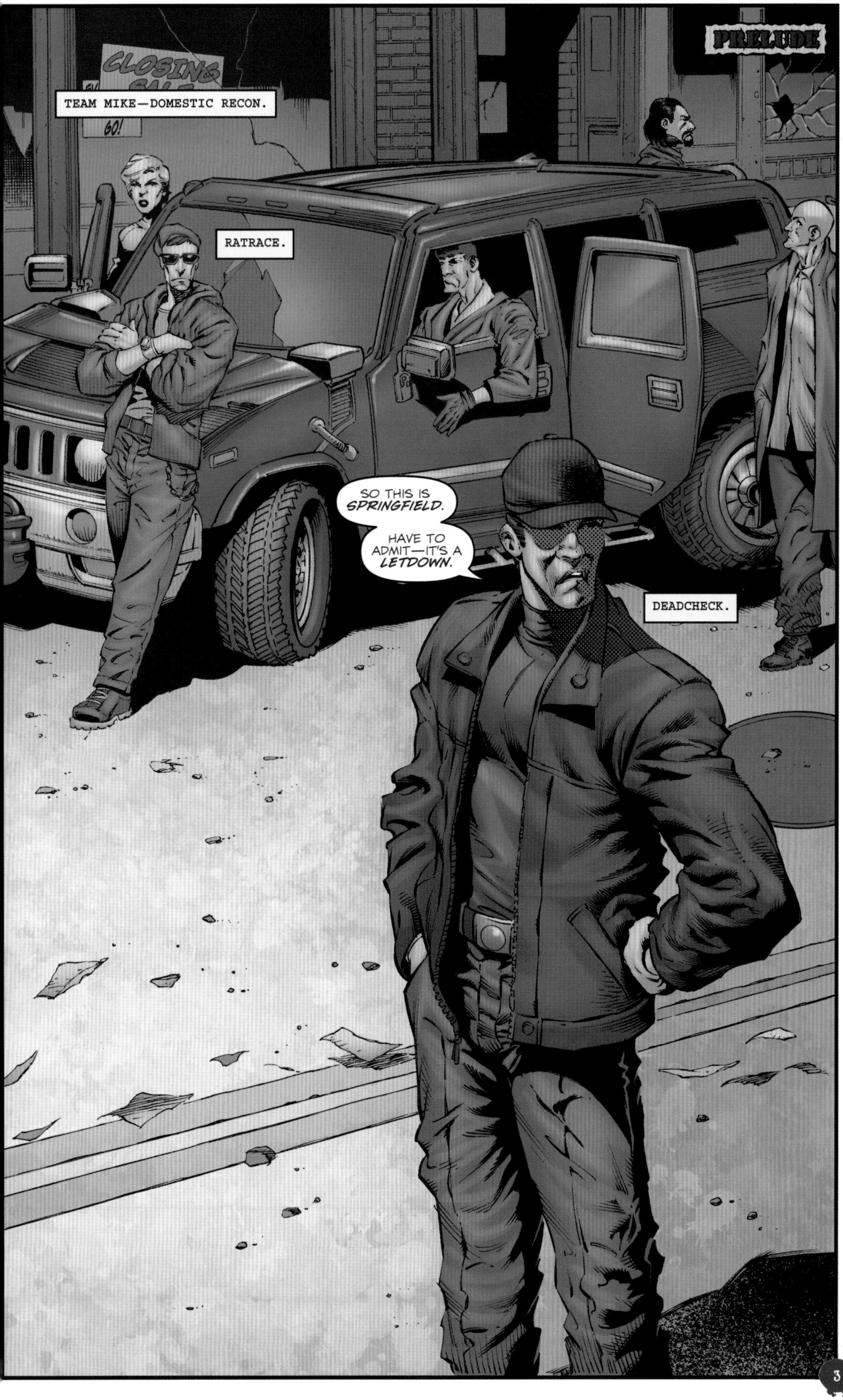
PRELUDE
CLOSING SALE
GO!
TEAM MIKE—DOMESTIC RECON.
RATRACE.
SO THIS IS SPRINGFIELD.
HAVE TO ADMIT—IT'S A LETDOWN.
DEADCHECK.

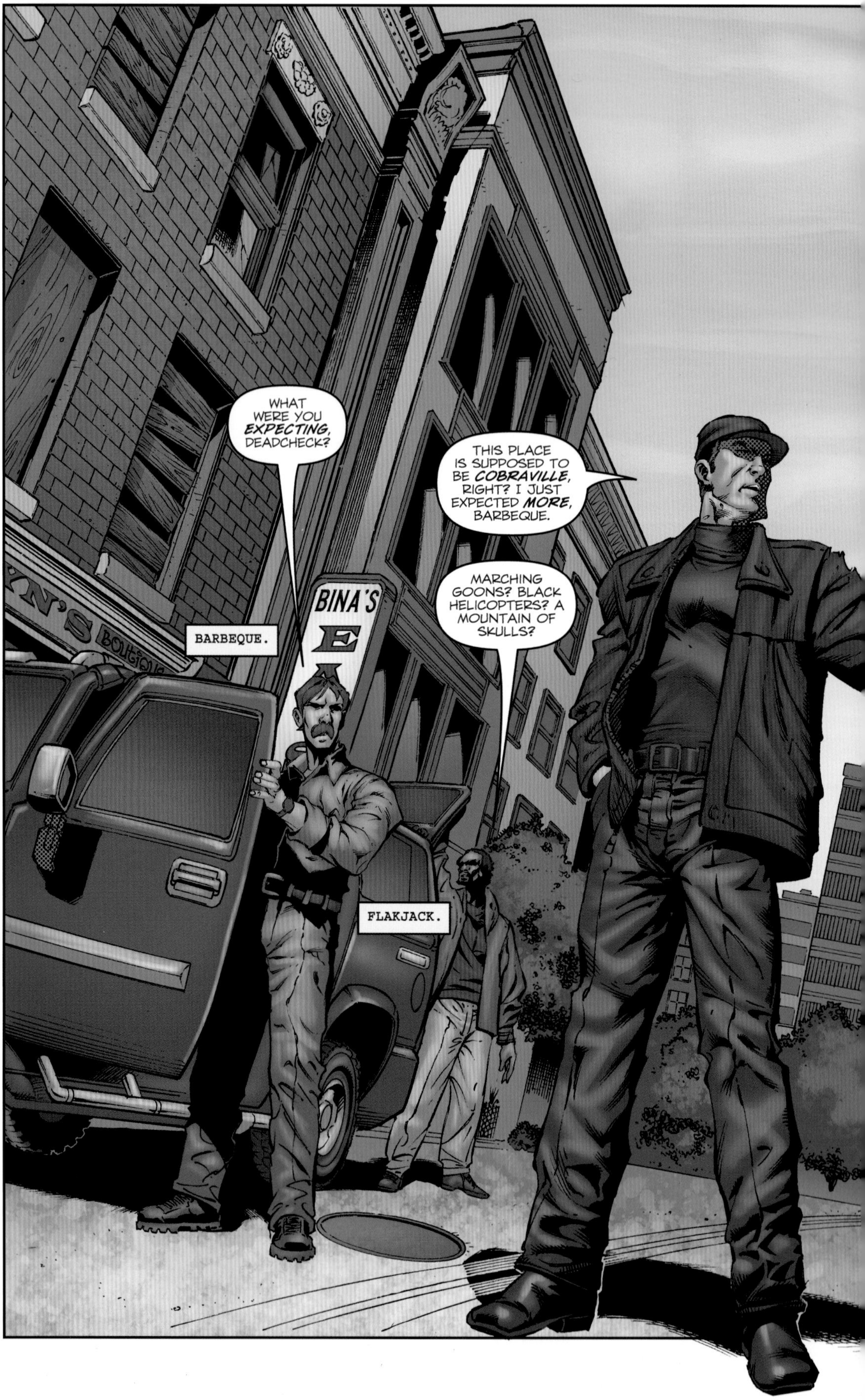
BARBEQUE.
WHAT WERE YOU EXPECTING, DEADCHECK?
THIS PLACE IS SUPPOSED TO BE COBRAVILLE, RIGHT? I JUST EXPECTED MORE, BARBEQUE.
MARCHING GOONS? BLACK HELICOPTERS? A MOUNTAIN OF SKULLS?
FLAKJACK.
BINA'S
BOUTIQUE

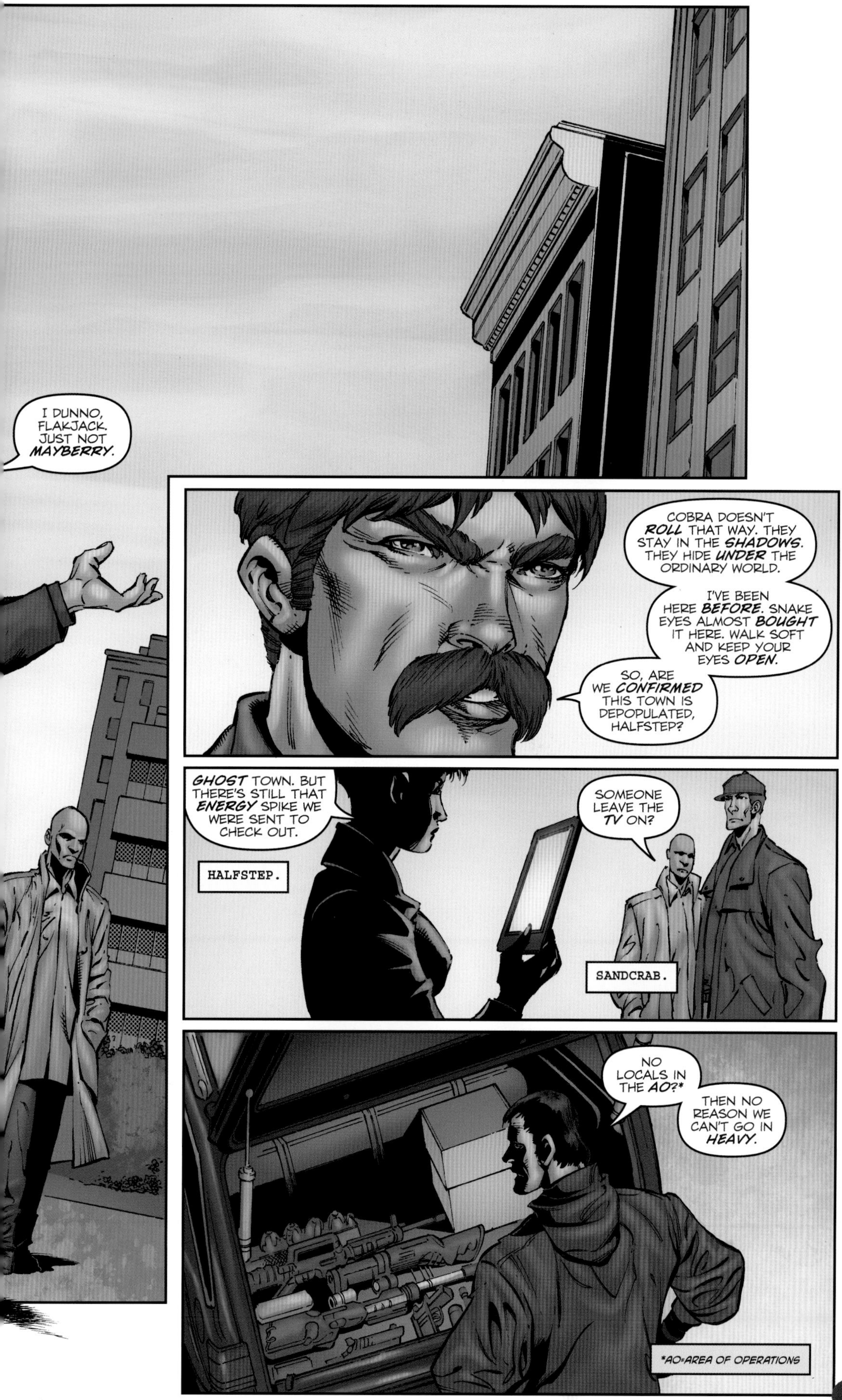
I DUNNO, FLAKJACK. JUST NOT MAYBERRY.
COBRA DOESN'T ROLL THAT WAY. THEY STAY IN THE SHADOWS. THEY HIDE UNDER THE ORDINARY WORLD.
I'VE BEEN HERE BEFORE. SNAKE EYES ALMOST BOUGHT IT HERE. WALK SOFT AND KEEP YOUR EYES OPEN.
SO, ARE WE CONFIRMED THIS TOWN IS DEPOPULATED, HALFSTEP?
GHOST TOWN. BUT THERE'S STILL THAT ENERGY SPIKE WE WERE SENT TO CHECK OUT.
HALFSTEP.
SOMEONE LEAVE THE TV ON?
SANDCRAB.
NO LOCALS IN THE AO?*
THEN NO REASON WE CAN'T GO IN HEAVY.
*AO=AREA OF OPERATIONS

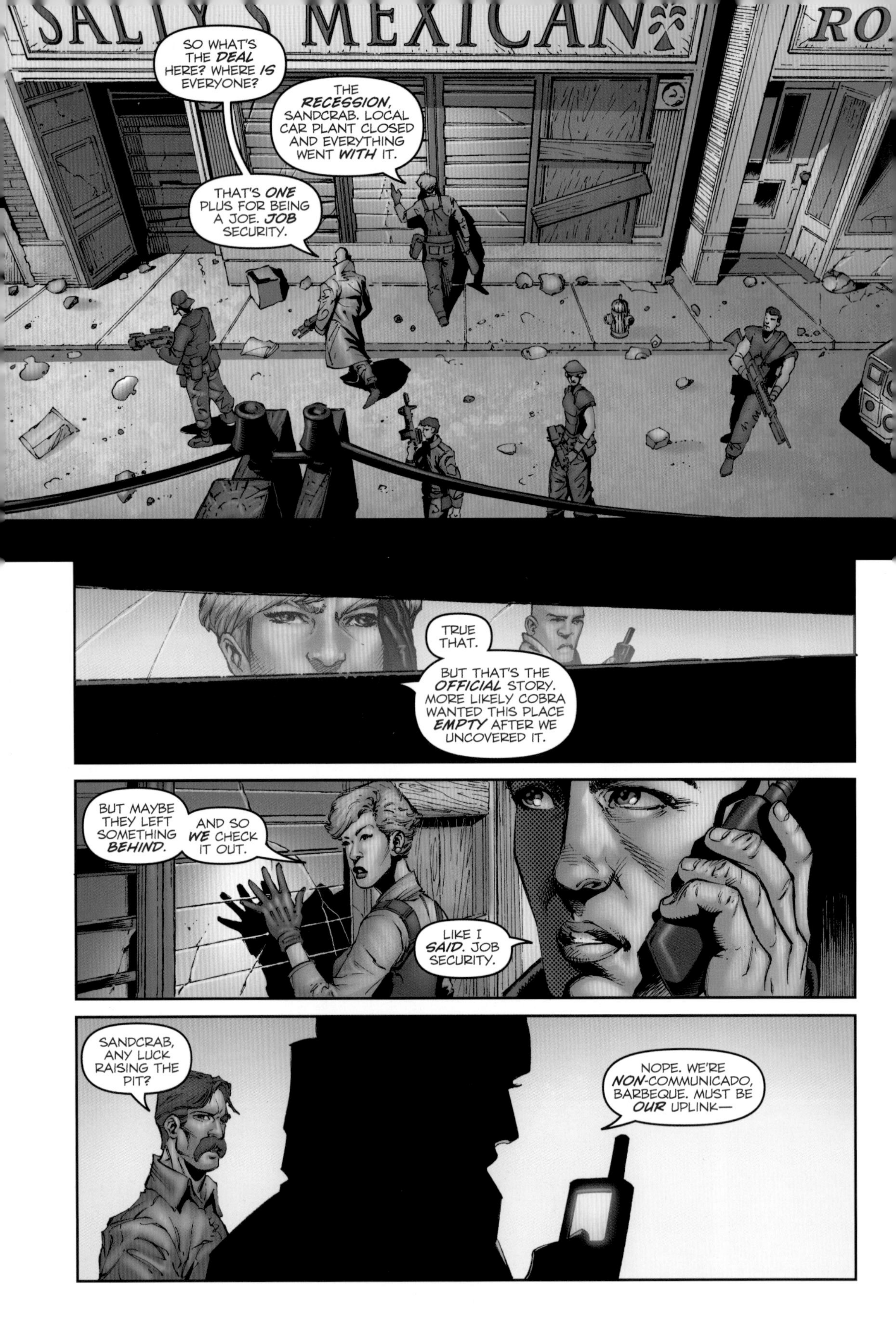
SALLY'S MEXICAN
RO
SO WHAT'S THE DEAL HERE? WHERE IS EVERYONE?
THE RECESSION, SANDCRAB. LOCAL CAR PLANT CLOSED AND EVERYTHING WENT WITH IT.
THAT'S ONE PLUS FOR BEING A JOE. JOB SECURITY.
TRUE THAT.
BUT THAT'S THE OFFICIAL STORY. MORE LIKELY COBRA WANTED THIS PLACE EMPTY AFTER WE UNCOVERED IT.
BUT MAYBE THEY LEFT SOMETHING BEHIND.
AND SO WE CHECK IT OUT.
LIKE I SAID. JOB SECURITY.
SANDCRAB, ANY LUCK RAISING THE PIT?
NOPE. WE'RE NON-COMMUNICADO, BARBEQUE. MUST BE OUR UPLINK—

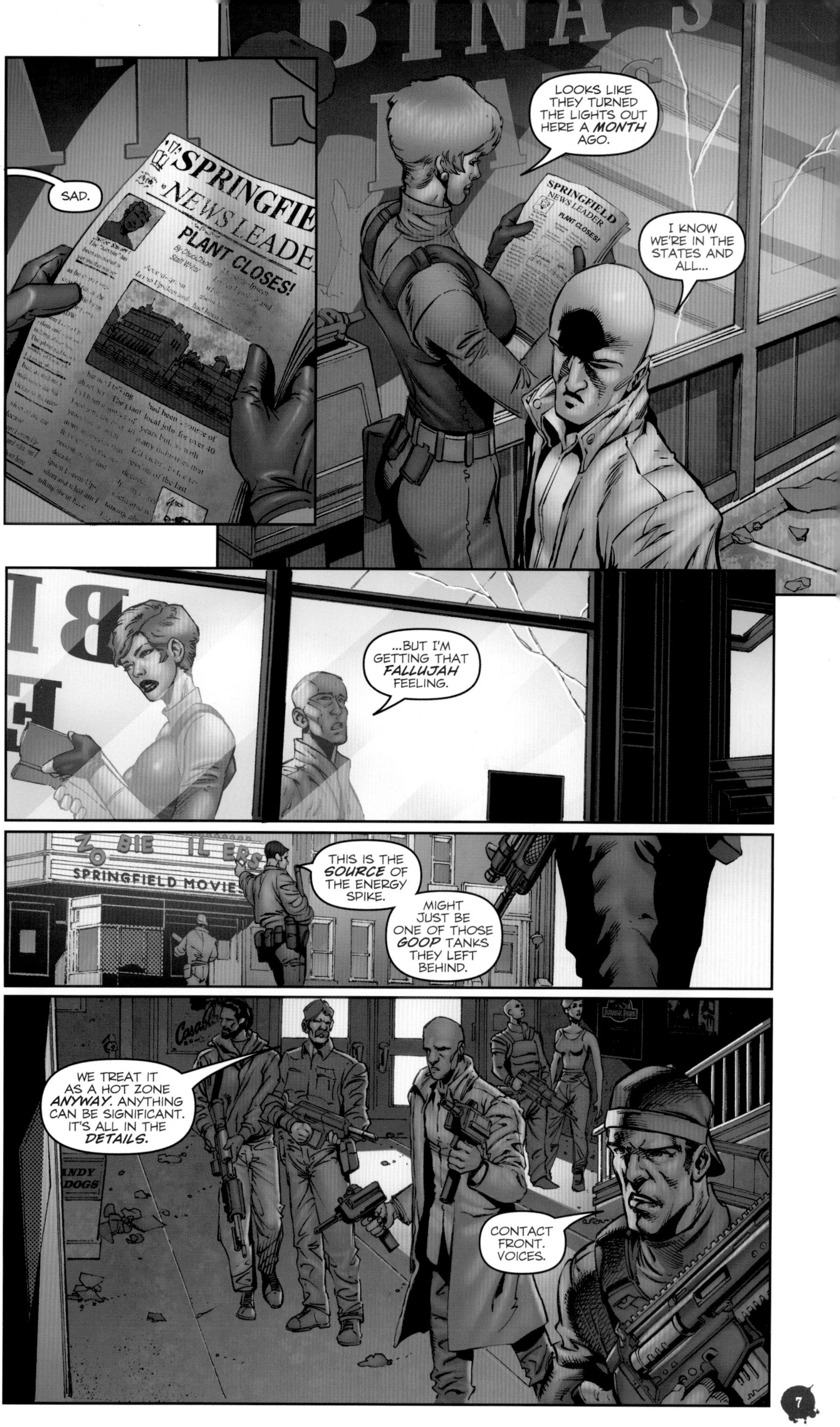
SPRINGFIELD NEWS LEADER
PLANT CLOSES!
SAD.
LOOKS LIKE THEY TURNED THE LIGHTS OUT HERE A *MONTH* AGO.
I KNOW WE'RE IN THE STATES AND ALL...
...BUT I'M GETTING THAT *FALLUJAH* FEELING.
SPRINGFIELD MOVIES
THIS IS THE *SOURCE* OF THE ENERGY SPIKE.
MIGHT JUST BE ONE OF THOSE *GOOP* TANKS THEY LEFT BEHIND.
WE TREAT IT AS A HOT ZONE *ANYWAY*. ANYTHING CAN BE SIGNIFICANT. IT'S ALL IN THE *DETAILS*.
JURASSIC PARK
CONTACT FRONT. VOICES.

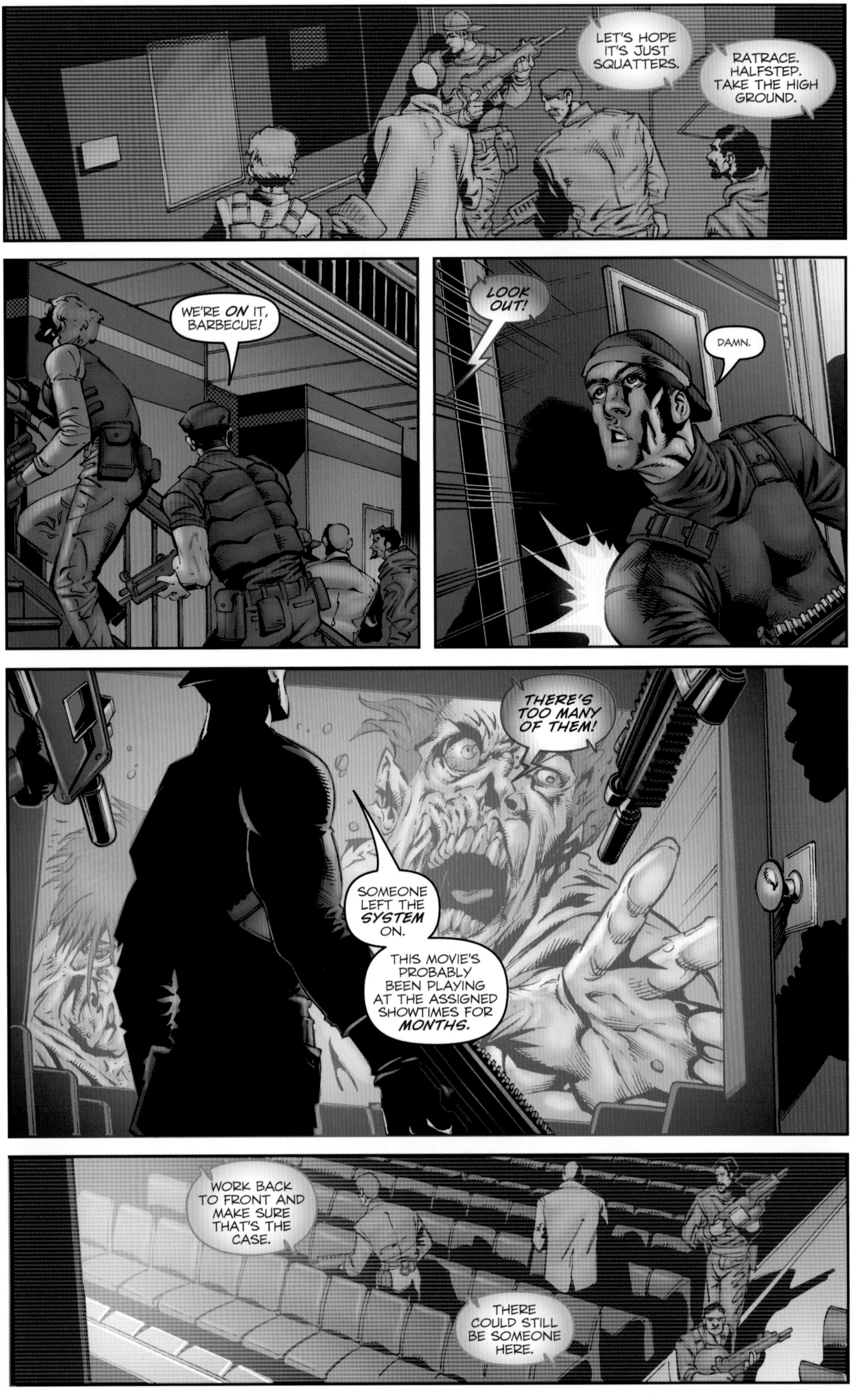
LET'S HOPE IT'S JUST SQUATTERS.
RATRACE. HALFSTEP. TAKE THE HIGH GROUND.
WE'RE ON IT, BARBECUE!
LOOK OUT!
DAMN.
THERE'S TOO MANY OF THEM!
SOMEONE LEFT THE SYSTEM ON.
THIS MOVIE'S PROBABLY BEEN PLAYING AT THE ASSIGNED SHOWTIMES FOR MONTHS.
WORK BACK TO FRONT AND MAKE SURE THAT'S THE CASE.
THERE COULD STILL BE SOMEONE HERE.

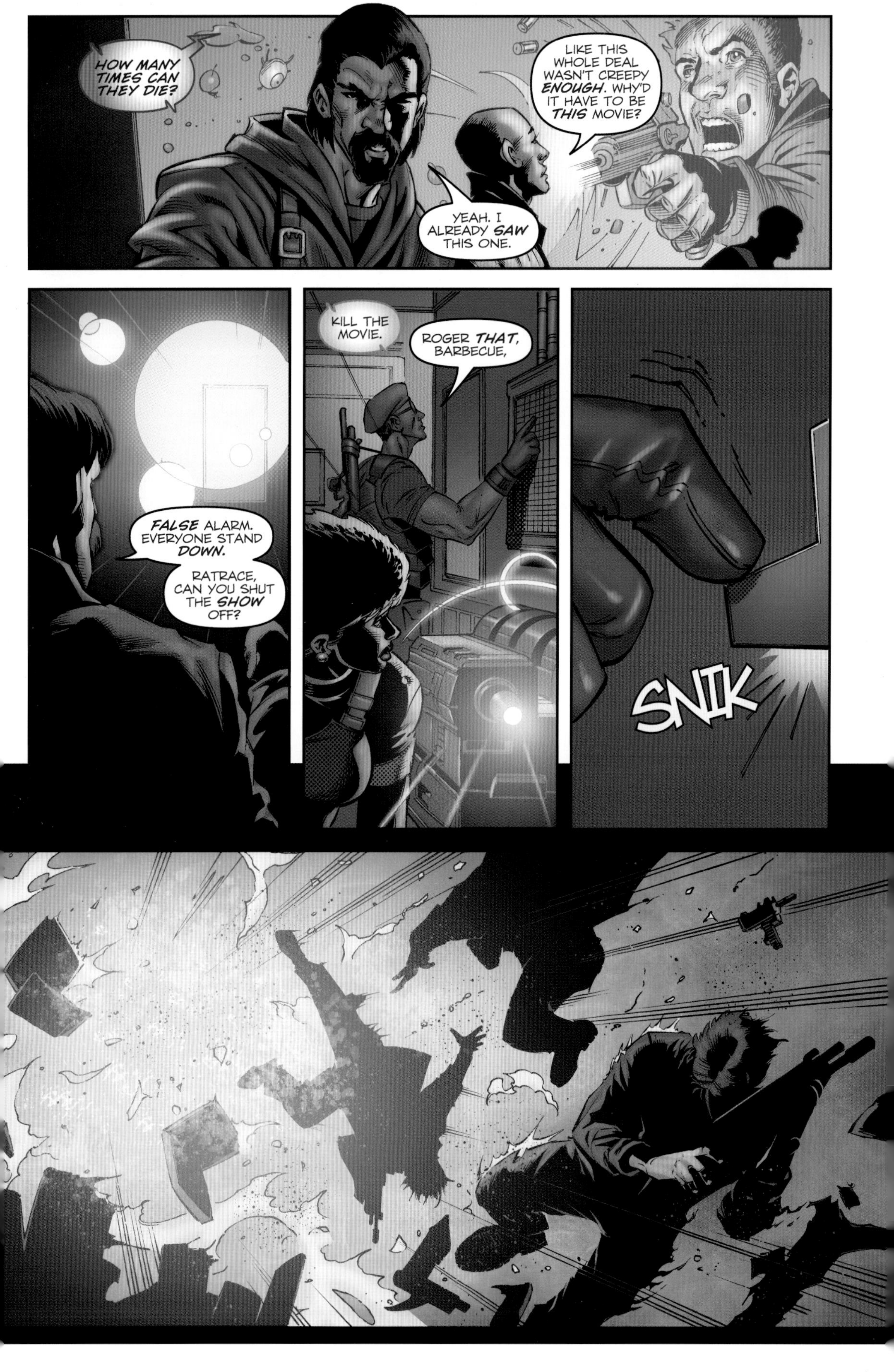
HOW MANY TIMES CAN THEY DIE?
LIKE THIS WHOLE DEAL WASN'T CREEPY ENOUGH. WHY'D IT HAVE TO BE THIS MOVIE?
YEAH. I ALREADY SAW THIS ONE.
FALSE ALARM. EVERYONE STAND DOWN.
RATRACE, CAN YOU SHUT THE SHOW OFF?
KILL THE MOVIE.
ROGER THAT, BARBECUE,
SNIK

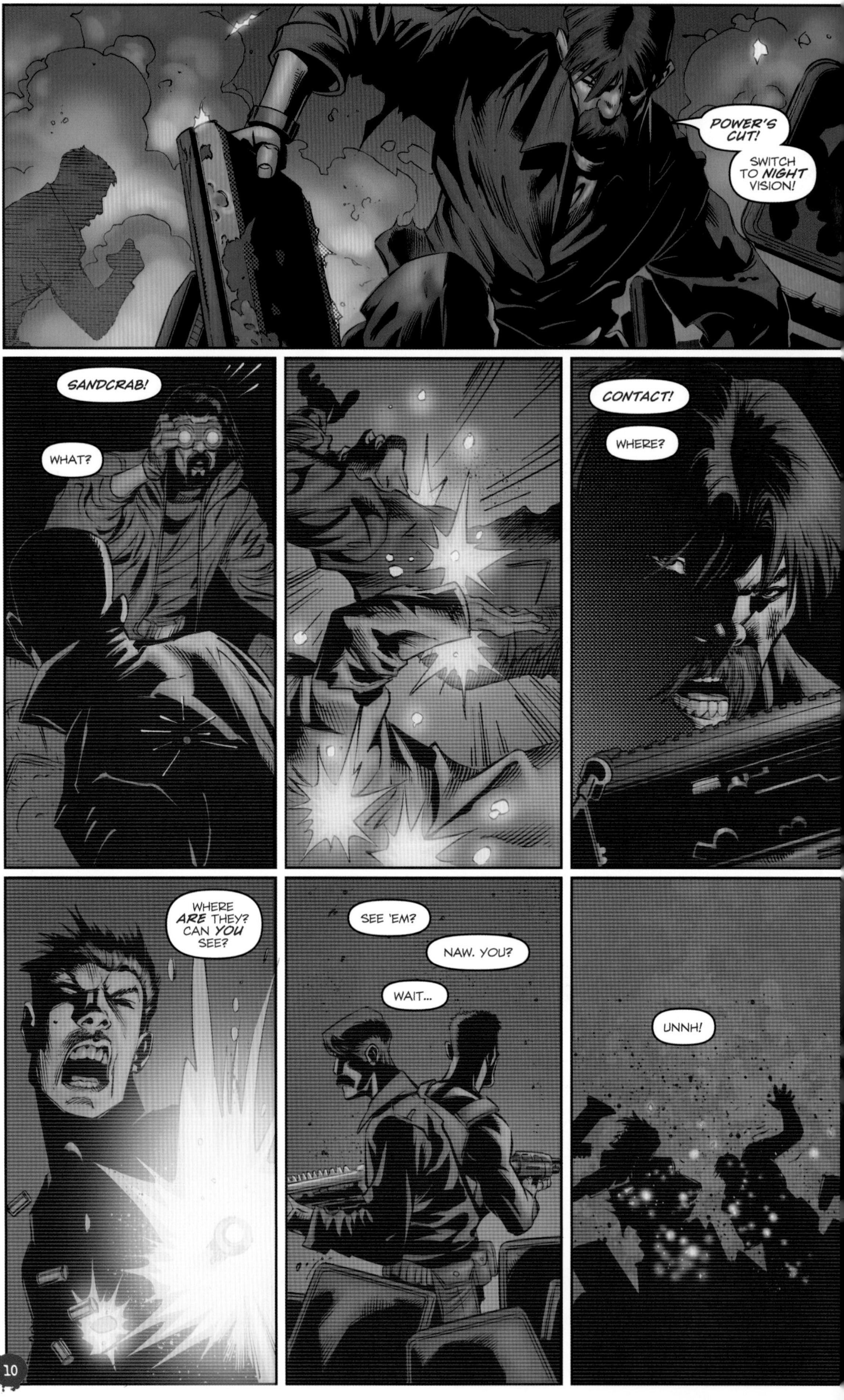
POWER'S CUT!
SWITCH TO NIGHT VISION!
SANDCRAB!
WHAT?
CONTACT!
WHERE?
WHERE ARE THEY? CAN YOU SEE?
SEE 'EM?
NAW. YOU?
WAIT...
UNNH!

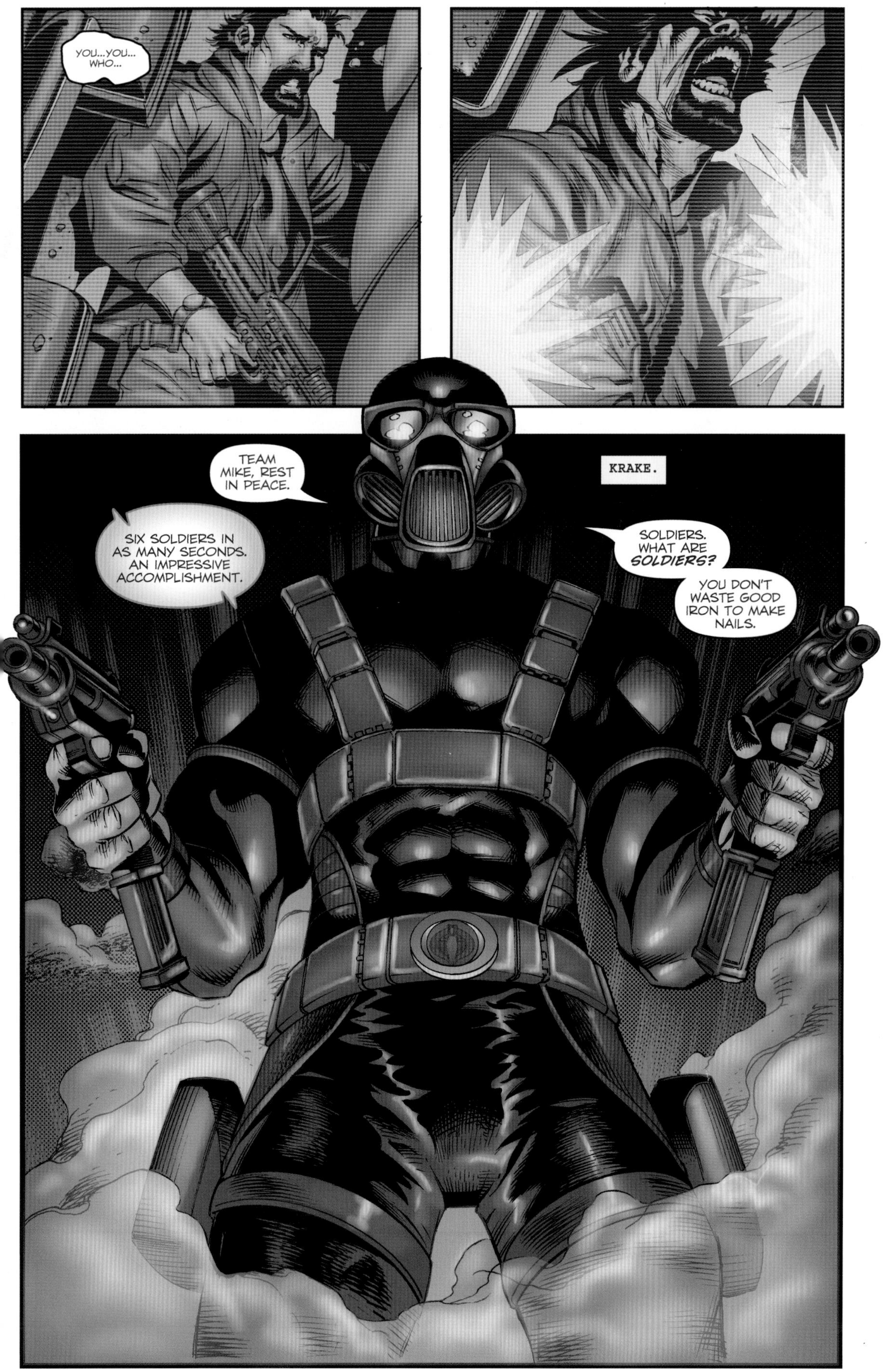
YOU...YOU... WHO...
TEAM MIKE, REST IN PEACE.
SIX SOLDIERS IN AS MANY SECONDS. AN IMPRESSIVE ACCOMPLISHMENT.
KRAKE.
SOLDIERS. WHAT ARE *SOLDIERS?*
YOU DON'T WASTE GOOD IRON TO MAKE NAILS.

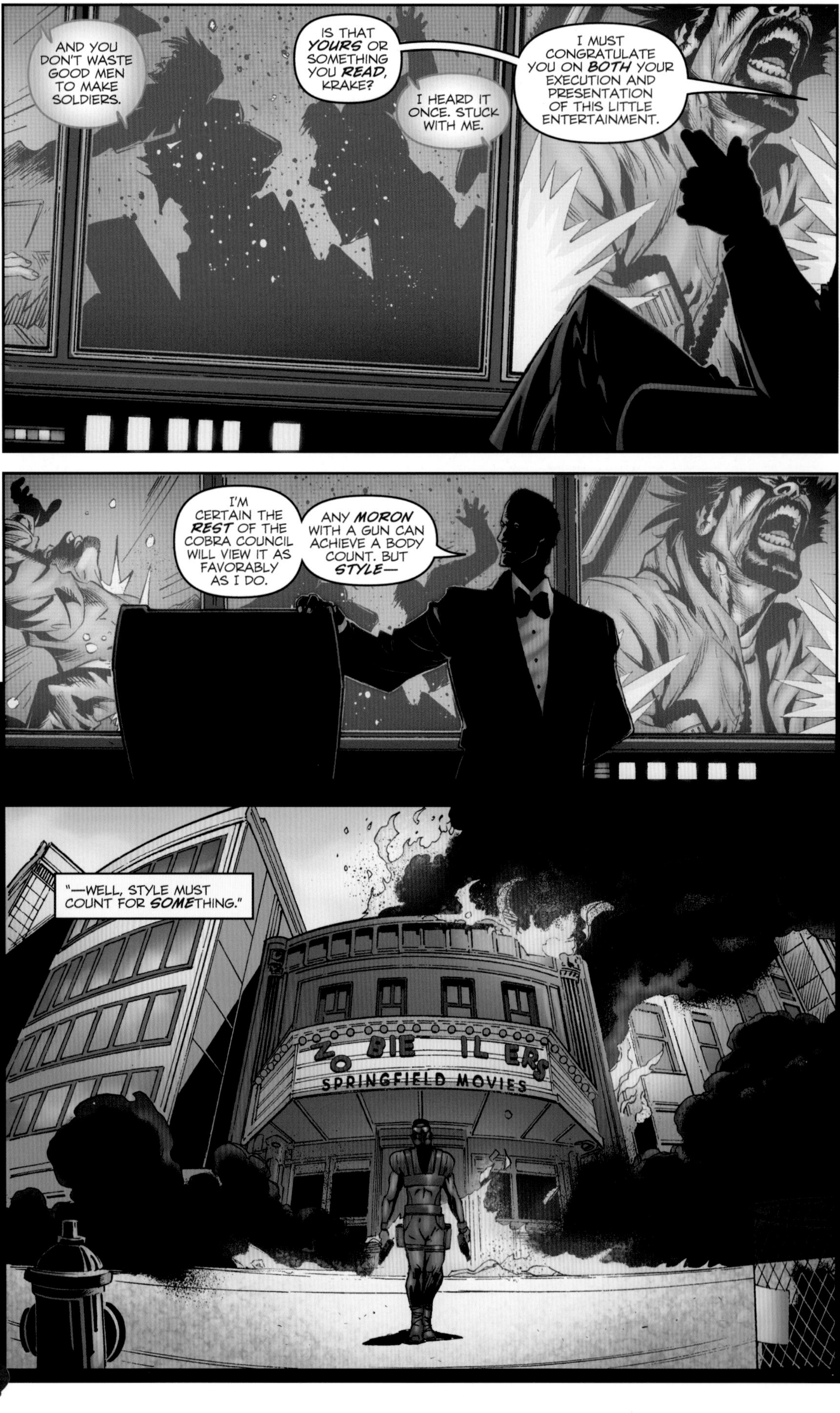
AND YOU DON'T WASTE GOOD MEN TO MAKE SOLDIERS.
IS THAT YOURS OR SOMETHING YOU READ, KRAKE?
I HEARD IT ONCE. STUCK WITH ME.
I MUST CONGRATULATE YOU ON BOTH YOUR EXECUTION AND PRESENTATION OF THIS LITTLE ENTERTAINMENT.
I'M CERTAIN THE REST OF THE COBRA COUNCIL WILL VIEW IT AS FAVORABLY AS I DO.
ANY MORON WITH A GUN CAN ACHIEVE A BODY COUNT. BUT STYLE—
"—WELL, STYLE MUST COUNT FOR SOMETHING."
ZO BIE IL ERS
SPRINGFIELD MOVIES

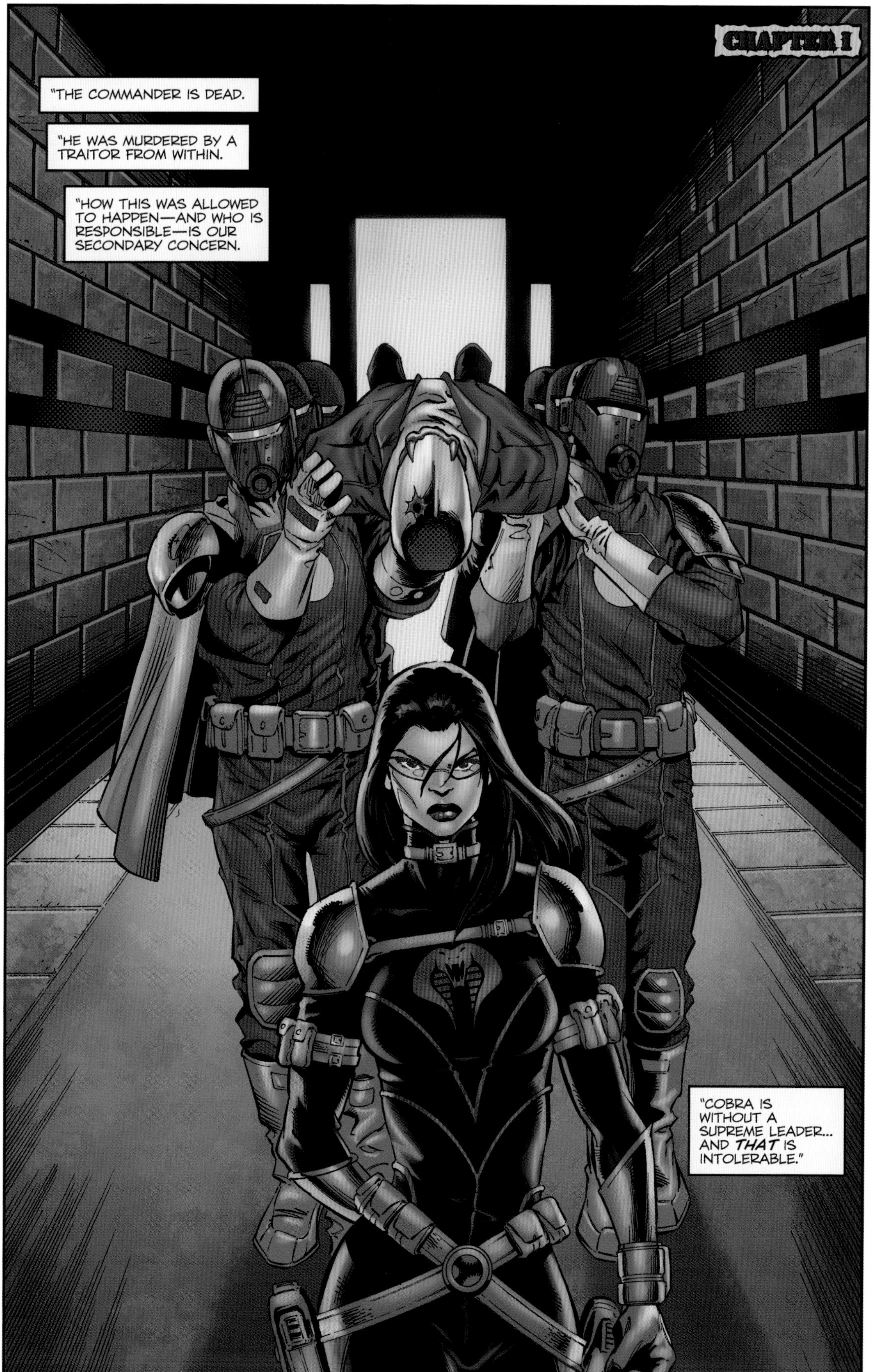
CHAPTER 1
"THE COMMANDER IS DEAD.
"HE WAS MURDERED BY A TRAITOR FROM WITHIN.
"HOW THIS WAS ALLOWED TO HAPPEN—AND WHO IS RESPONSIBLE—IS OUR SECONDARY CONCERN.
"COBRA IS WITHOUT A SUPREME LEADER... AND *THAT* IS INTOLERABLE."

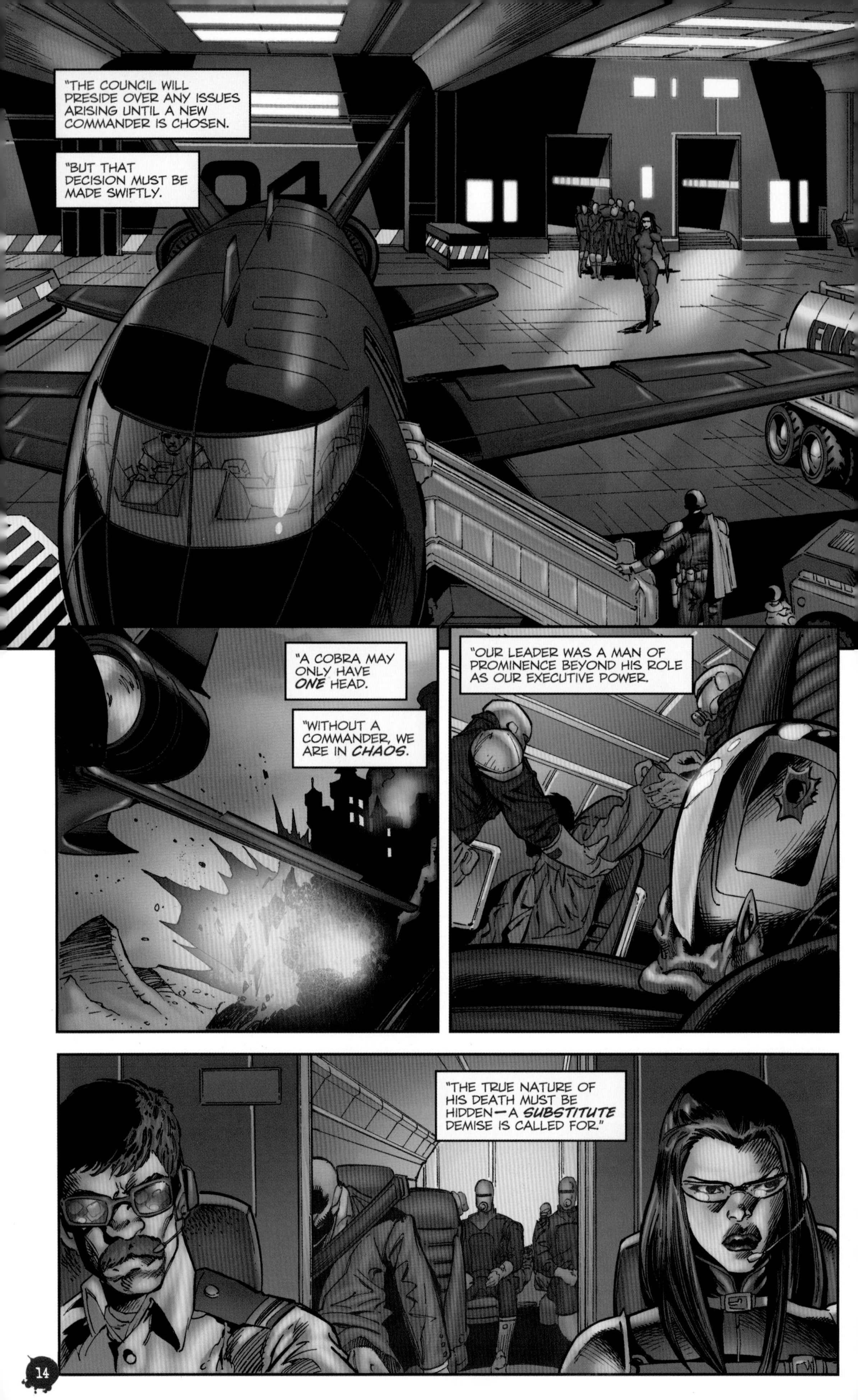
"THE COUNCIL WILL PRESIDE OVER ANY ISSUES ARISING UNTIL A NEW COMMANDER IS CHOSEN.
"BUT THAT DECISION MUST BE MADE SWIFTLY.
"A COBRA MAY ONLY HAVE *ONE* HEAD.
"WITHOUT A COMMANDER, WE ARE IN *CHAOS*.
"OUR LEADER WAS A MAN OF PROMINENCE BEYOND HIS ROLE AS OUR EXECUTIVE POWER.
"THE TRUE NATURE OF HIS DEATH MUST BE HIDDEN—A *SUBSTITUTE* DEMISE IS CALLED FOR."

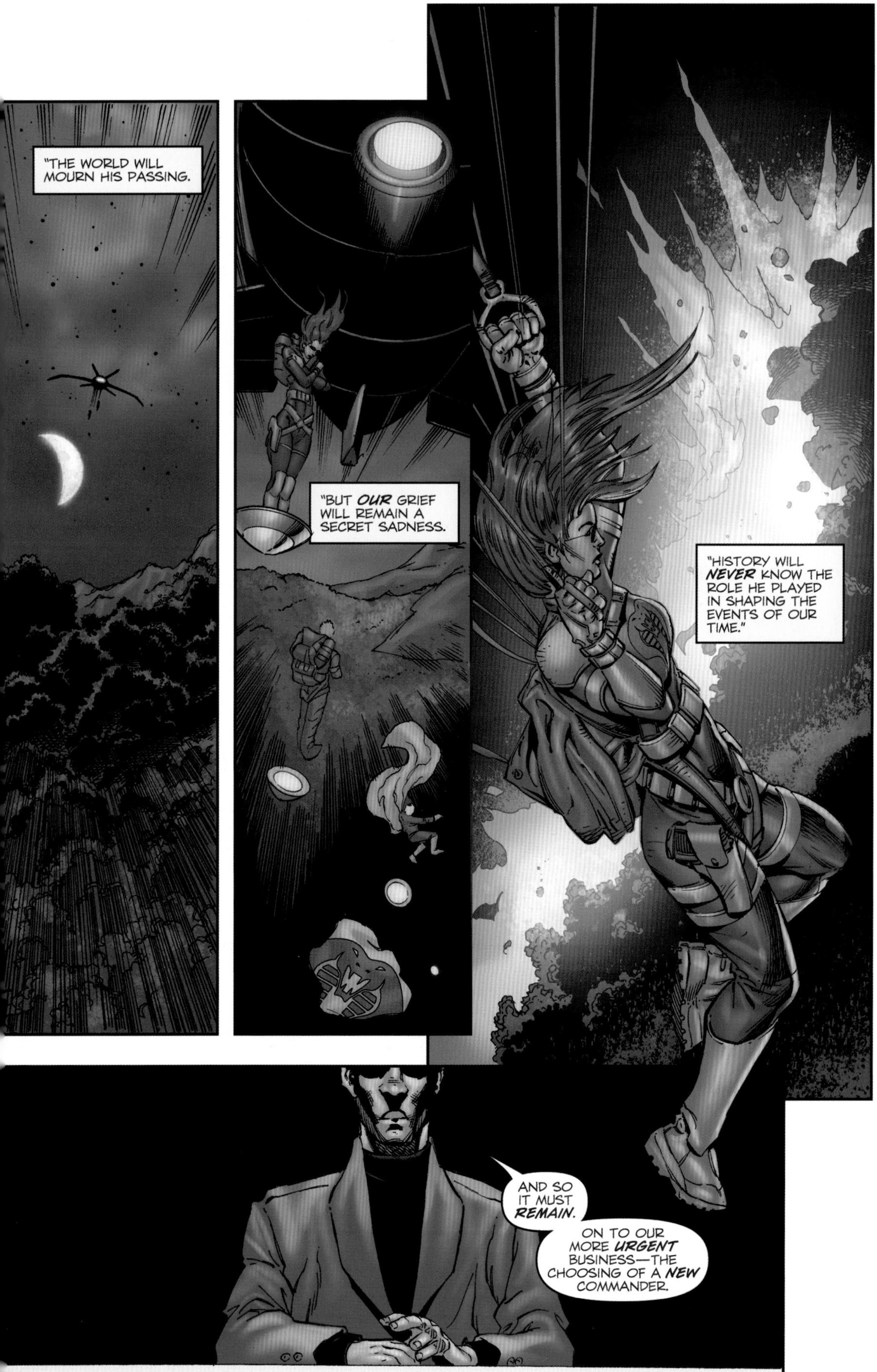
"THE WORLD WILL MOURN HIS PASSING.
"BUT OUR GRIEF WILL REMAIN A SECRET SADNESS.
"HISTORY WILL NEVER KNOW THE ROLE HE PLAYED IN SHAPING THE EVENTS OF OUR TIME."
AND SO IT MUST REMAIN.
ON TO OUR MORE URGENT BUSINESS—THE CHOOSING OF A NEW COMMANDER.

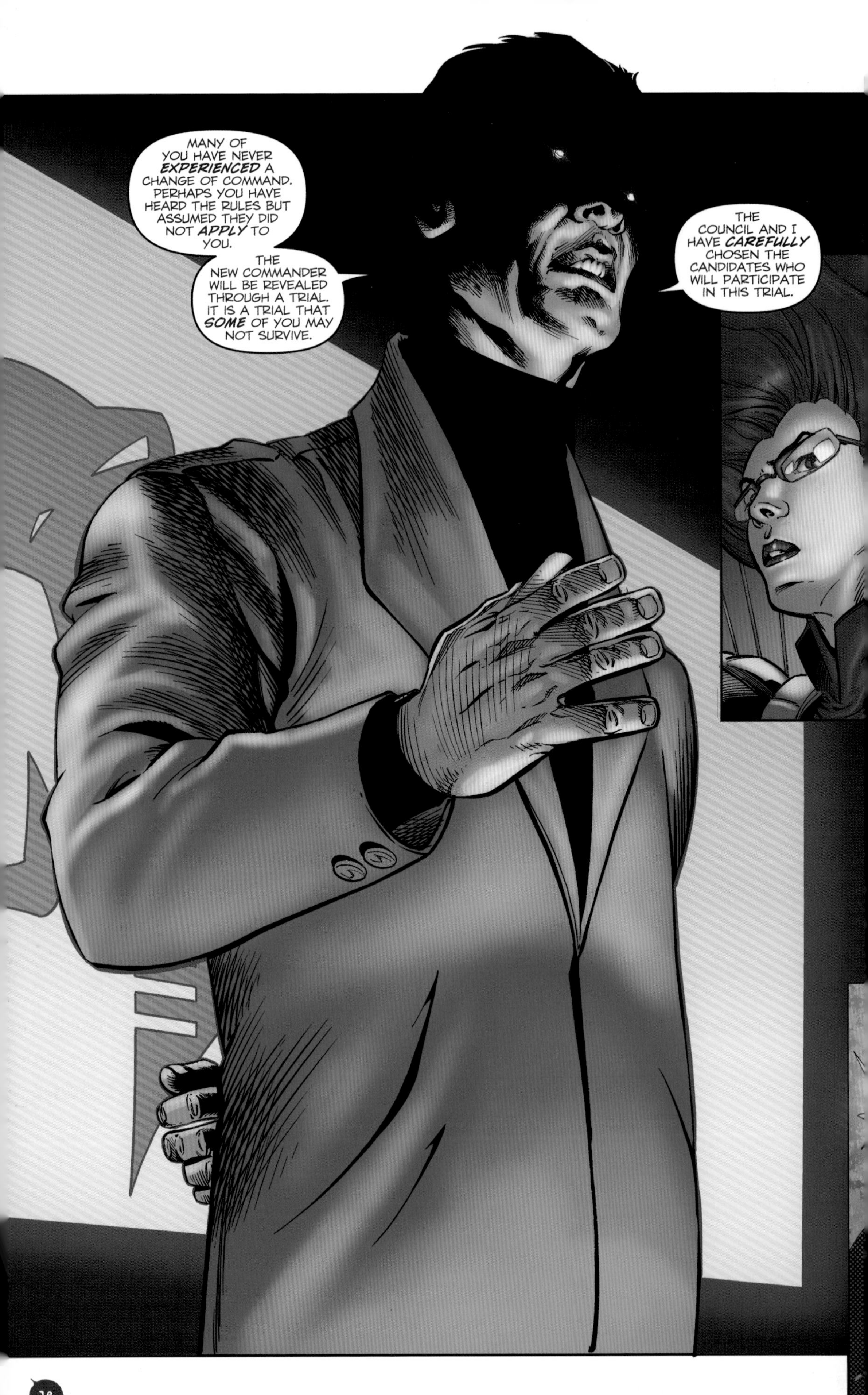
MANY OF YOU HAVE NEVER EXPERIENCED A CHANGE OF COMMAND. PERHAPS YOU HAVE HEARD THE RULES BUT ASSUMED THEY DID NOT APPLY TO YOU.
THE NEW COMMANDER WILL BE REVEALED THROUGH A TRIAL. IT IS A TRIAL THAT SOME OF YOU MAY NOT SURVIVE.
THE COUNCIL AND I HAVE CAREFULLY CHOSEN THE CANDIDATES WHO WILL PARTICIPATE IN THIS TRIAL.

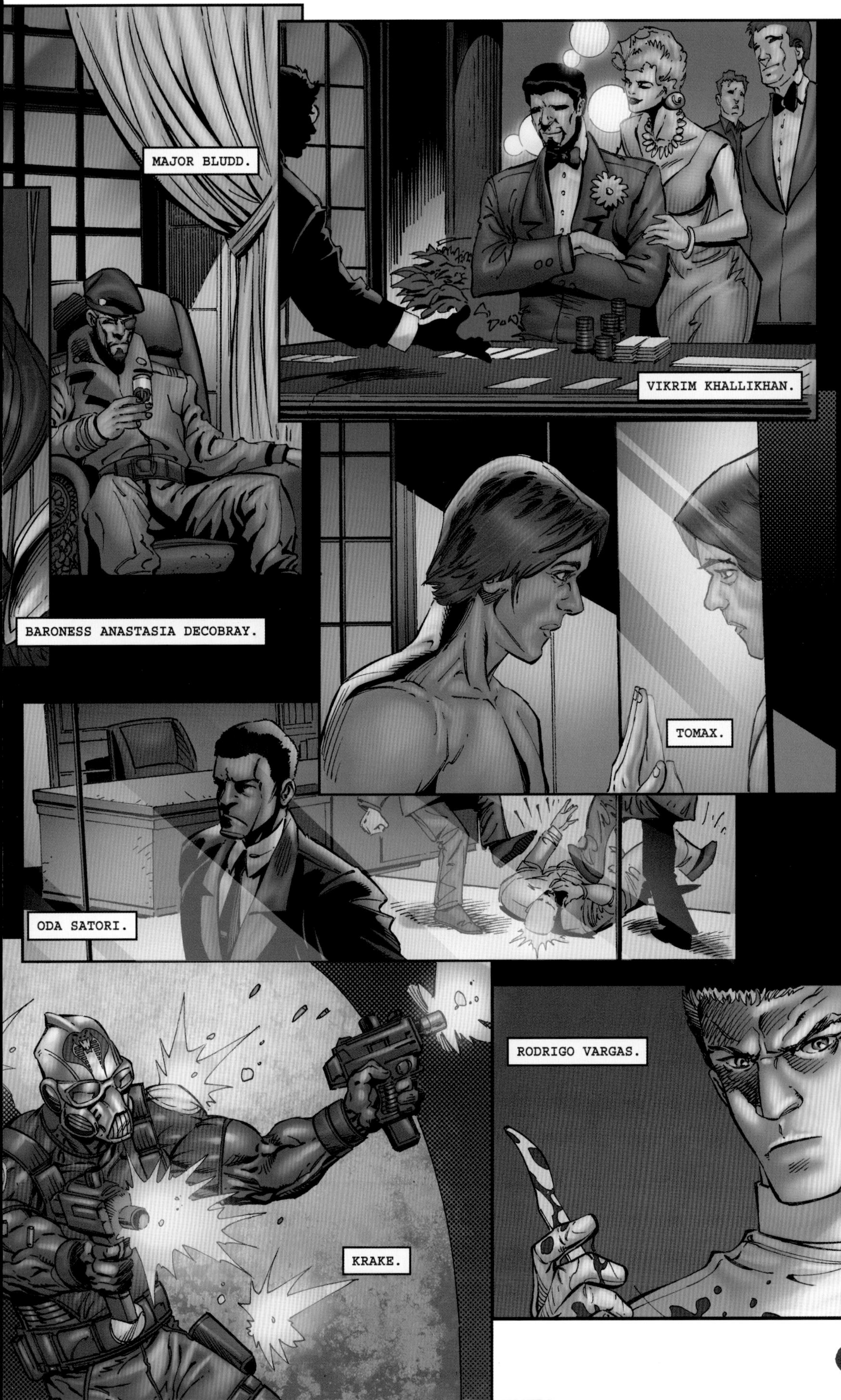

MAJOR BLUDD.
VIKRIM KHALLIKHAN.
BARONESS ANASTASIA DECOBRAY.
TOMAX.
ODA SATORI.
RODRIGO VARGAS.
KRAKE.

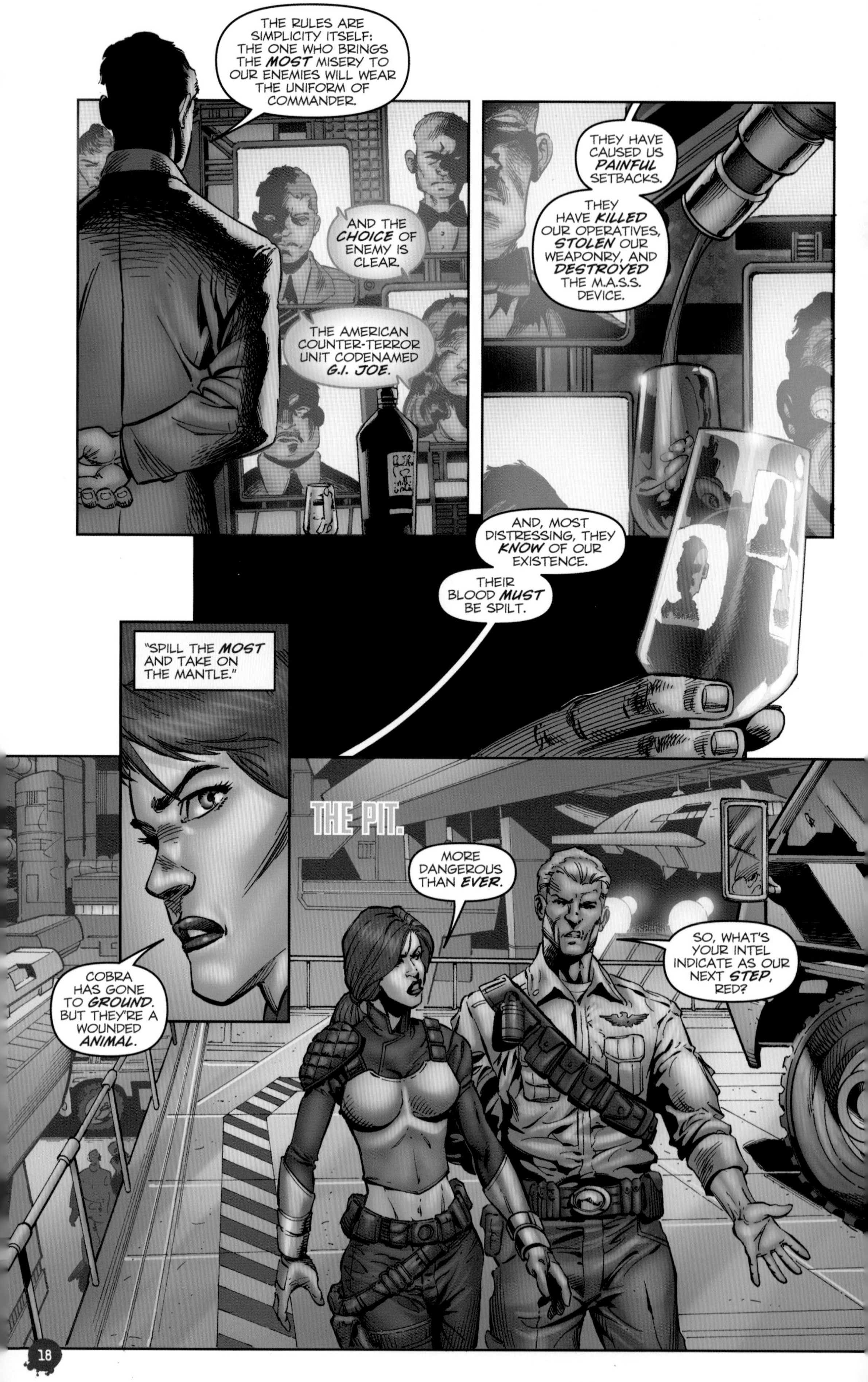
THE RULES ARE SIMPLICITY ITSELF: THE ONE WHO BRINGS THE MOST MISERY TO OUR ENEMIES WILL WEAR THE UNIFORM OF COMMANDER.
AND THE CHOICE OF ENEMY IS CLEAR.
THE AMERICAN COUNTER-TERROR UNIT CODENAMED G.I. JOE.
THEY HAVE CAUSED US PAINFUL SETBACKS.
THEY HAVE KILLED OUR OPERATIVES, STOLEN OUR WEAPONRY, AND DESTROYED THE M.A.S.S. DEVICE.
AND, MOST DISTRESSING, THEY KNOW OF OUR EXISTENCE.
THEIR BLOOD MUST BE SPILT.
"SPILL THE MOST AND TAKE ON THE MANTLE."
THE PIT.
MORE DANGEROUS THAN EVER.
SO, WHAT'S YOUR INTEL INDICATE AS OUR NEXT STEP, RED?
COBRA HAS GONE TO GROUND. BUT THEY'RE A WOUNDED ANIMAL.

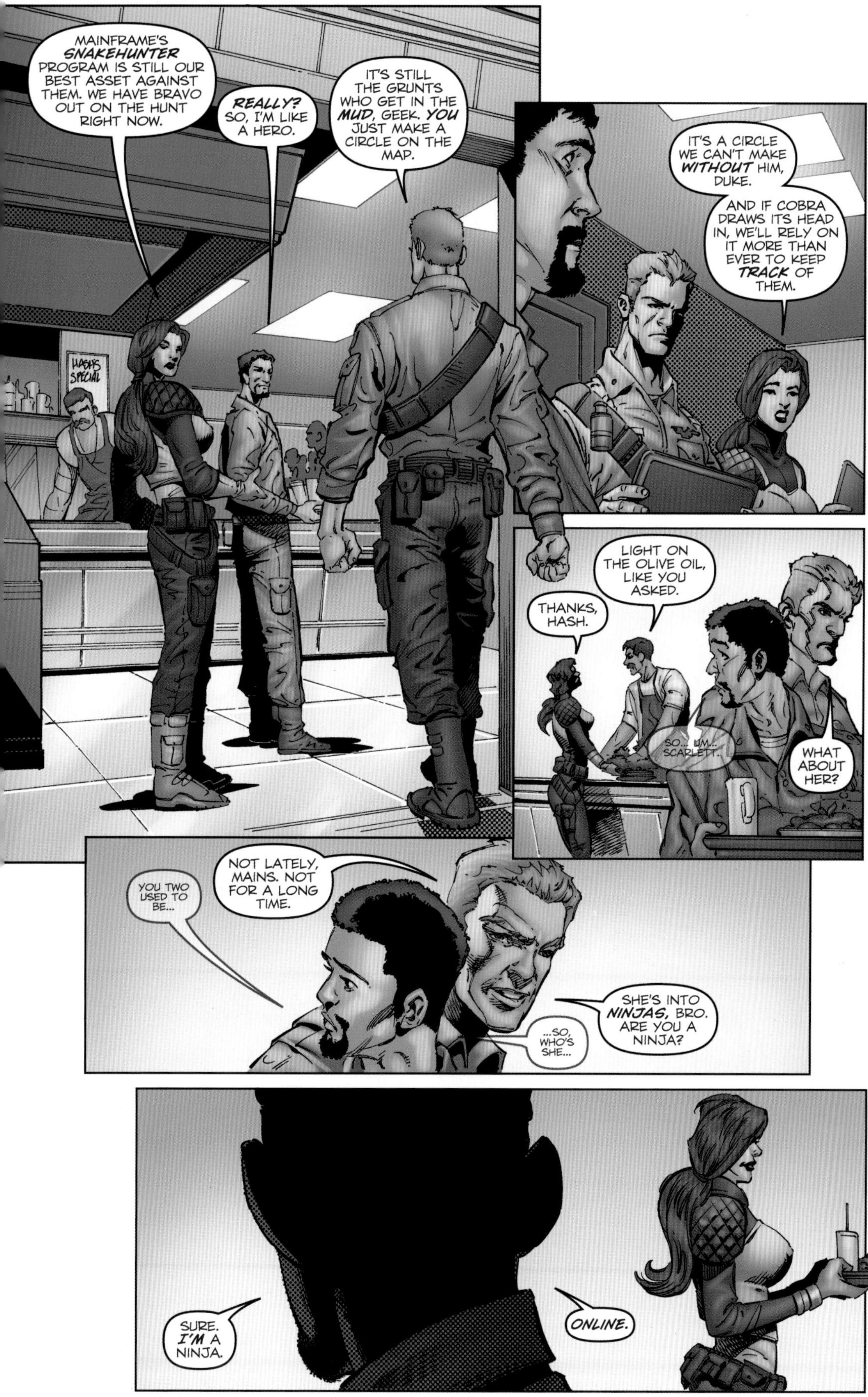

MAINFRAME'S SNAKEHUNTER PROGRAM IS STILL OUR BEST ASSET AGAINST THEM. WE HAVE BRAVO OUT ON THE HUNT RIGHT NOW.
REALLY? SO, I'M LIKE A HERO.
IT'S STILL THE GRUNTS WHO GET IN THE MUD, GEEK. YOU JUST MAKE A CIRCLE ON THE MAP.
HASH'S SPECIAL
IT'S A CIRCLE WE CAN'T MAKE WITHOUT HIM, DUKE.
AND IF COBRA DRAWS ITS HEAD IN, WE'LL RELY ON IT MORE THAN EVER TO KEEP TRACK OF THEM.
LIGHT ON THE OLIVE OIL, LIKE YOU ASKED.
THANKS, HASH.
SO... UM... SCARLETT.
WHAT ABOUT HER?
YOU TWO USED TO BE...
NOT LATELY, MAINS. NOT FOR A LONG TIME.
SHE'S INTO NINJAS, BRO. ARE YOU A NINJA?
...SO, WHO'S SHE...
SURE. I'M A NINJA.
ONLINE.

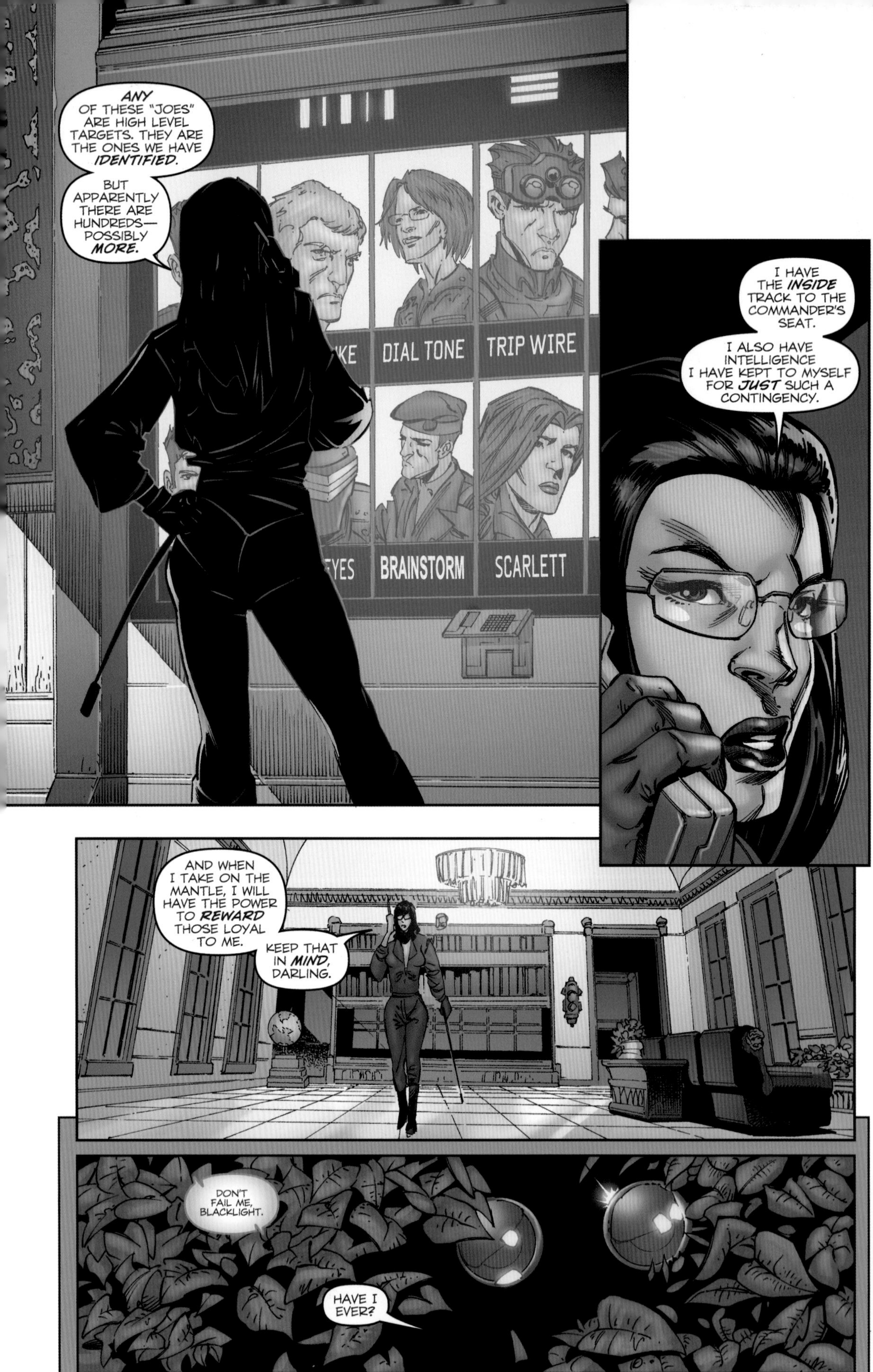
ANY OF THESE "JOES" ARE HIGH LEVEL TARGETS. THEY ARE THE ONES WE HAVE IDENTIFIED.
BUT APPARENTLY THERE ARE HUNDREDS— POSSIBLY MORE.
KE
DIAL TONE
TRIP WIRE
EYES
BRAINSTORM
SCARLETT
I HAVE THE INSIDE TRACK TO THE COMMANDER'S SEAT.
I ALSO HAVE INTELLIGENCE I HAVE KEPT TO MYSELF FOR JUST SUCH A CONTINGENCY.
AND WHEN I TAKE ON THE MANTLE, I WILL HAVE THE POWER TO REWARD THOSE LOYAL TO ME.
KEEP THAT IN MIND, DARLING.
DON'T FAIL ME, BLACKLIGHT.
HAVE I EVER?

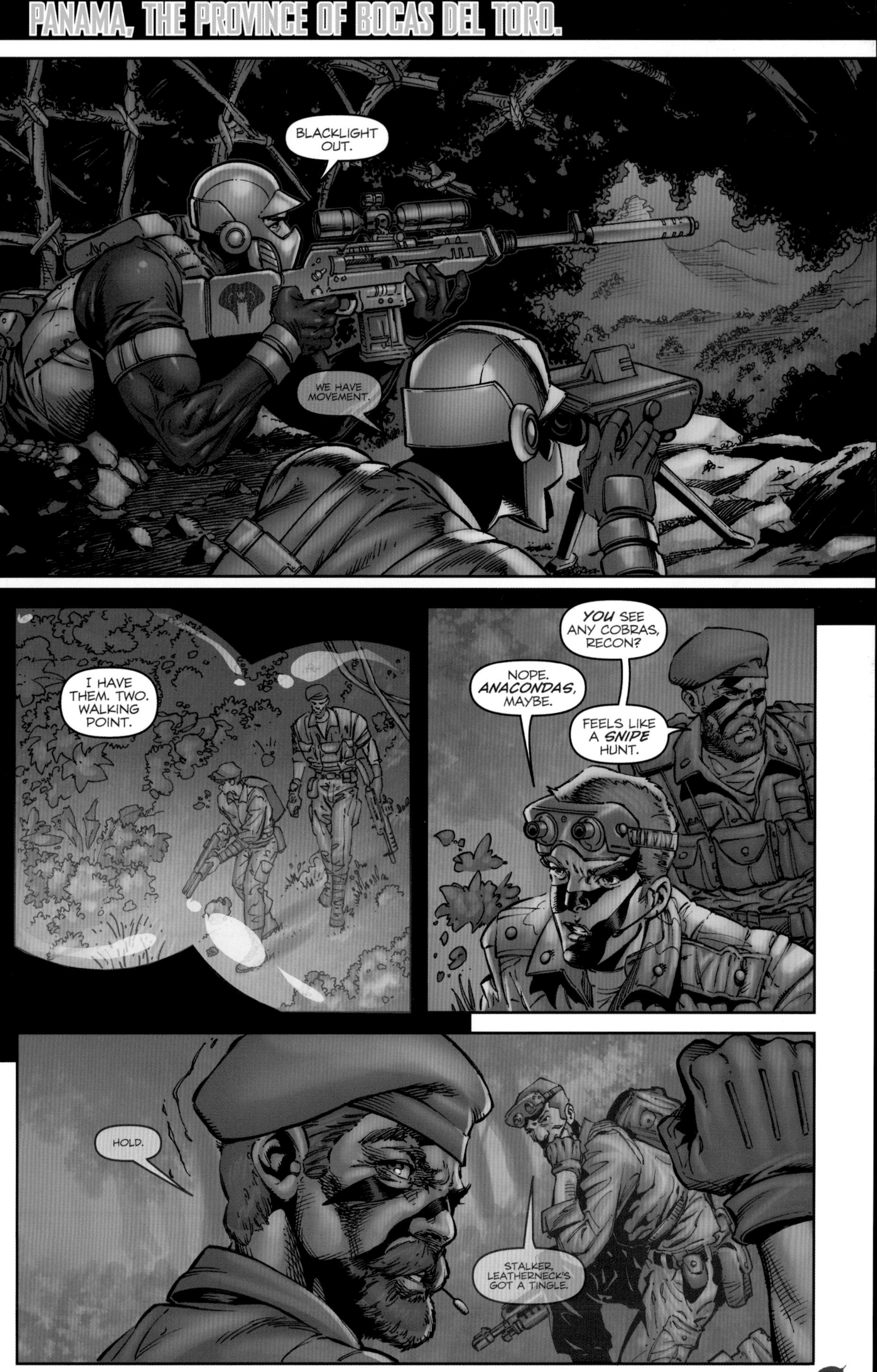
PANAMA, THE PROVINCE OF BOCAS DEL TORO.
BLACKLIGHT OUT.
WE HAVE MOVEMENT.
I HAVE THEM. TWO. WALKING POINT.
YOU SEE ANY COBRAS, RECON?
NOPE. ANACONDAS, MAYBE.
FEELS LIKE A SNIPE HUNT.
HOLD.
STALKER, LEATHERNECK'S GOT A TINGLE.

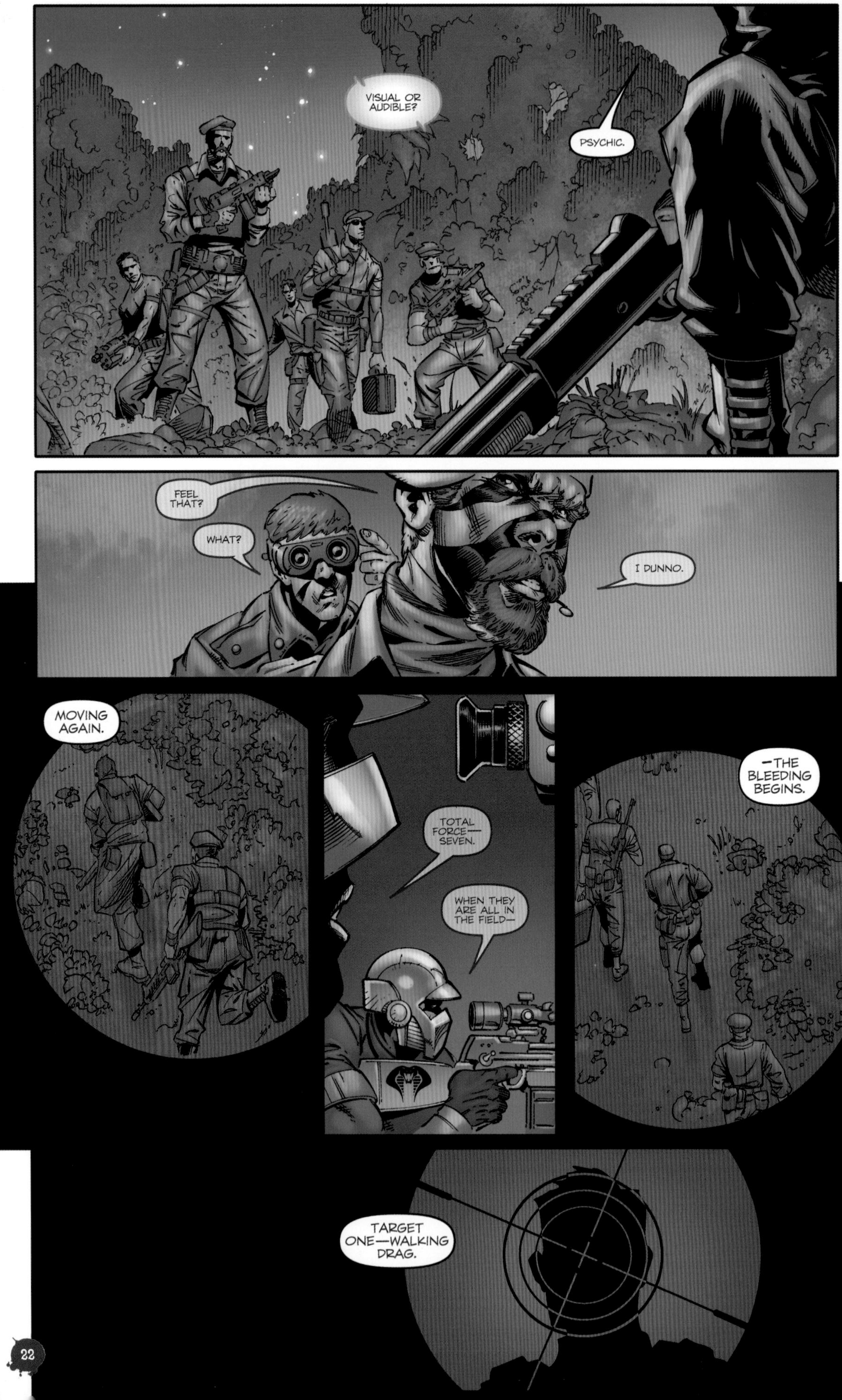
VISUAL OR AUDIBLE?
PSYCHIC.
FEEL THAT?
WHAT?
I DUNNO.
MOVING AGAIN.
TOTAL FORCE— SEVEN.
WHEN THEY ARE ALL IN THE FIELD—
—THE BLEEDING BEGINS.
TARGET ONE—WALKING DRAG.

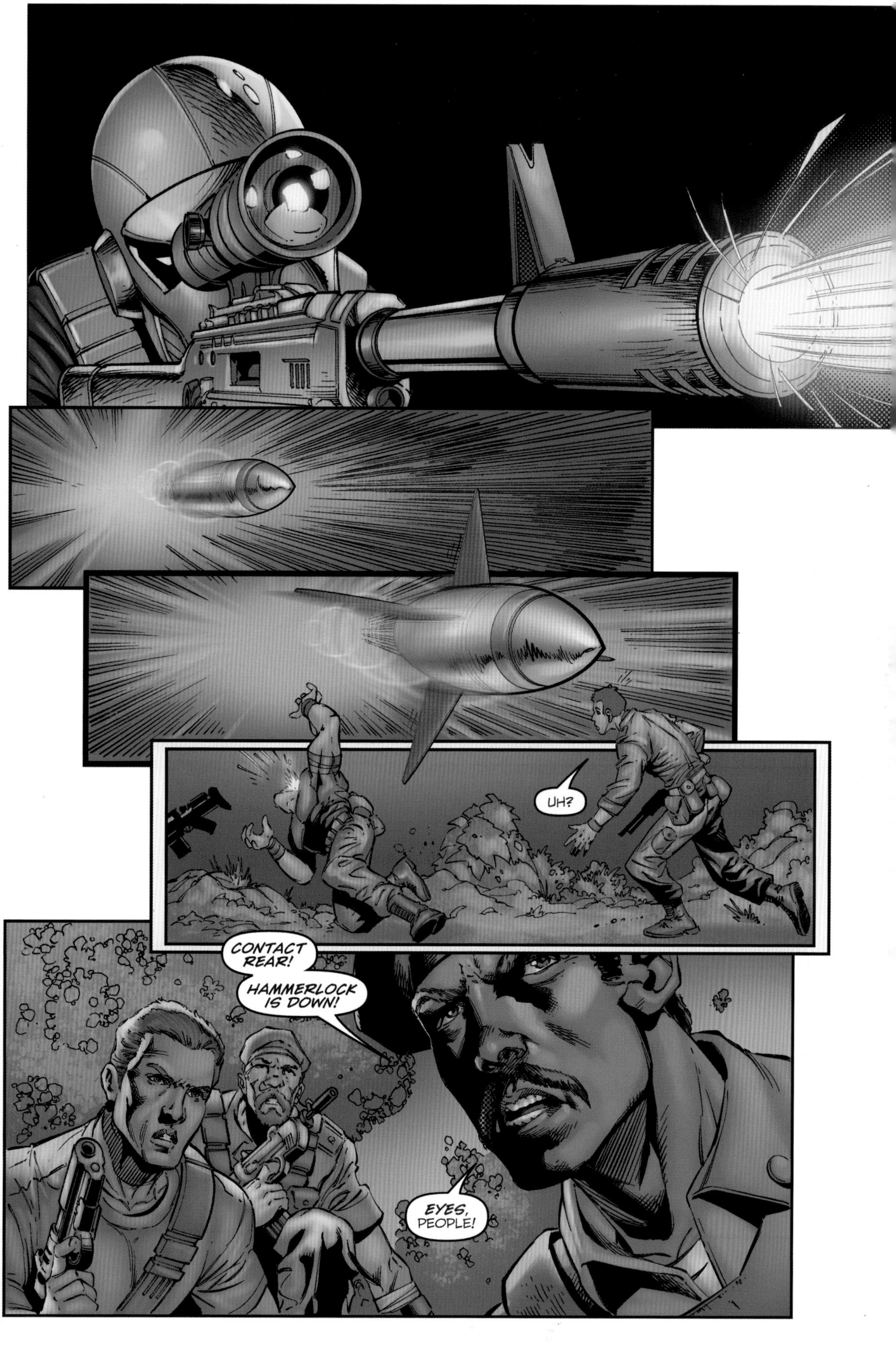
UH?
CONTACT REAR!
HAMMERLOCK IS DOWN!
EYES, PEOPLE!

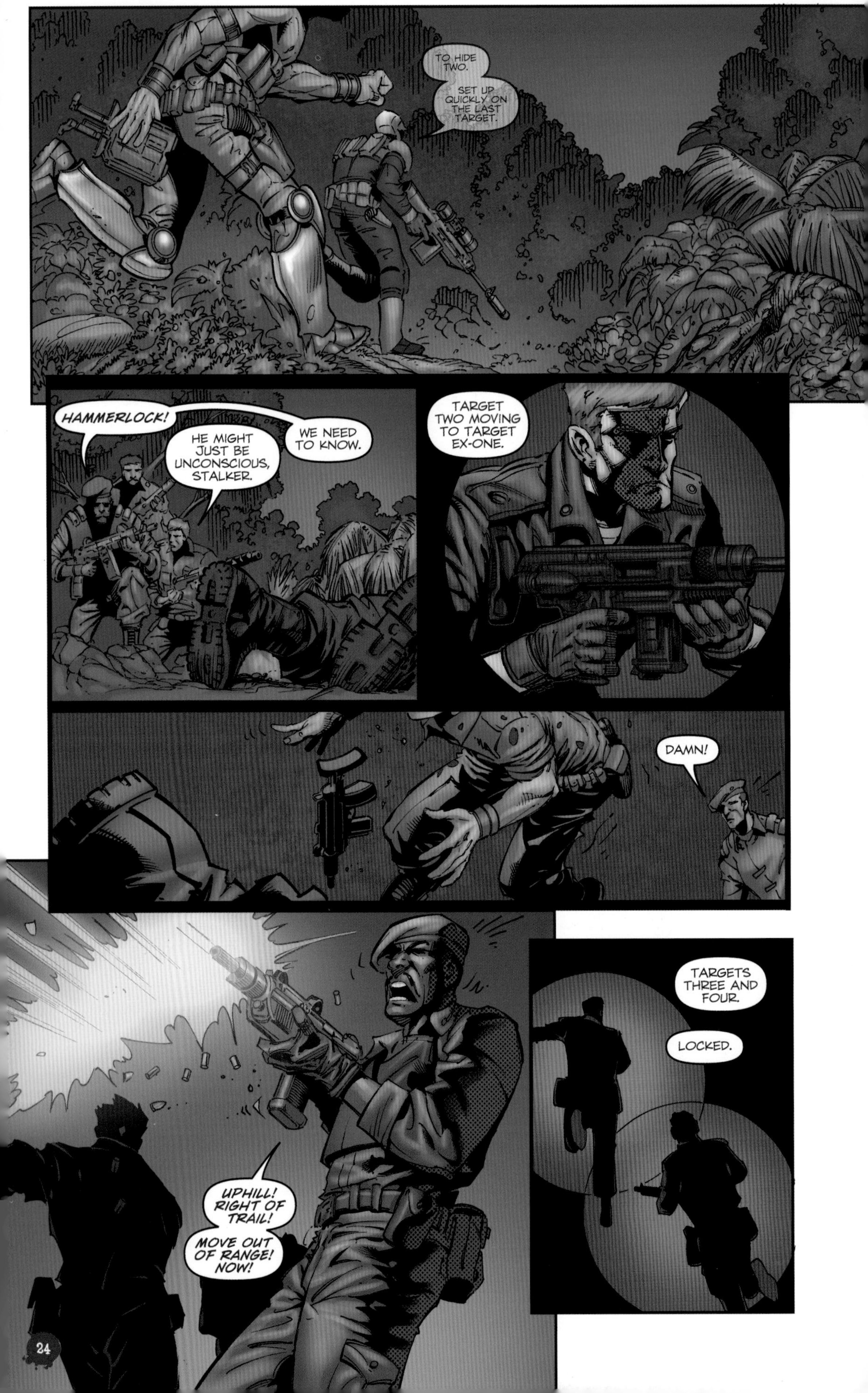
TO HIDE TWO.
SET UP QUICKLY ON THE LAST TARGET.
HAMMERLOCK!
HE MIGHT JUST BE UNCONSCIOUS, STALKER.
WE NEED TO KNOW.
TARGET TWO MOVING TO TARGET EX-ONE.
DAMN!
UPHILL! RIGHT OF TRAIL!
MOVE OUT OF RANGE! NOW!
TARGETS THREE AND FOUR.
LOCKED.

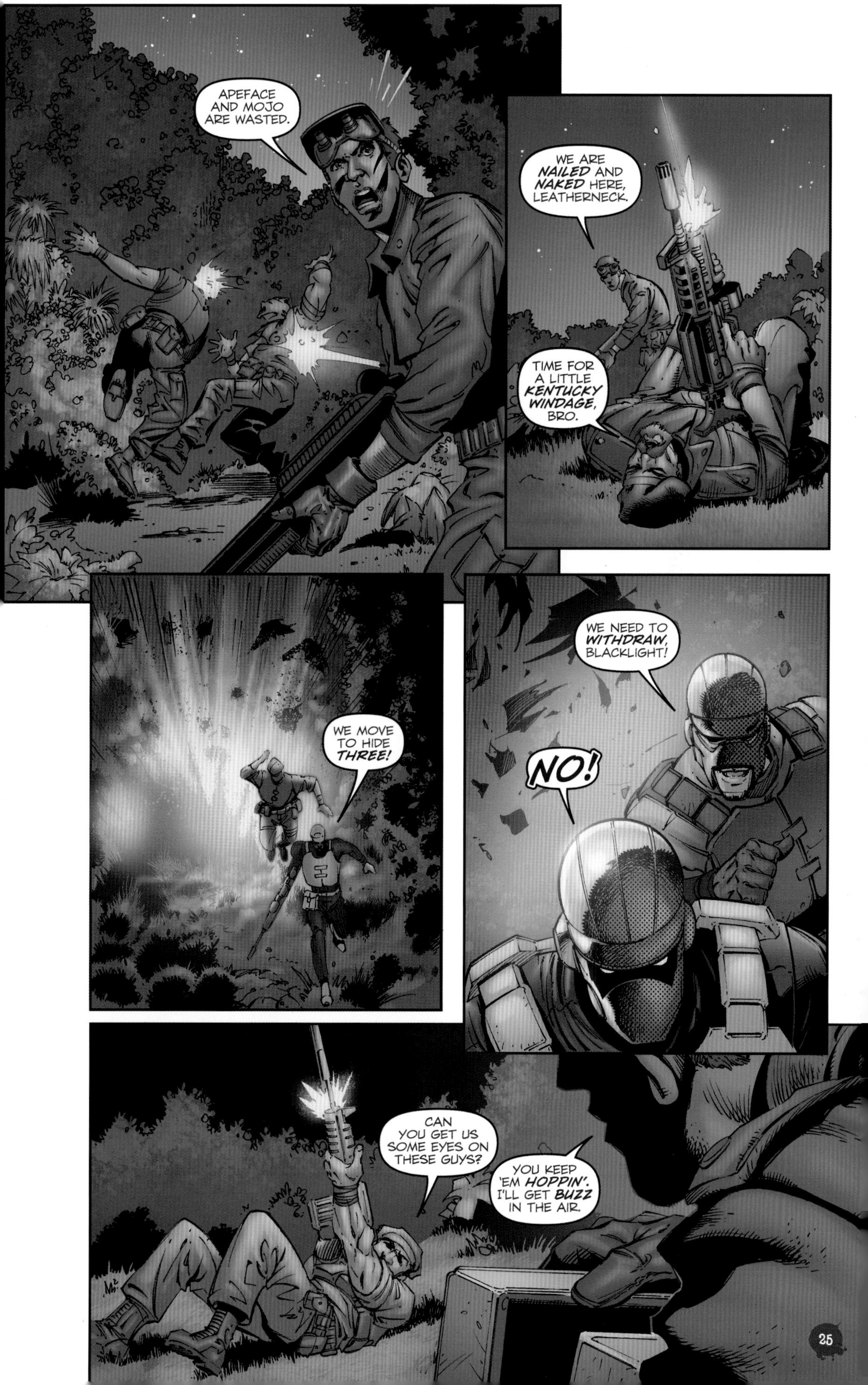
APEFACE AND MOJO ARE WASTED.
WE ARE NAILED AND NAKED HERE, LEATHERNECK.
TIME FOR A LITTLE KENTUCKY WINDAGE, BRO.
WE MOVE TO HIDE THREE!
WE NEED TO WITHDRAW, BLACKLIGHT!
NO!
CAN YOU GET US SOME EYES ON THESE GUYS?
YOU KEEP 'EM HOPPIN'. I'LL GET BUZZ IN THE AIR.

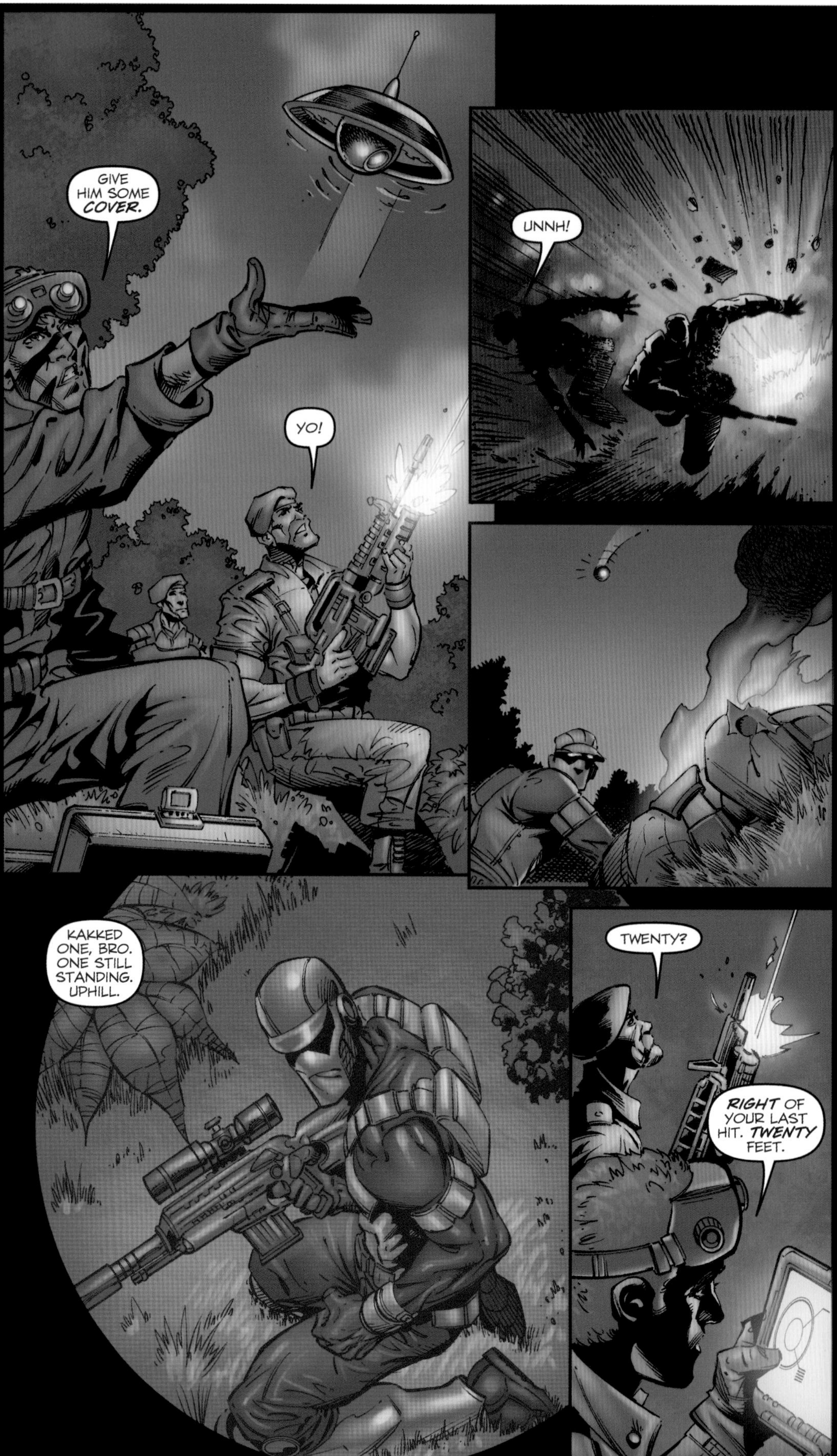
GIVE HIM SOME **COVER.**
YO!
UNNH!
KAKKED ONE, BRO. ONE STILL STANDING. UPHILL.
TWENTY?
RIGHT OF YOUR LAST HIT. **TWENTY** FEET.

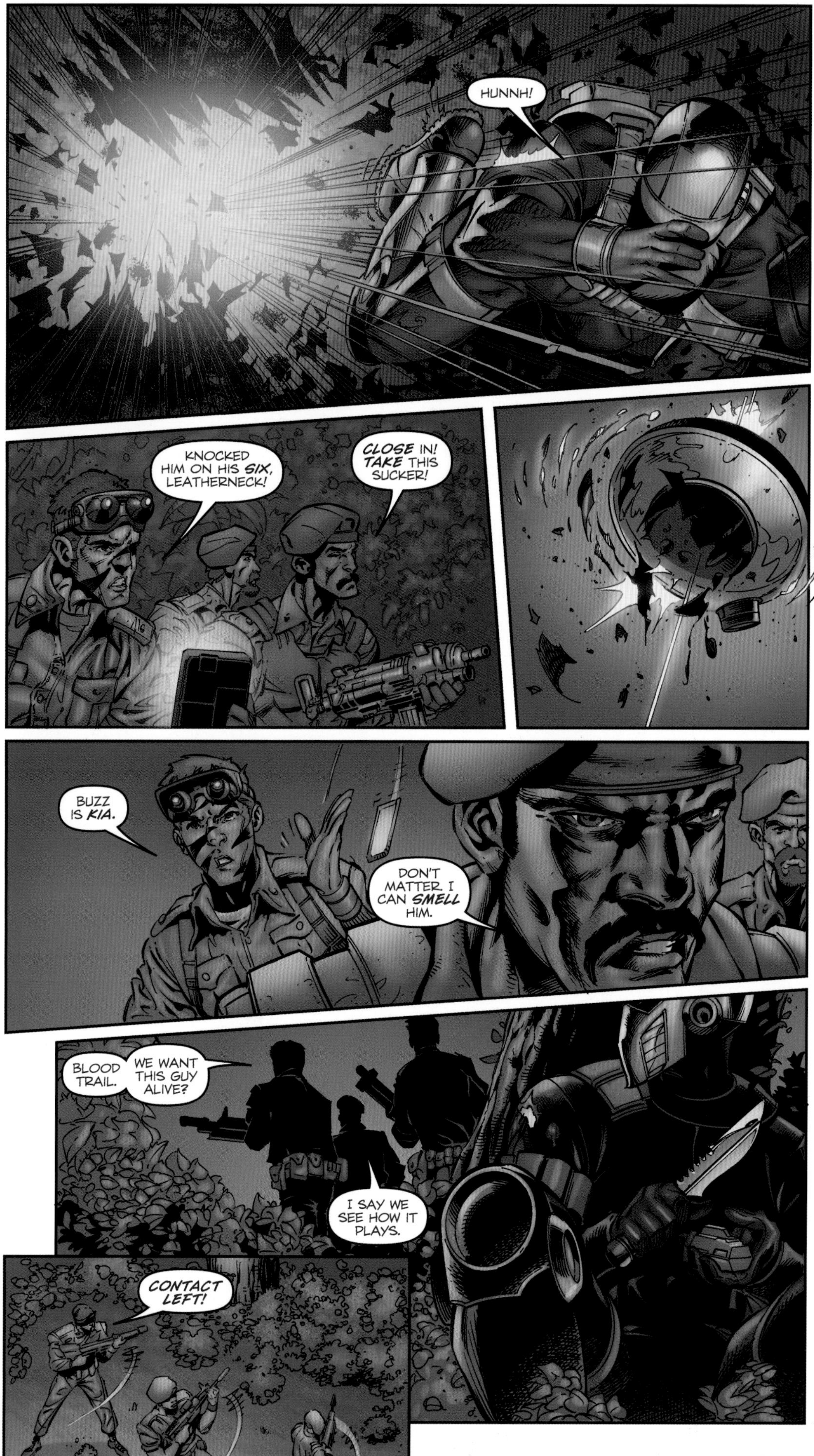
HUNNH!
KNOCKED HIM ON HIS SIX, LEATHERNECK!
CLOSE IN! TAKE THIS SUCKER!
BUZZ IS KIA.
DON'T MATTER. I CAN SMELL HIM.
BLOOD TRAIL.
WE WANT THIS GUY ALIVE?
I SAY WE SEE HOW IT PLAYS.
CONTACT LEFT!

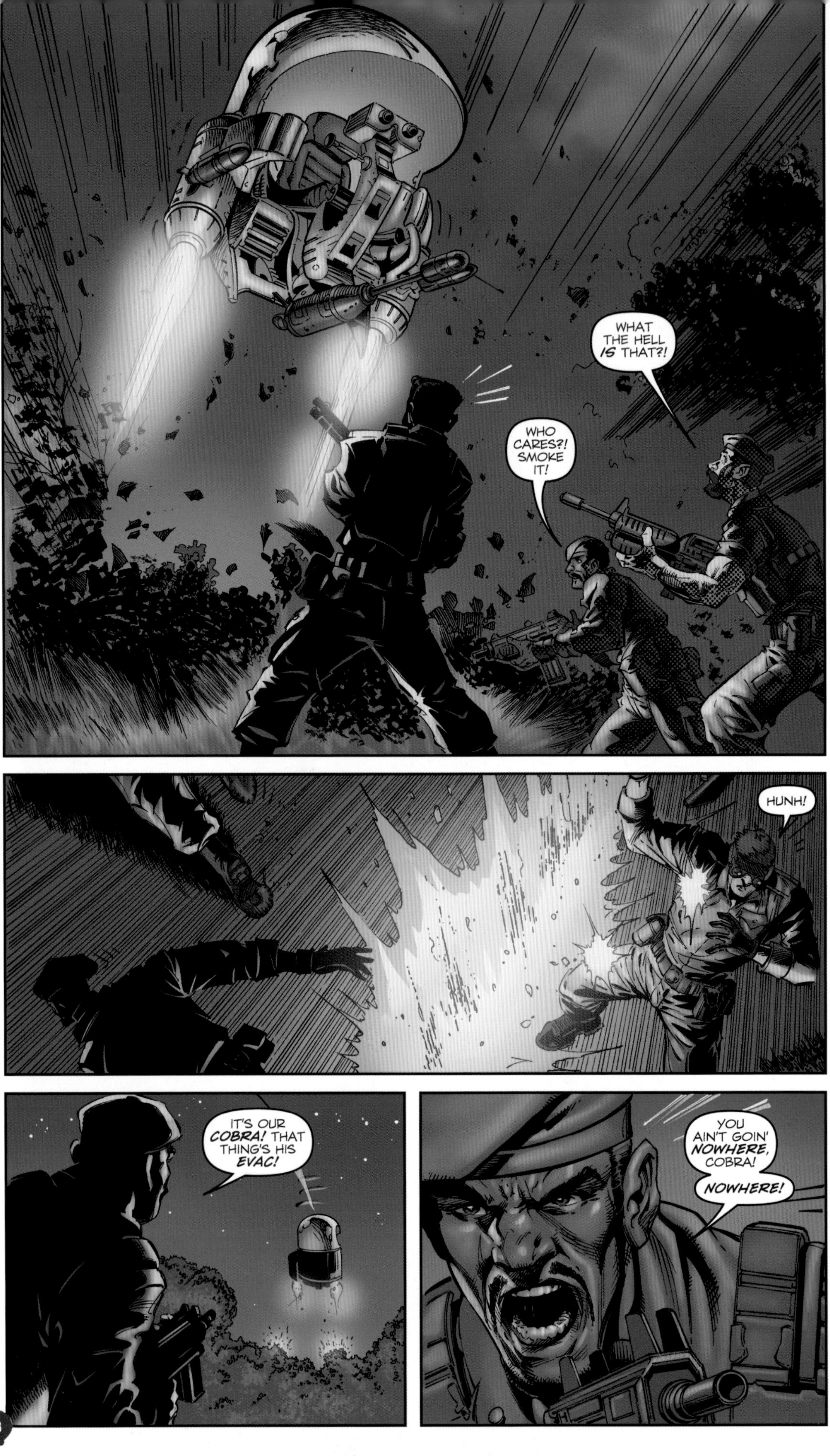
WHAT THE HELL IS THAT?!
WHO CARES?! SMOKE IT!
HUNH!
IT'S OUR COBRA! THAT THING'S HIS EVAC!
YOU AIN'T GOIN' NOWHERE, COBRA!
NOWHERE!

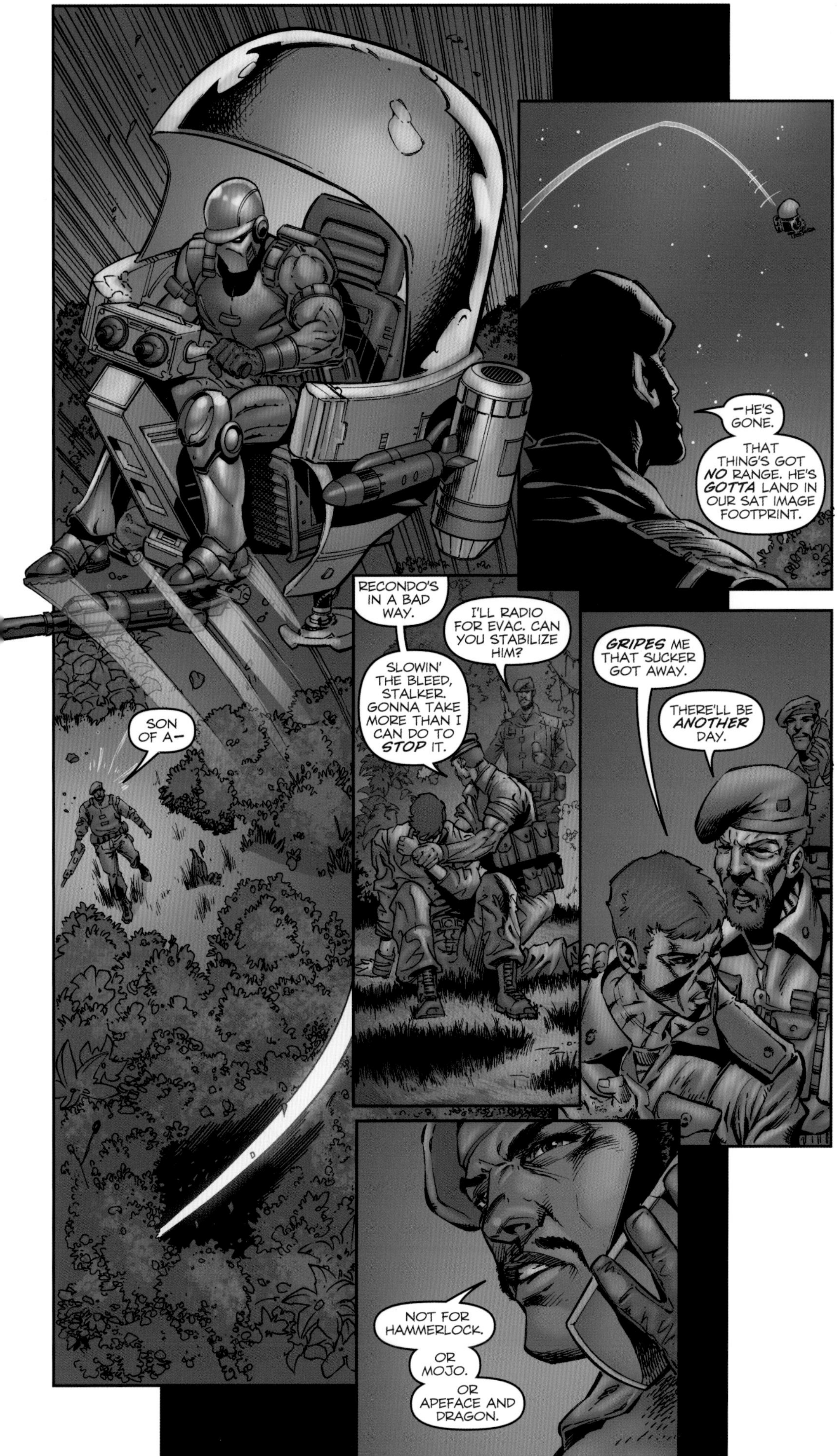

—HE'S GONE.
THAT THING'S GOT NO RANGE. HE'S GOTTA LAND IN OUR SAT IMAGE FOOTPRINT.
SON OF A—
RECONDO'S IN A BAD WAY.
I'LL RADIO FOR EVAC. CAN YOU STABILIZE HIM?
SLOWIN' THE BLEED, STALKER. GONNA TAKE MORE THAN I CAN DO TO STOP IT.
GRIPES ME THAT SUCKER GOT AWAY.
THERE'LL BE ANOTHER DAY.
NOT FOR HAMMERLOCK.
OR MOJO.
OR APEFACE AND DRAGON.

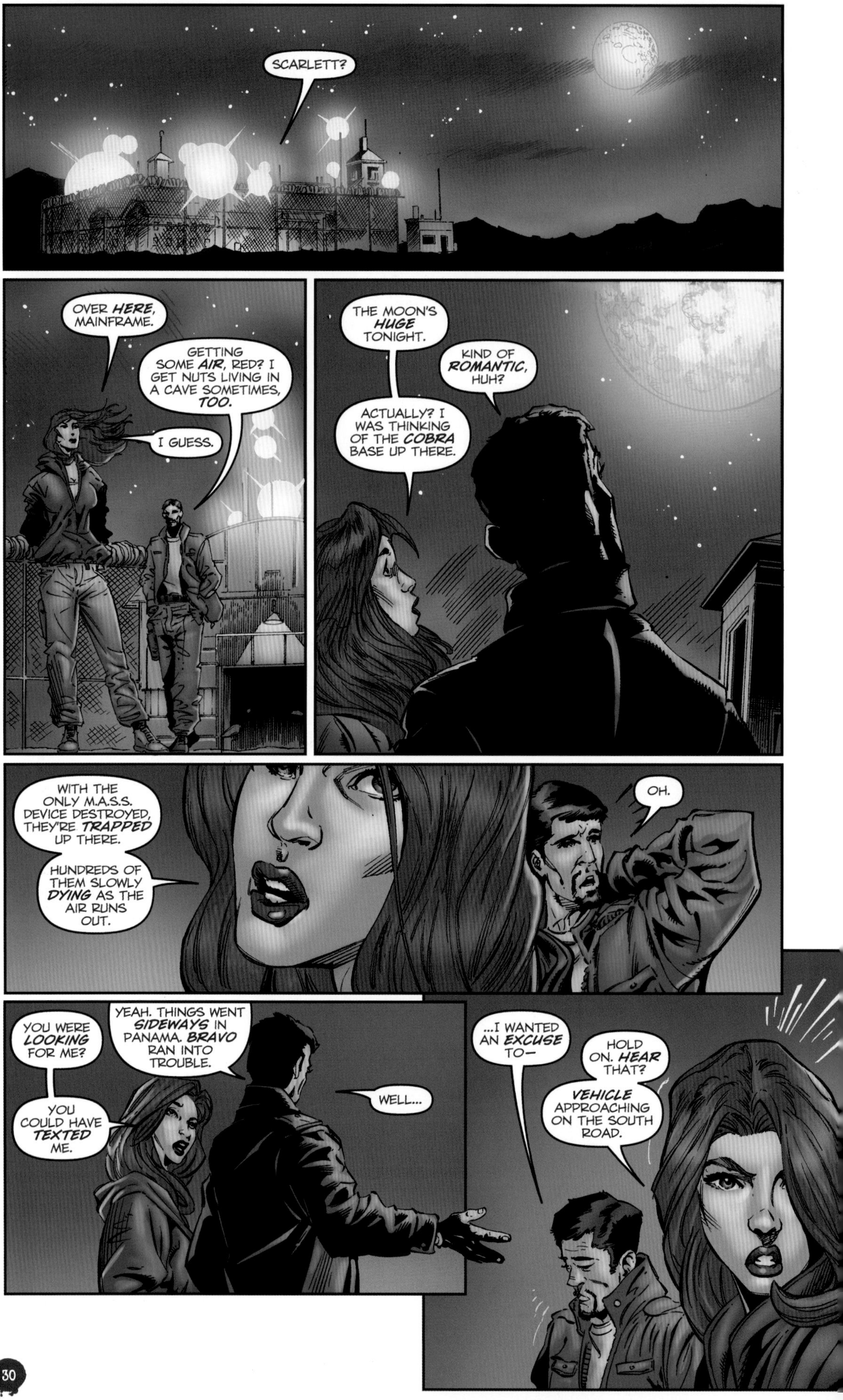

SCARLETT?
OVER HERE, MAINFRAME.
GETTING SOME AIR, RED? I GET NUTS LIVING IN A CAVE SOMETIMES, TOO.
I GUESS.
THE MOON'S HUGE TONIGHT.
KIND OF ROMANTIC, HUH?
ACTUALLY? I WAS THINKING OF THE COBRA BASE UP THERE.
WITH THE ONLY M.A.S.S. DEVICE DESTROYED, THEY'RE TRAPPED UP THERE.
HUNDREDS OF THEM SLOWLY DYING AS THE AIR RUNS OUT.
OH.
YOU WERE LOOKING FOR ME?
YEAH. THINGS WENT SIDEWAYS IN PANAMA. BRAVO RAN INTO TROUBLE.
YOU COULD HAVE TEXTED ME.
WELL...
...I WANTED AN EXCUSE TO—
HOLD ON. HEAR THAT?
VEHICLE APPROACHING ON THE SOUTH ROAD.

"WHO'S COMING IN AT THIS HOUR?"

FACIAL RECOGNITION POSITIVE FOR GENERAL HAWK.

ACCESS GRANTED.

M. HAWK

CONFIRMED

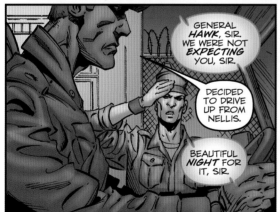

GENERAL *HAWK*, SIR. WE WERE NOT *EXPECTING* YOU, SIR.

DECIDED TO DRIVE UP FROM NELLIS.

BEAUTIFUL *NIGHT* FOR IT, SIR.

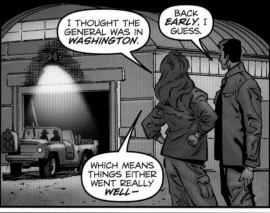

I THOUGHT THE GENERAL WAS IN *WASHINGTON*.

BACK *EARLY*, I GUESS.

WHICH MEANS THINGS EITHER WENT REALLY *WELL—*

"—OR REALLY *BAD*."

WELCOME BACK TO *THE PIT*, SIR!

31

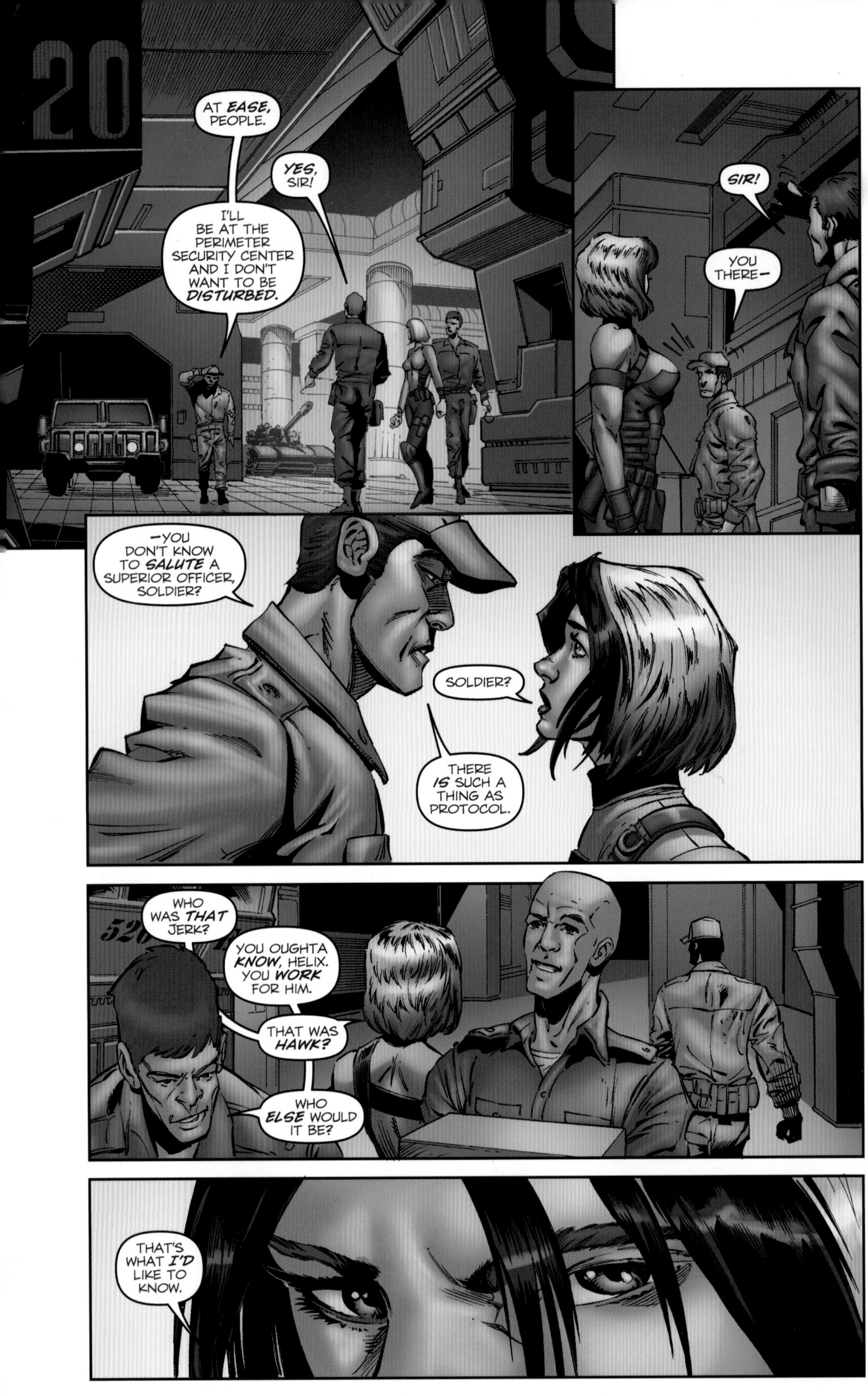
20
AT EASE, PEOPLE.
YES, SIR!
I'LL BE AT THE PERIMETER SECURITY CENTER AND I DON'T WANT TO BE DISTURBED.
SIR!
YOU THERE—
—YOU DON'T KNOW TO SALUTE A SUPERIOR OFFICER, SOLDIER?
SOLDIER?
THERE IS SUCH A THING AS PROTOCOL.
WHO WAS THAT JERK?
YOU OUGHTA KNOW, HELIX. YOU WORK FOR HIM.
THAT WAS HAWK?
WHO ELSE WOULD IT BE?
THAT'S WHAT I'D LIKE TO KNOW.

GENERAL!

RELAX, SOLDIER.

I NEED YOU TO CHECK ON SOMETHING ON THE NORTHERN PERIMETER.

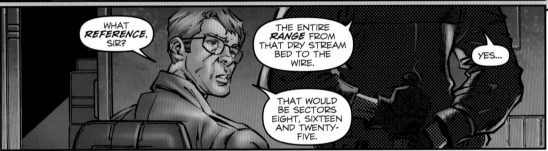

WHAT *REFERENCE*, SIR?

THE ENTIRE *RANGE* FROM THAT DRY STREAM BED TO THE WIRE.

YES...

THAT WOULD BE SECTORS EIGHT, SIXTEEN AND TWENTY-FIVE.

...IT *WOULD*.

IH—

EIGHT... SIXTEEN... TWENTY-FIVE...

SEISMICS. MOTION. INFRA-RED.

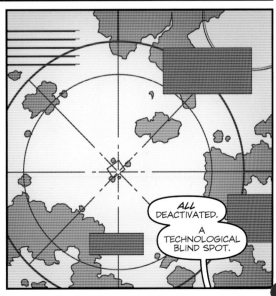

ALL DEACTIVATED.

A TECHNOLOGICAL BLIND SPOT.

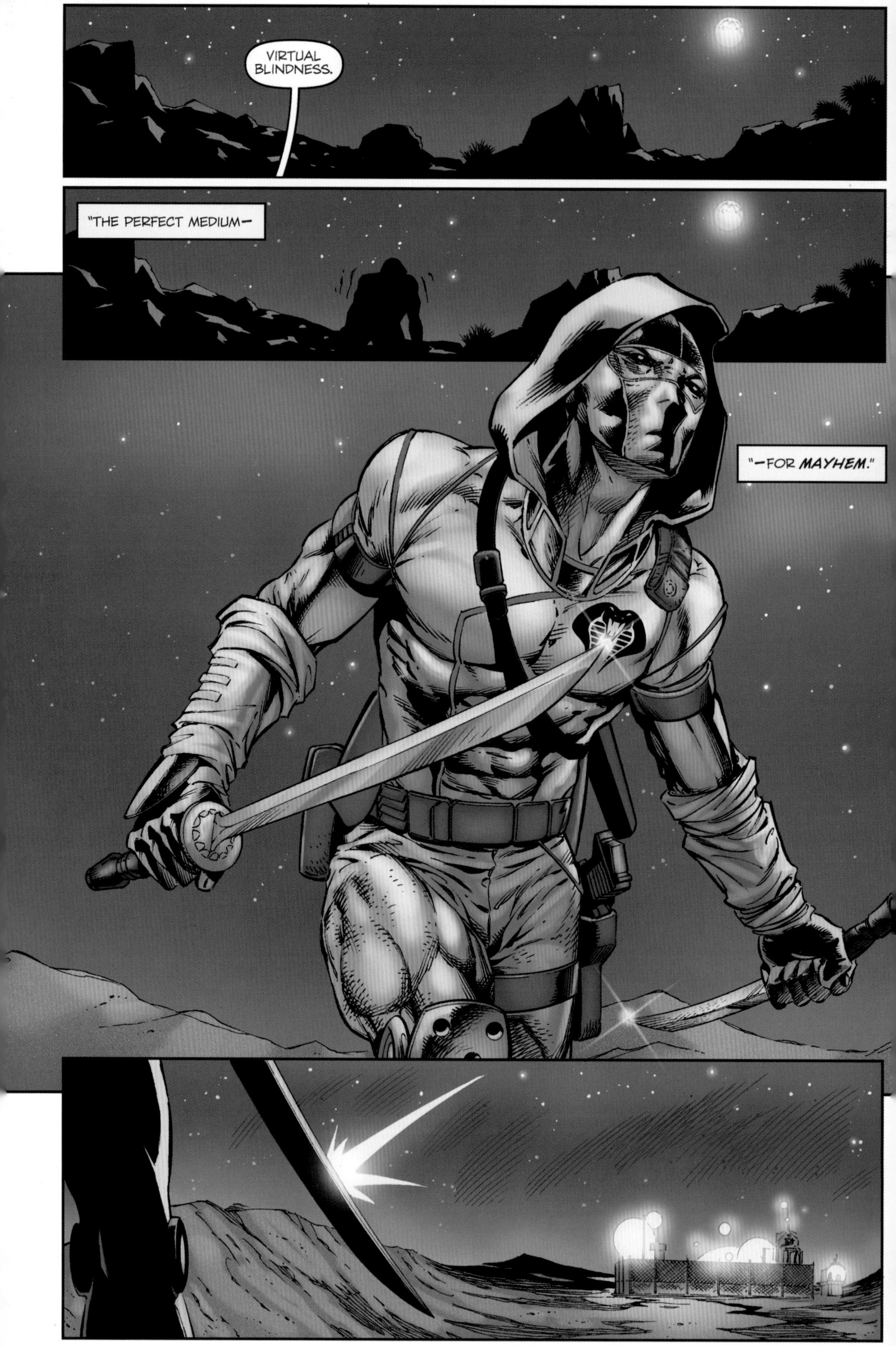

VIRTUAL BLINDNESS.
"THE PERFECT MEDIUM—
"—FOR MAYHEM."

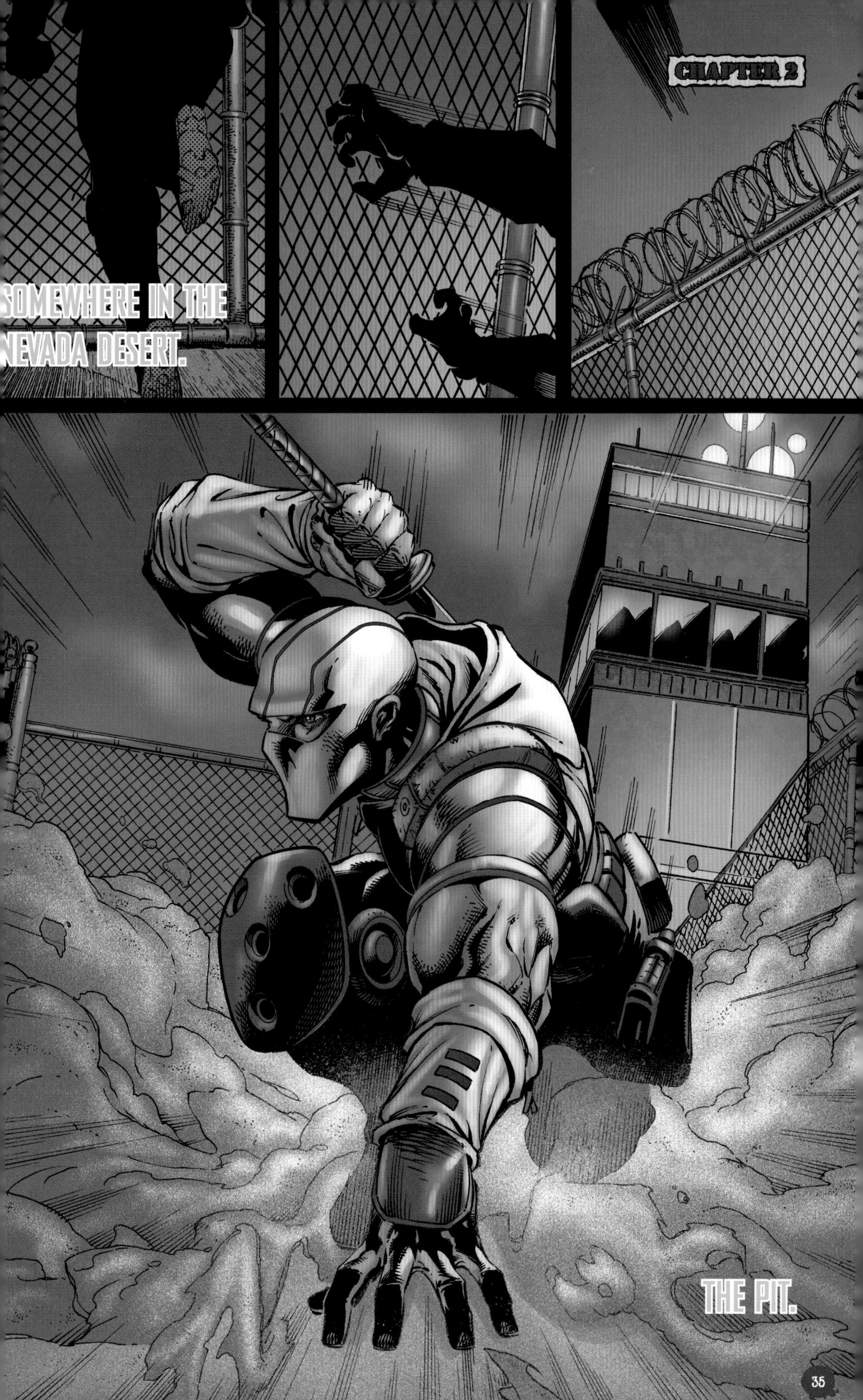
CHAPTER 2
SOMEWHERE IN THE NEVADA DESERT.
THE PIT.

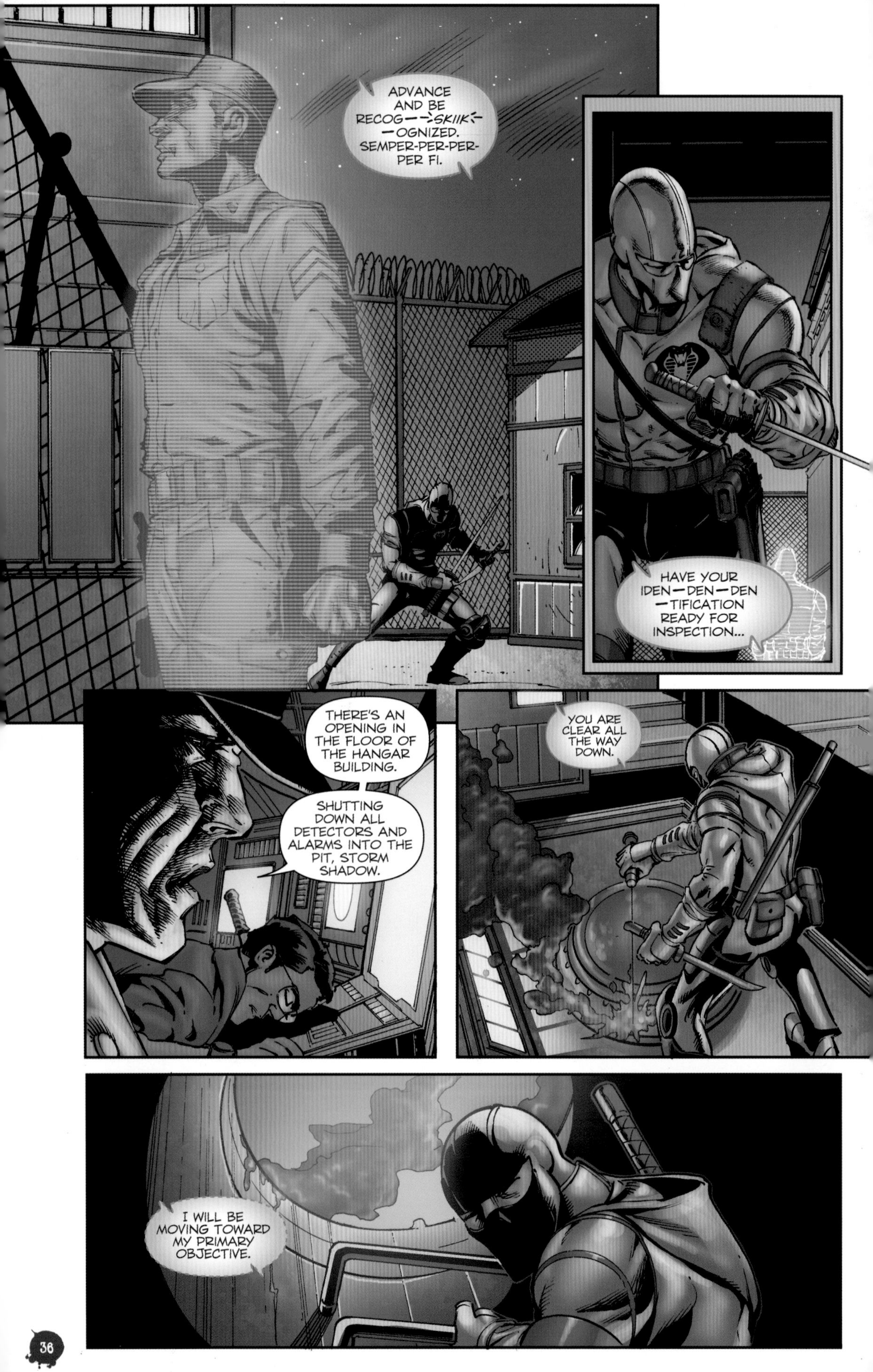
ADVANCE AND BE RECOG—SKIIK—OGNIZED. SEMPER-PER-PER-PER FI.
HAVE YOUR IDEN—DEN—DEN—TIFICATION READY FOR INSPECTION...
THERE'S AN OPENING IN THE FLOOR OF THE HANGAR BUILDING.
SHUTTING DOWN ALL DETECTORS AND ALARMS INTO THE PIT, STORM SHADOW.
YOU ARE CLEAR ALL THE WAY DOWN.
I WILL BE MOVING TOWARD MY PRIMARY OBJECTIVE.

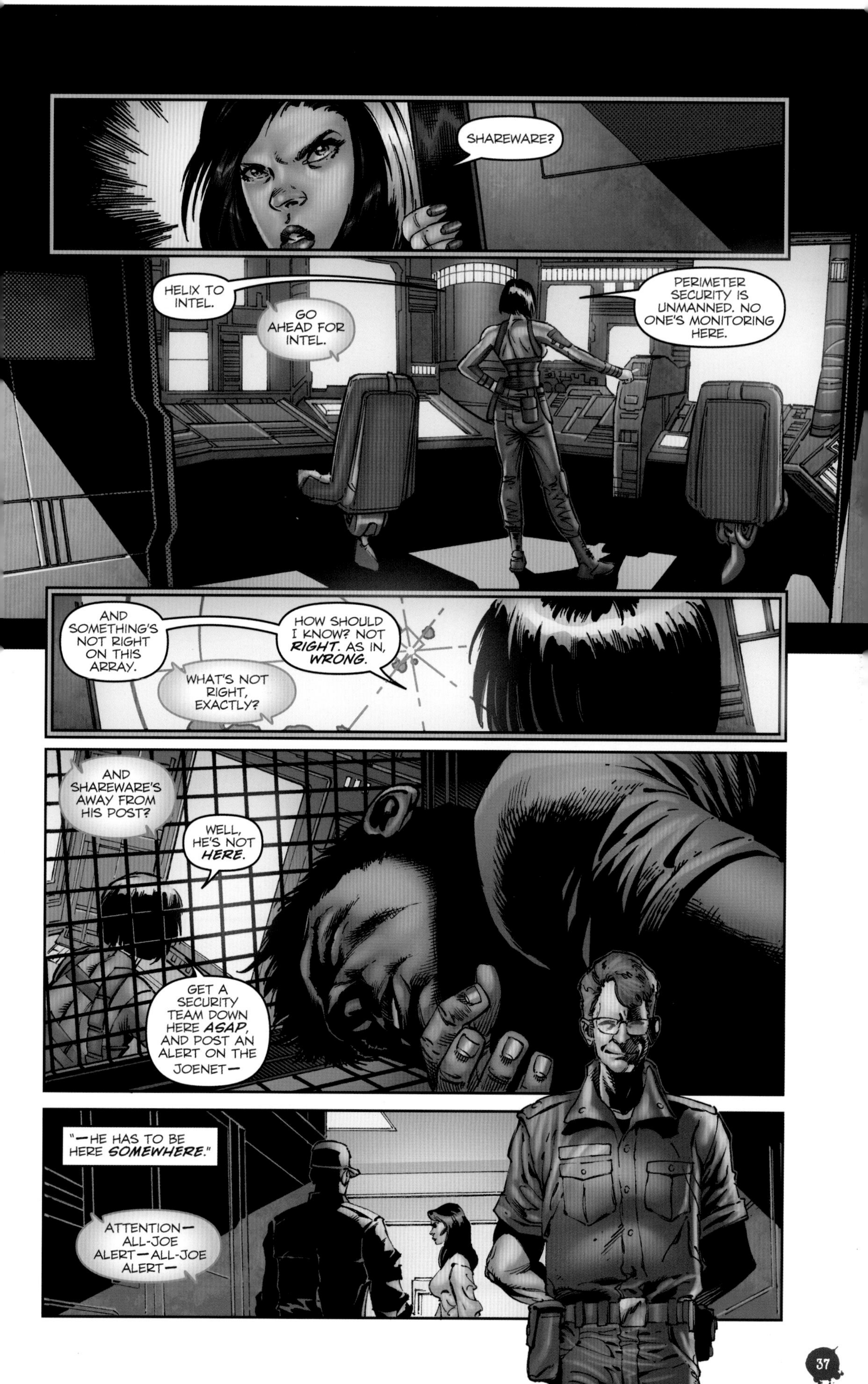

SHAREWARE?
HELIX TO INTEL.
GO AHEAD FOR INTEL.
PERIMETER SECURITY IS UNMANNED. NO ONE'S MONITORING HERE.
AND SOMETHING'S NOT RIGHT ON THIS ARRAY.
WHAT'S NOT RIGHT, EXACTLY?
HOW SHOULD I KNOW? NOT ***RIGHT***. AS IN, ***WRONG***.
AND SHAREWARE'S AWAY FROM HIS POST?
WELL, HE'S NOT ***HERE***.
GET A SECURITY TEAM DOWN HERE ***ASAP***, AND POST AN ALERT ON THE JOENET—
"—HE HAS TO BE HERE ***SOMEWHERE***."
ATTENTION— ALL-JOE ALERT— ALL-JOE ALERT—

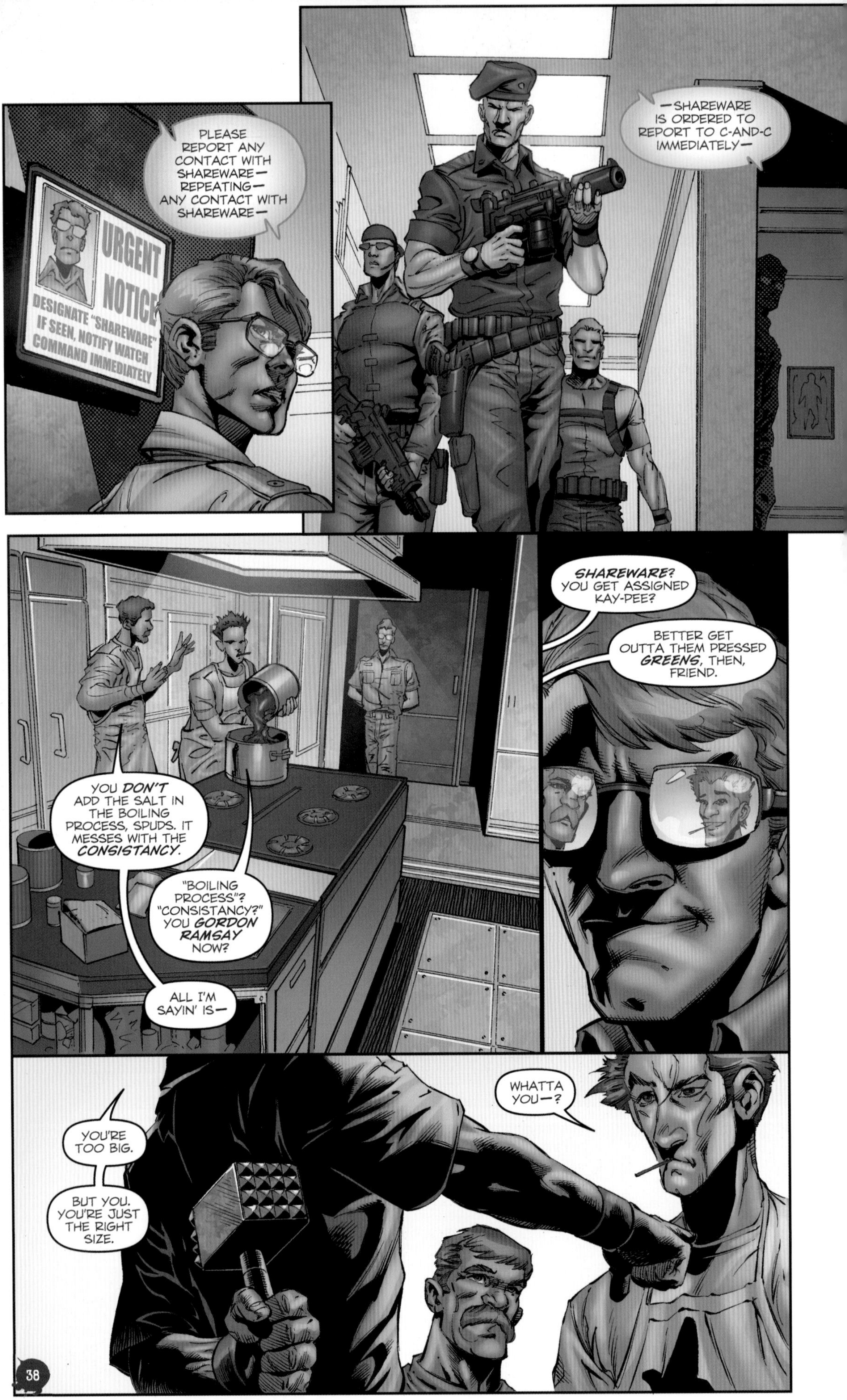

PLEASE REPORT ANY CONTACT WITH SHAREWARE— REPEATING— ANY CONTACT WITH SHAREWARE—
URGENT NOTICE
DESIGNATE "SHAREWARE" IF SEEN, NOTIFY WATCH COMMAND IMMEDIATELY
—SHAREWARE IS ORDERED TO REPORT TO C-AND-C IMMEDIATELY—
YOU DON'T ADD THE SALT IN THE BOILING PROCESS, SPUDS. IT MESSES WITH THE CONSISTANCY.
"BOILING PROCESS"? "CONSISTANCY?" YOU GORDON RAMSAY NOW?
ALL I'M SAYIN' IS—
SHAREWARE? YOU GET ASSIGNED KAY-PEE?
BETTER GET OUTTA THEM PRESSED GREENS, THEN, FRIEND.
WHATTA YOU—?
YOU'RE TOO BIG.
BUT YOU. YOU'RE JUST THE RIGHT SIZE.

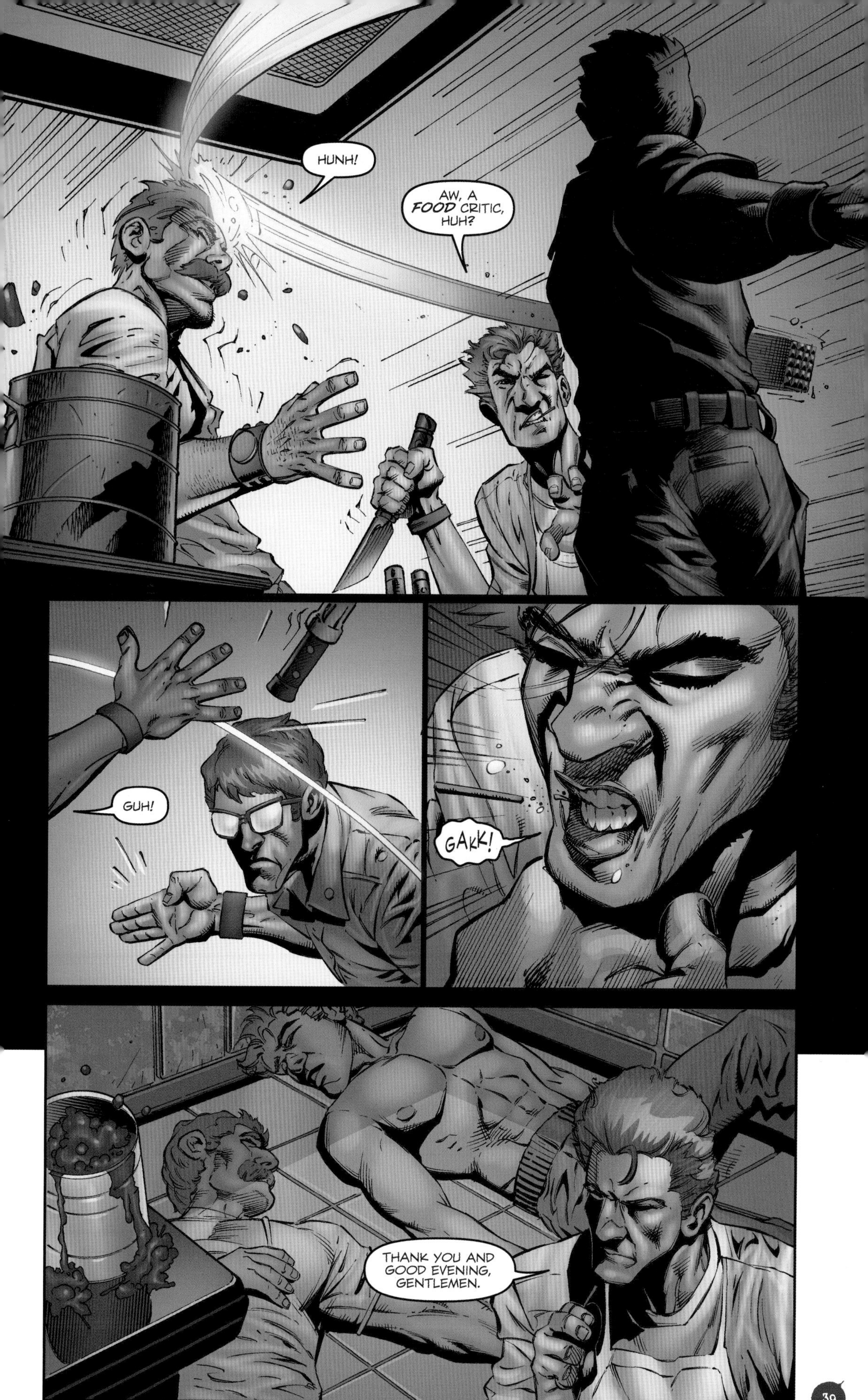
HUNH!
AW, A *FOOD* CRITIC, HUH?
GUH!
GAKK!
THANK YOU AND GOOD EVENING, GENTLEMEN.

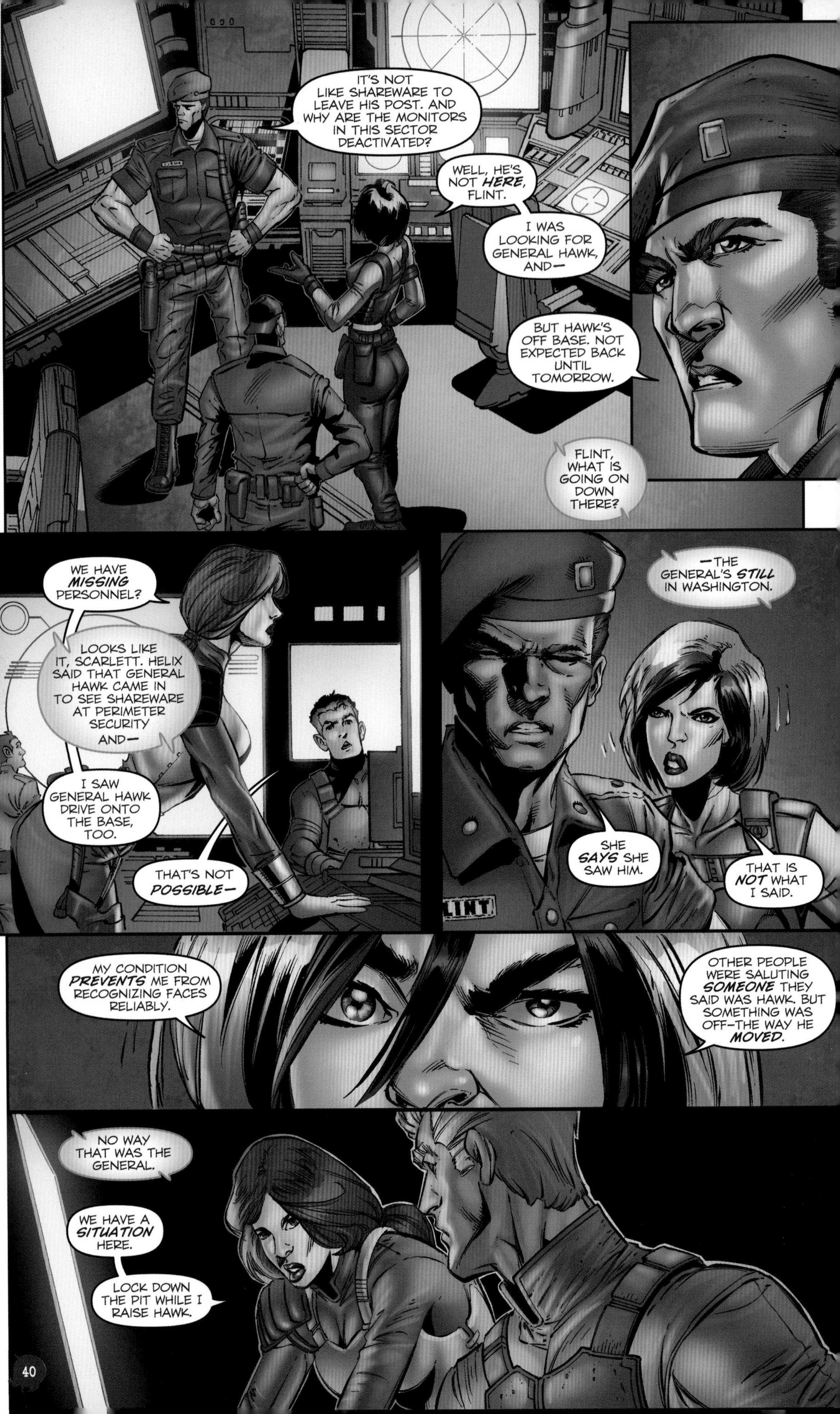
IT'S NOT LIKE SHAREWARE TO LEAVE HIS POST. AND WHY ARE THE MONITORS IN THIS SECTOR DEACTIVATED?
WELL, HE'S NOT *HERE*, FLINT.
I WAS LOOKING FOR GENERAL HAWK, AND—
BUT HAWK'S OFF BASE. NOT EXPECTED BACK UNTIL TOMORROW.
FLINT, WHAT IS GOING ON DOWN THERE?
WE HAVE *MISSING* PERSONNEL?
LOOKS LIKE IT, SCARLETT. HELIX SAID THAT GENERAL HAWK CAME IN TO SEE SHAREWARE AT PERIMETER SECURITY AND—
I SAW GENERAL HAWK DRIVE ONTO THE BASE, TOO.
THAT'S NOT *POSSIBLE*—
—THE GENERAL'S *STILL* IN WASHINGTON.
SHE *SAYS* SHE SAW HIM.
THAT IS *NOT* WHAT I SAID.
FLINT
MY CONDITION *PREVENTS* ME FROM RECOGNIZING FACES RELIABLY.
OTHER PEOPLE WERE SALUTING *SOMEONE* THEY SAID WAS HAWK. BUT SOMETHING WAS OFF—THE WAY HE *MOVED*.
NO WAY THAT WAS THE GENERAL.
WE HAVE A *SITUATION* HERE.
LOCK DOWN THE PIT WHILE I RAISE HAWK.

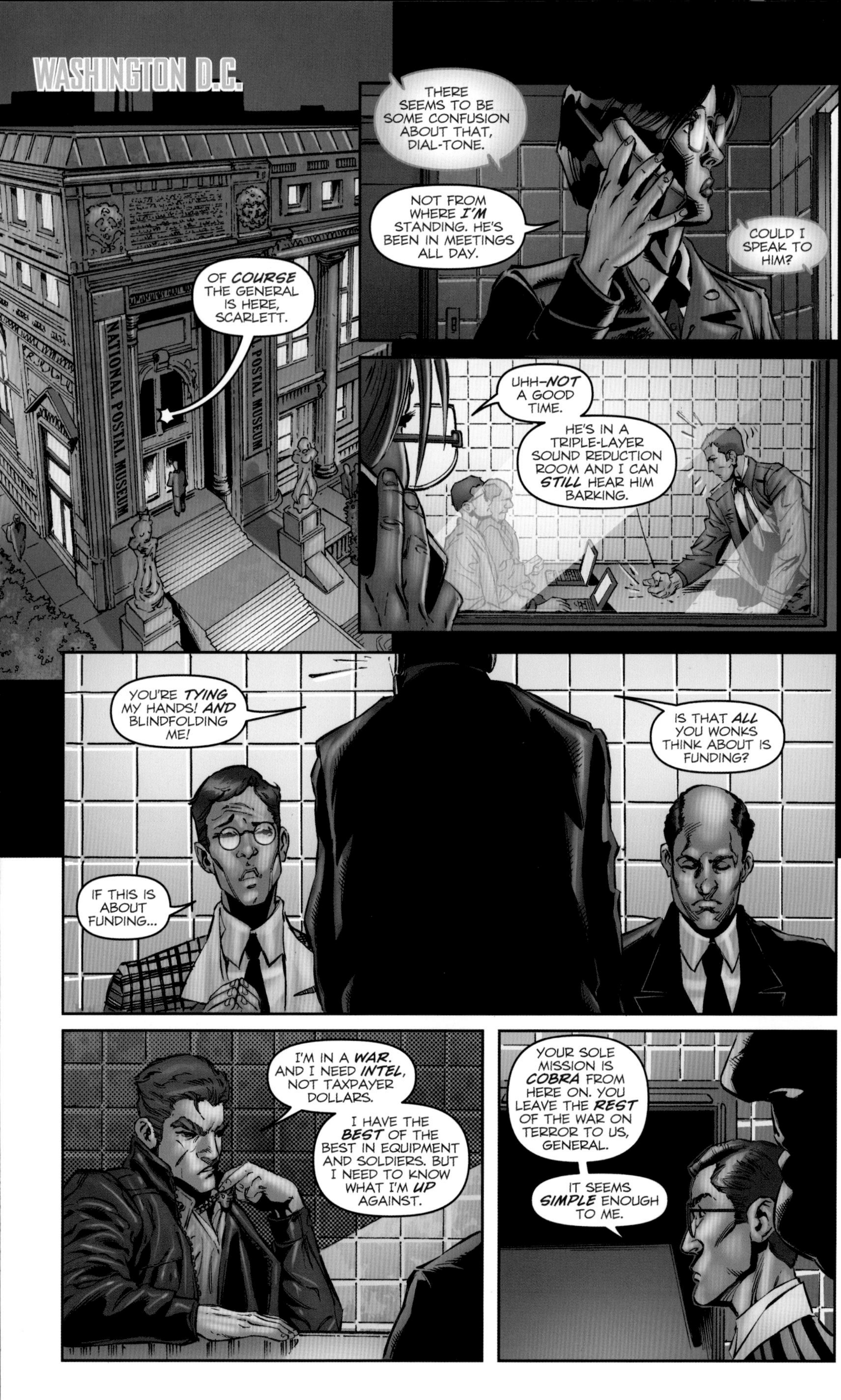
WASHINGTON D.C.
THERE SEEMS TO BE SOME CONFUSION ABOUT THAT, DIAL-TONE.
NOT FROM WHERE I'M STANDING. HE'S BEEN IN MEETINGS ALL DAY.
COULD I SPEAK TO HIM?
OF COURSE THE GENERAL IS HERE, SCARLETT.
NATIONAL POSTAL MUSEUM
POSTAL MUSEUM
UHH--NOT A GOOD TIME.
HE'S IN A TRIPLE-LAYER SOUND REDUCTION ROOM AND I CAN STILL HEAR HIM BARKING.
YOU'RE TYING MY HANDS! AND BLINDFOLDING ME!
IS THAT ALL YOU WONKS THINK ABOUT IS FUNDING?
IF THIS IS ABOUT FUNDING...
I'M IN A WAR. AND I NEED INTEL, NOT TAXPAYER DOLLARS.
I HAVE THE BEST OF THE BEST IN EQUIPMENT AND SOLDIERS. BUT I NEED TO KNOW WHAT I'M UP AGAINST.
YOUR SOLE MISSION IS COBRA FROM HERE ON. YOU LEAVE THE REST OF THE WAR ON TERROR TO US, GENERAL.
IT SEEMS SIMPLE ENOUGH TO ME.

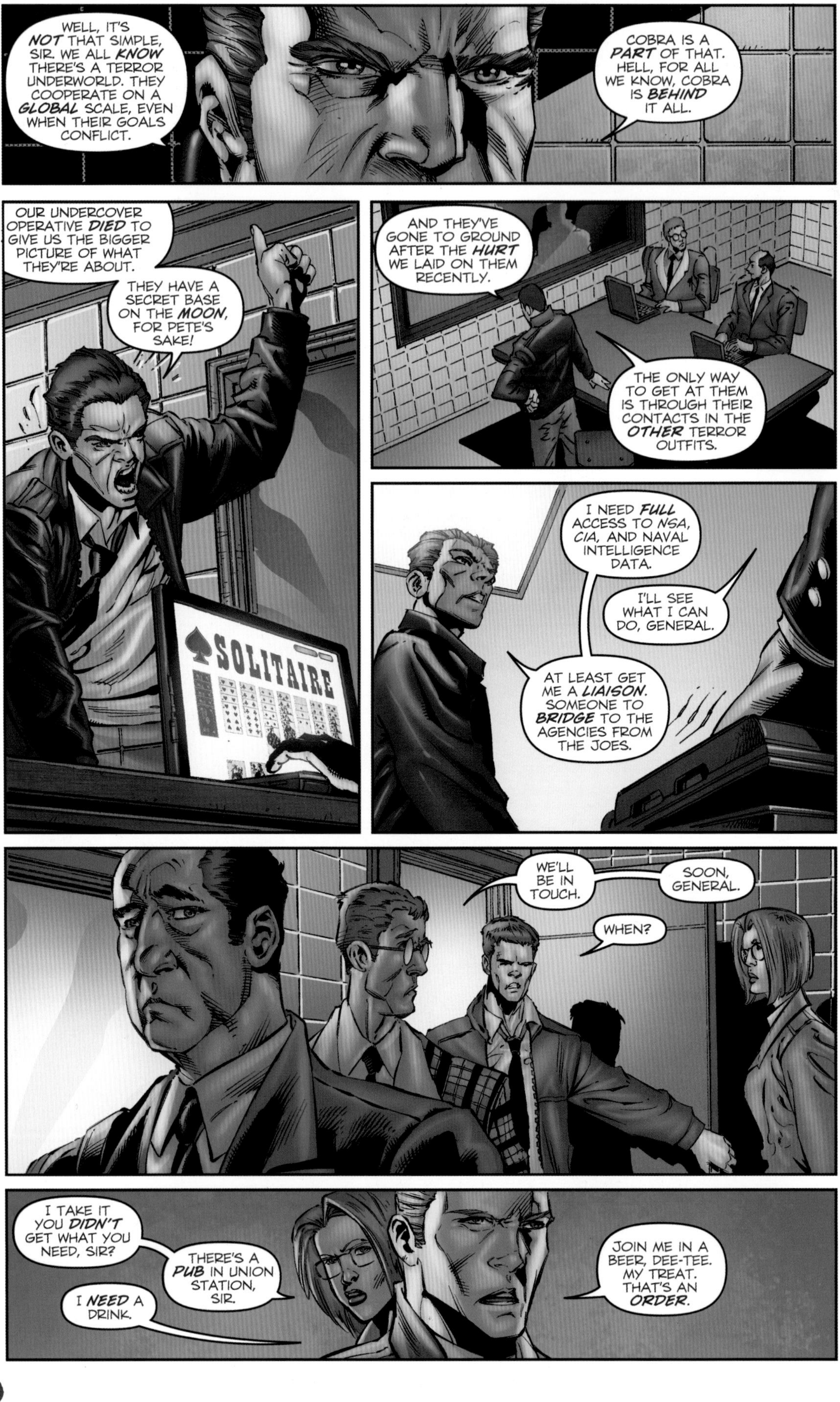
WELL, IT'S NOT THAT SIMPLE, SIR. WE ALL KNOW THERE'S A TERROR UNDERWORLD. THEY COOPERATE ON A GLOBAL SCALE, EVEN WHEN THEIR GOALS CONFLICT.
COBRA IS A PART OF THAT. HELL, FOR ALL WE KNOW, COBRA IS BEHIND IT ALL.
OUR UNDERCOVER OPERATIVE DIED TO GIVE US THE BIGGER PICTURE OF WHAT THEY'RE ABOUT.
THEY HAVE A SECRET BASE ON THE MOON, FOR PETE'S SAKE!
SOLITAIRE
AND THEY'VE GONE TO GROUND AFTER THE HURT WE LAID ON THEM RECENTLY.
THE ONLY WAY TO GET AT THEM IS THROUGH THEIR CONTACTS IN THE OTHER TERROR OUTFITS.
I NEED FULL ACCESS TO NSA, CIA, AND NAVAL INTELLIGENCE DATA.
I'LL SEE WHAT I CAN DO, GENERAL.
AT LEAST GET ME A LIAISON. SOMEONE TO BRIDGE TO THE AGENCIES FROM THE JOES.
WE'LL BE IN TOUCH.
SOON, GENERAL.
WHEN?
I TAKE IT YOU DIDN'T GET WHAT YOU NEED, SIR?
I NEED A DRINK.
THERE'S A PUB IN UNION STATION, SIR.
JOIN ME IN A BEER, DEE-TEE. MY TREAT. THAT'S AN ORDER.

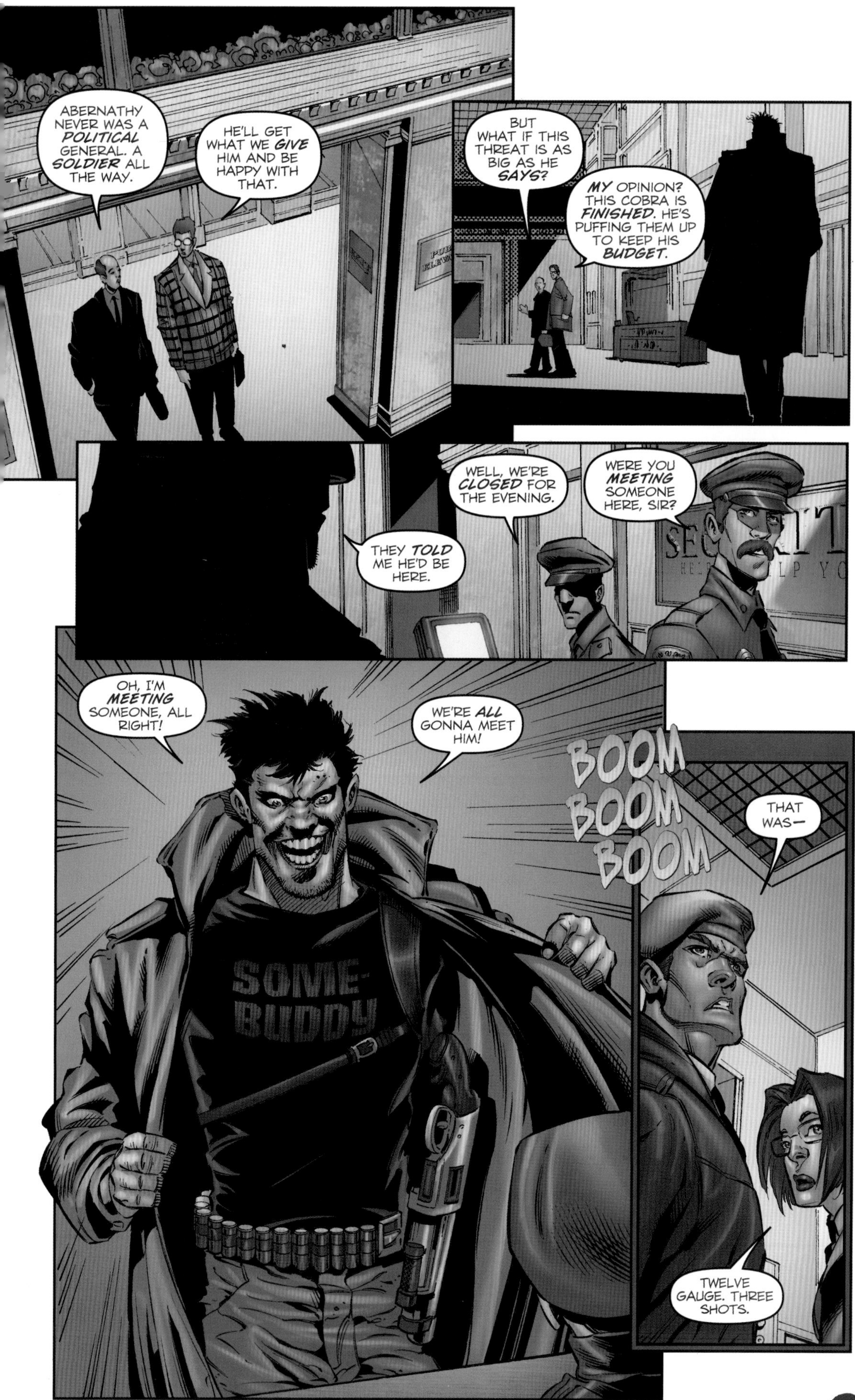
ABERNATHY NEVER WAS A POLITICAL GENERAL. A SOLDIER ALL THE WAY.
HE'LL GET WHAT WE GIVE HIM AND BE HAPPY WITH THAT.
BUT WHAT IF THIS THREAT IS AS BIG AS HE SAYS?
MY OPINION? THIS COBRA IS FINISHED. HE'S PUFFING THEM UP TO KEEP HIS BUDGET.
WELL, WE'RE CLOSED FOR THE EVENING.
WERE YOU MEETING SOMEONE HERE, SIR?
THEY TOLD ME HE'D BE HERE.
OH, I'M MEETING SOMEONE, ALL RIGHT!
WE'RE ALL GONNA MEET HIM!
SOME-BUDDY
BOOM BOOM BOOM
THAT WAS—
TWELVE GAUGE. THREE SHOTS.

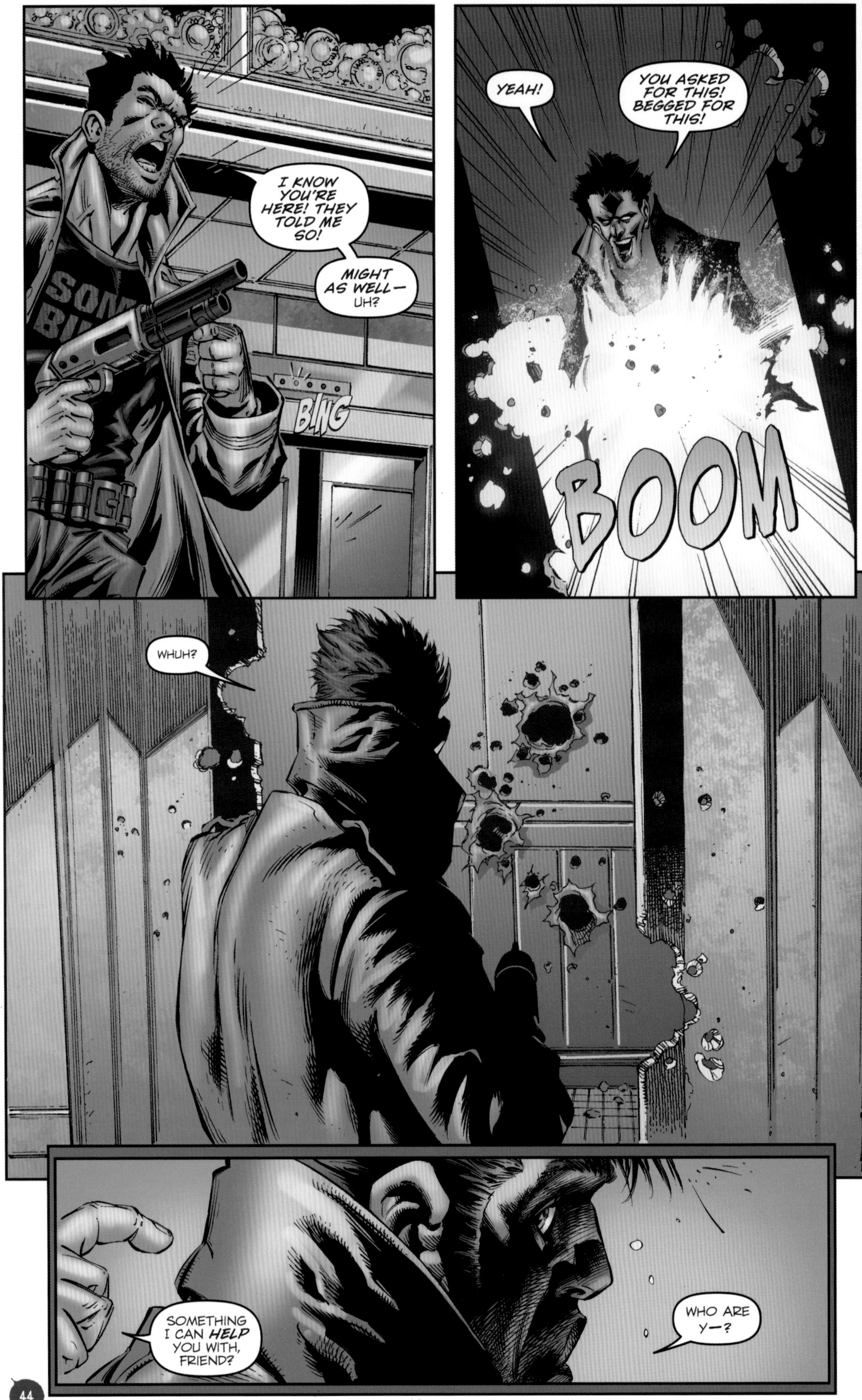
I KNOW YOU'RE HERE! THEY TOLD ME SO!
MIGHT AS WELL— UH?
BING
YEAH!
YOU ASKED FOR THIS! BEGGED FOR THIS!
BOOM
WHUH?
SOMETHING I CAN HELP YOU WITH, FRIEND?
WHO ARE Y—?

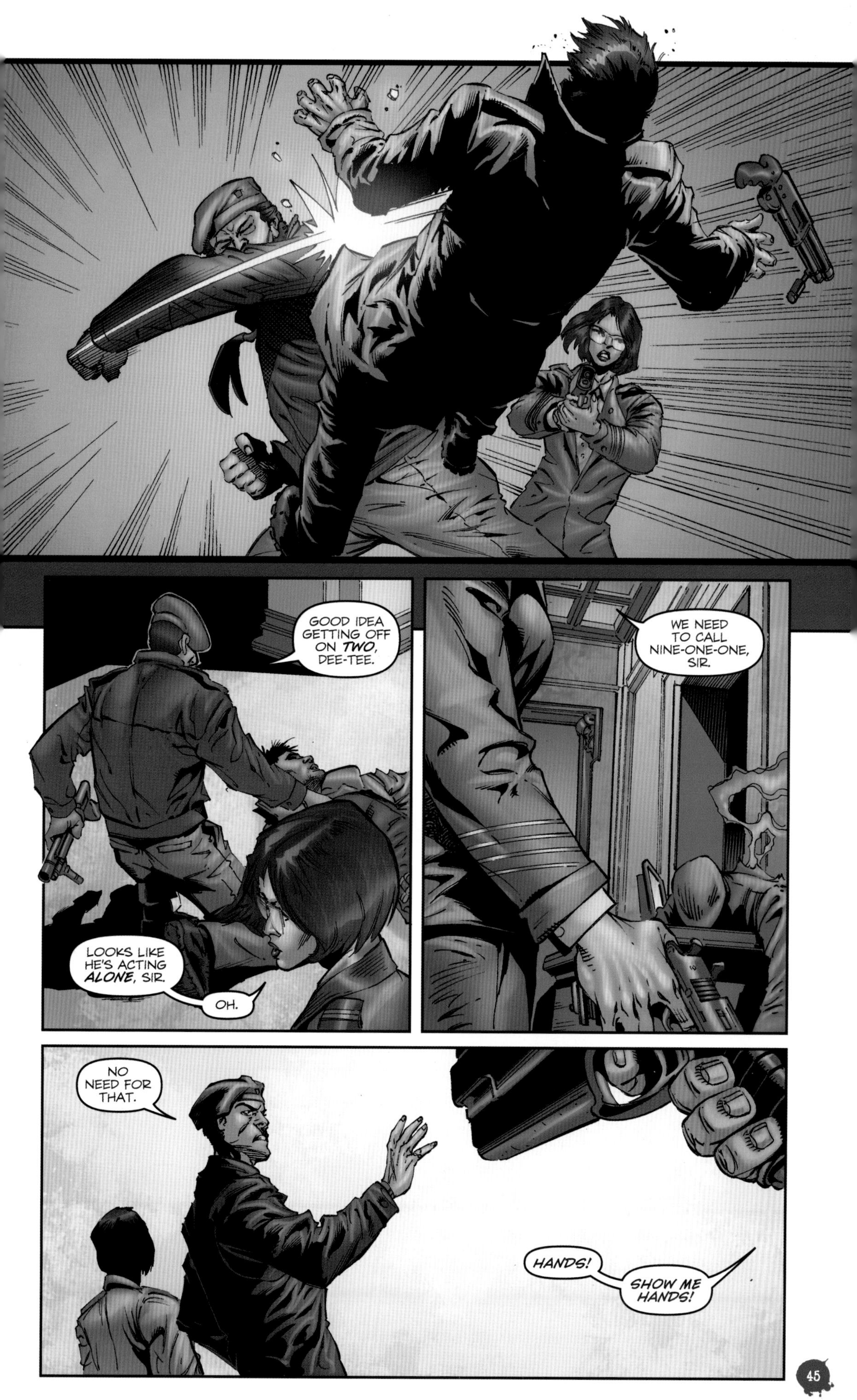
GOOD IDEA GETTING OFF ON TWO, DEE-TEE.
LOOKS LIKE HE'S ACTING ALONE, SIR.
OH.
WE NEED TO CALL NINE-ONE-ONE, SIR.
NO NEED FOR THAT.
HANDS!
SHOW ME HANDS!

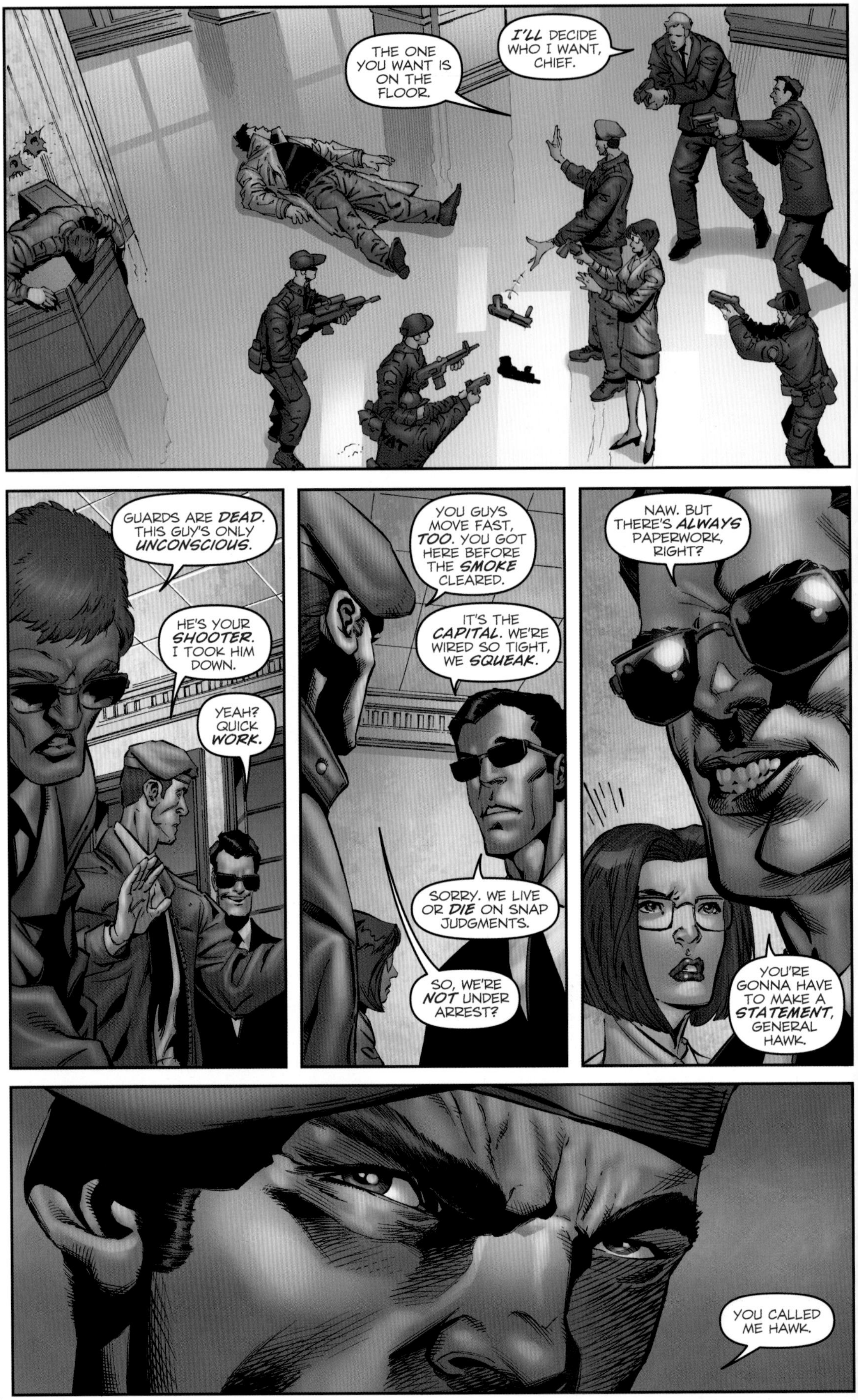
THE ONE YOU WANT IS ON THE FLOOR.
I'LL DECIDE WHO I WANT, CHIEF.
GUARDS ARE *DEAD*. THIS GUY'S ONLY *UNCONSCIOUS*.
HE'S YOUR *SHOOTER*. I TOOK HIM DOWN.
YEAH? QUICK *WORK*.
YOU GUYS MOVE FAST, *TOO*. YOU GOT HERE BEFORE THE *SMOKE* CLEARED.
IT'S THE *CAPITAL*. WE'RE WIRED SO TIGHT, WE *SQUEAK*.
SORRY. WE LIVE OR *DIE* ON SNAP JUDGMENTS.
SO, WE'RE *NOT* UNDER ARREST?
NAW. BUT THERE'S *ALWAYS* PAPERWORK, RIGHT?
YOU'RE GONNA HAVE TO MAKE A *STATEMENT*, GENERAL HAWK.
YOU CALLED ME HAWK.

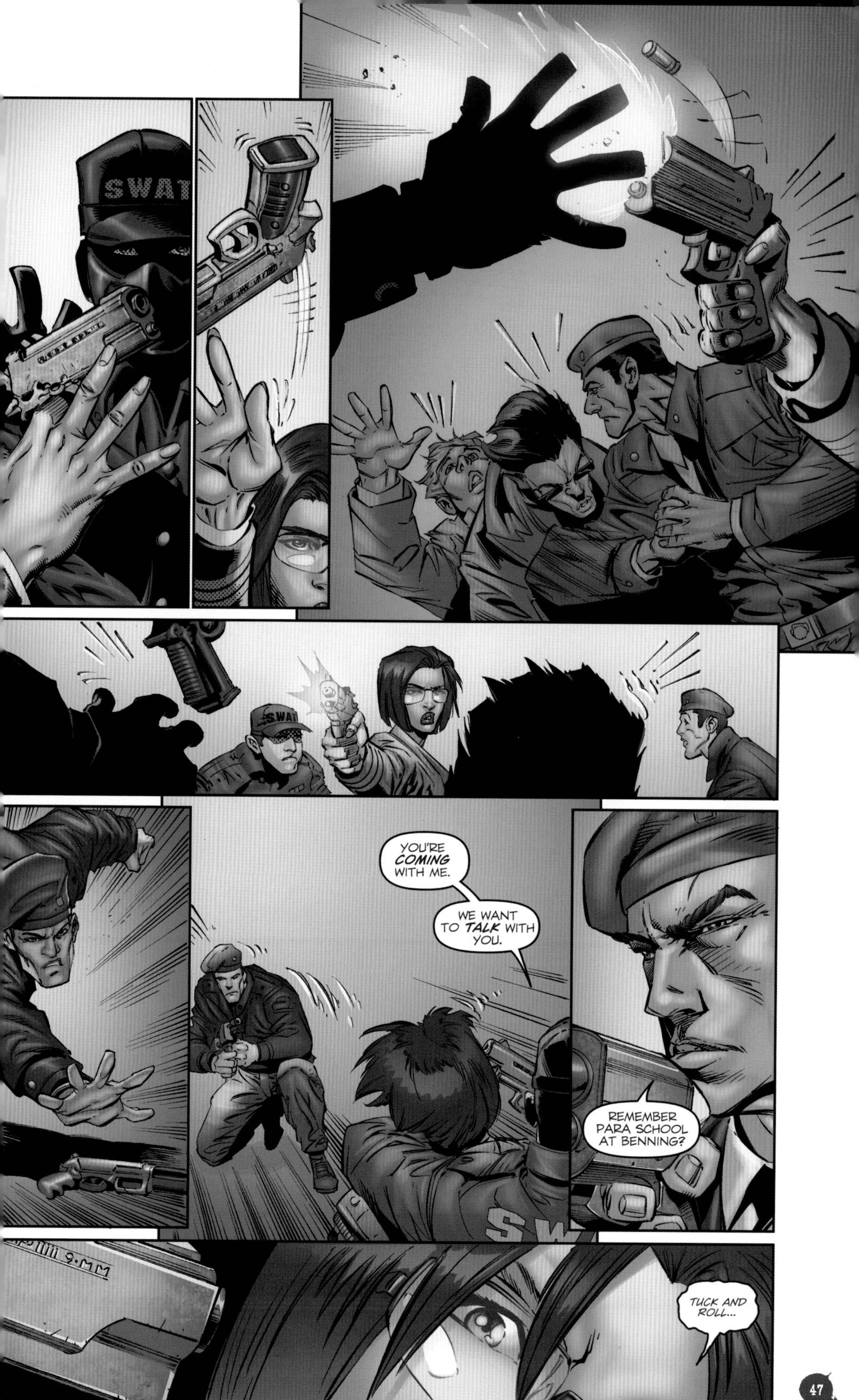
SWAT
YOU'RE COMING WITH ME.
WE WANT TO TALK WITH YOU.
REMEMBER PARA SCHOOL AT BENNING?
9·MM
TUCK AND ROLL...

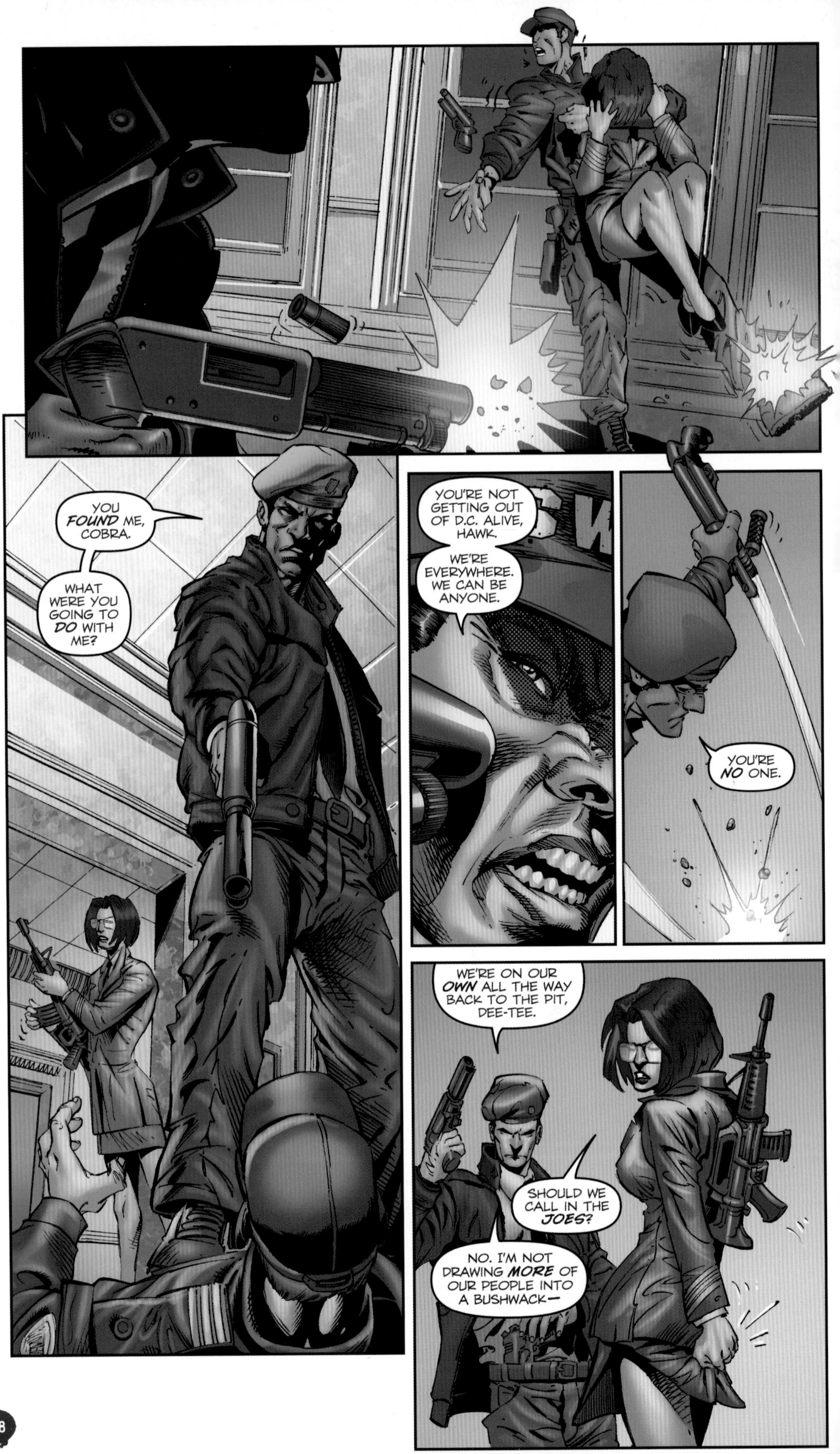

YOU FOUND ME, COBRA.
WHAT WERE YOU GOING TO DO WITH ME?
YOU'RE NOT GETTING OUT OF D.C. ALIVE, HAWK.
WE'RE EVERYWHERE. WE CAN BE ANYONE.
YOU'RE NO ONE.
WE'RE ON OUR OWN ALL THE WAY BACK TO THE PIT, DEE-TEE.
SHOULD WE CALL IN THE JOES?
NO. I'M NOT DRAWING MORE OF OUR PEOPLE INTO A BUSHWACK—

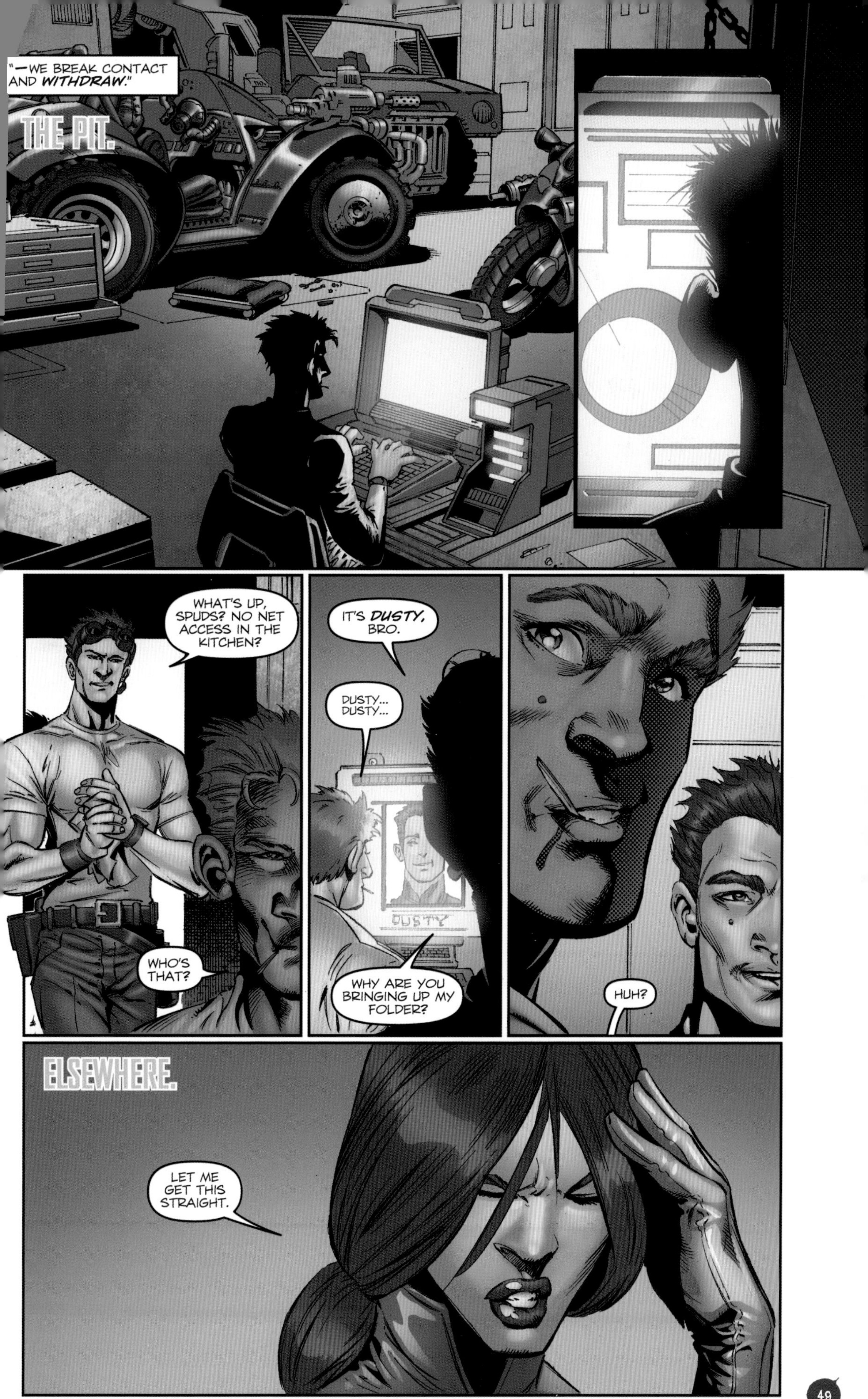
"—WE BREAK CONTACT AND WITHDRAW."
THE PIT.
WHAT'S UP, SPUDS? NO NET ACCESS IN THE KITCHEN?
WHO'S THAT?
IT'S DUSTY, BRO.
DUSTY... DUSTY...
DUSTY
WHY ARE YOU BRINGING UP MY FOLDER?
HUH?
ELSEWHERE.
LET ME GET THIS STRAIGHT.

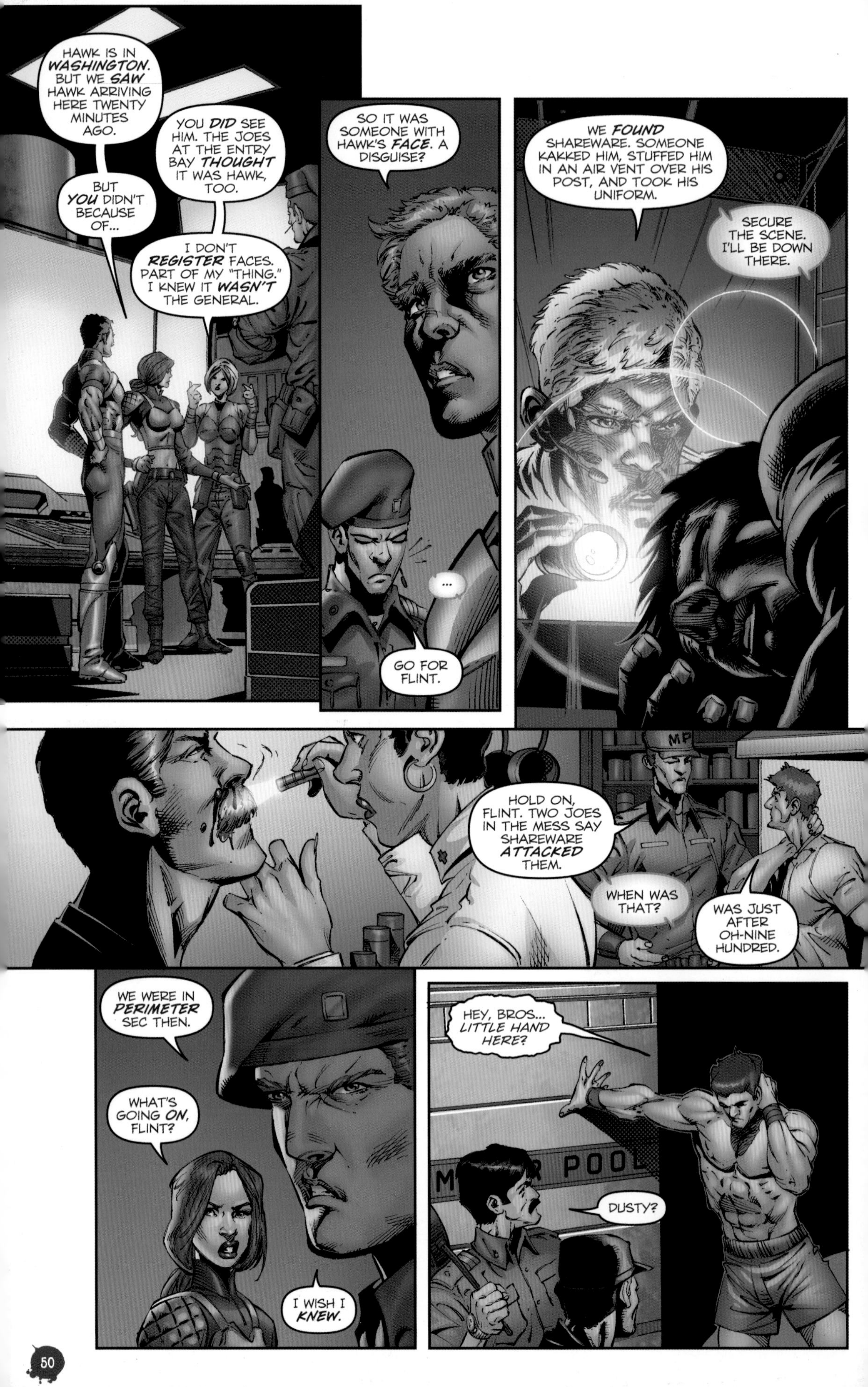
HAWK IS IN WASHINGTON. BUT WE SAW HAWK ARRIVING HERE TWENTY MINUTES AGO.
YOU DID SEE HIM. THE JOES AT THE ENTRY BAY THOUGHT IT WAS HAWK, TOO.
BUT YOU DIDN'T BECAUSE OF...
I DON'T REGISTER FACES. PART OF MY "THING." I KNEW IT WASN'T THE GENERAL.
SO IT WAS SOMEONE WITH HAWK'S FACE. A DISGUISE?
...
GO FOR FLINT.
WE FOUND SHAREWARE. SOMEONE KAKKED HIM, STUFFED HIM IN AN AIR VENT OVER HIS POST, AND TOOK HIS UNIFORM.
SECURE THE SCENE. I'LL BE DOWN THERE.
MP
HOLD ON, FLINT. TWO JOES IN THE MESS SAY SHAREWARE ATTACKED THEM.
WHEN WAS THAT?
WAS JUST AFTER OH-NINE HUNDRED.
WE WERE IN PERIMETER SEC THEN.
WHAT'S GOING ON, FLINT?
I WISH I KNEW.
HEY, BROS... LITTLE HAND HERE?
DUSTY?

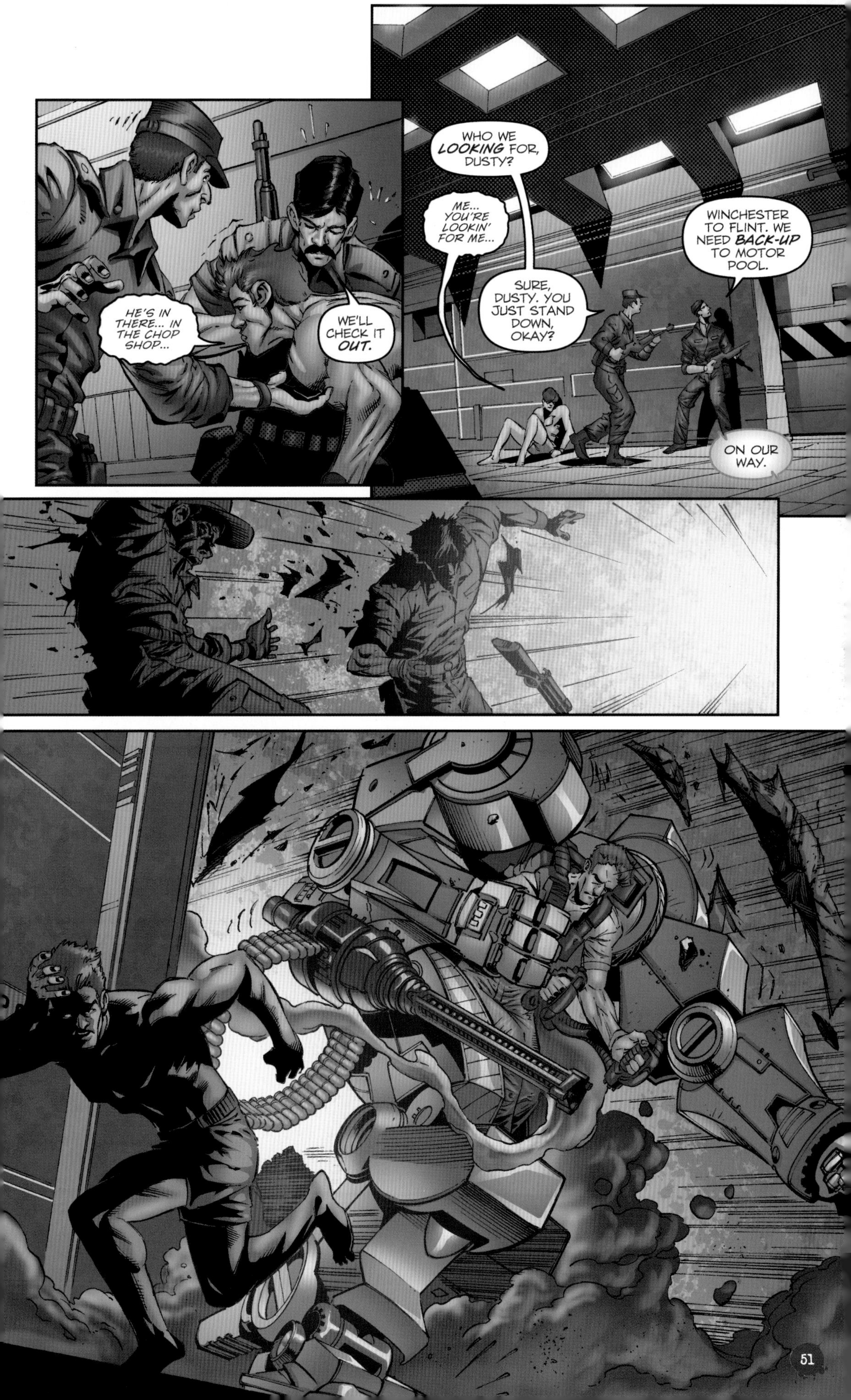
HE'S IN THERE... IN THE CHOP SHOP...
WE'LL CHECK IT OUT.
WHO WE LOOKING FOR, DUSTY?
ME... YOU'RE LOOKIN' FOR ME...
SURE, DUSTY. YOU JUST STAND DOWN, OKAY?
WINCHESTER TO FLINT. WE NEED BACK-UP TO MOTOR POOL.
ON OUR WAY.

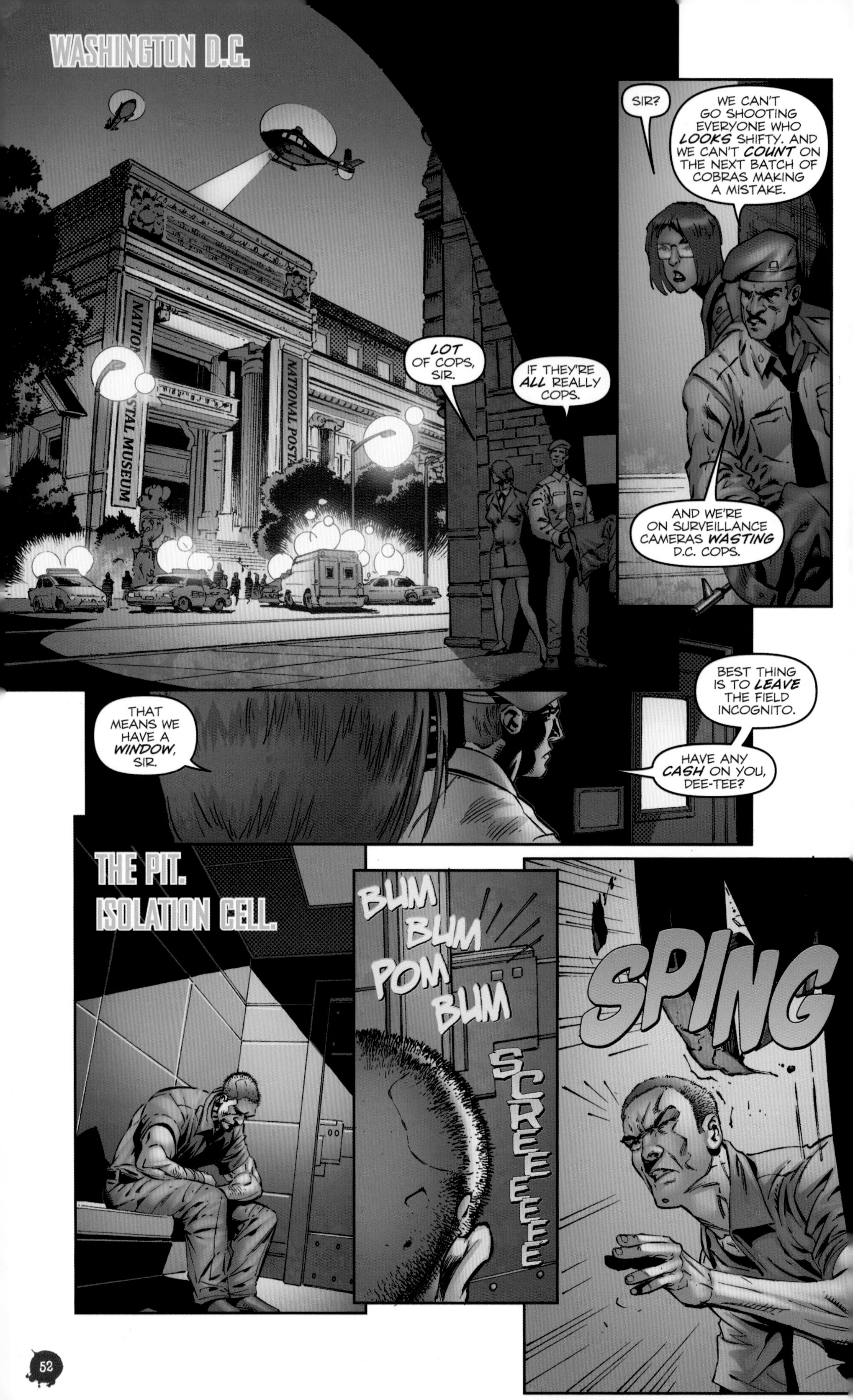
WASHINGTON D.C.
NATIONAL POSTAL MUSEUM
LOT OF COPS, SIR.
IF THEY'RE ALL REALLY COPS.
SIR?
WE CAN'T GO SHOOTING EVERYONE WHO LOOKS SHIFTY. AND WE CAN'T COUNT ON THE NEXT BATCH OF COBRAS MAKING A MISTAKE.
AND WE'RE ON SURVEILLANCE CAMERAS WASTING D.C. COPS.
THAT MEANS WE HAVE A WINDOW, SIR.
BEST THING IS TO LEAVE THE FIELD INCOGNITO.
HAVE ANY CASH ON YOU, DEE-TEE?
THE PIT. ISOLATION CELL.
BUM BUM POM BUM
SCREEEEEE
SPING

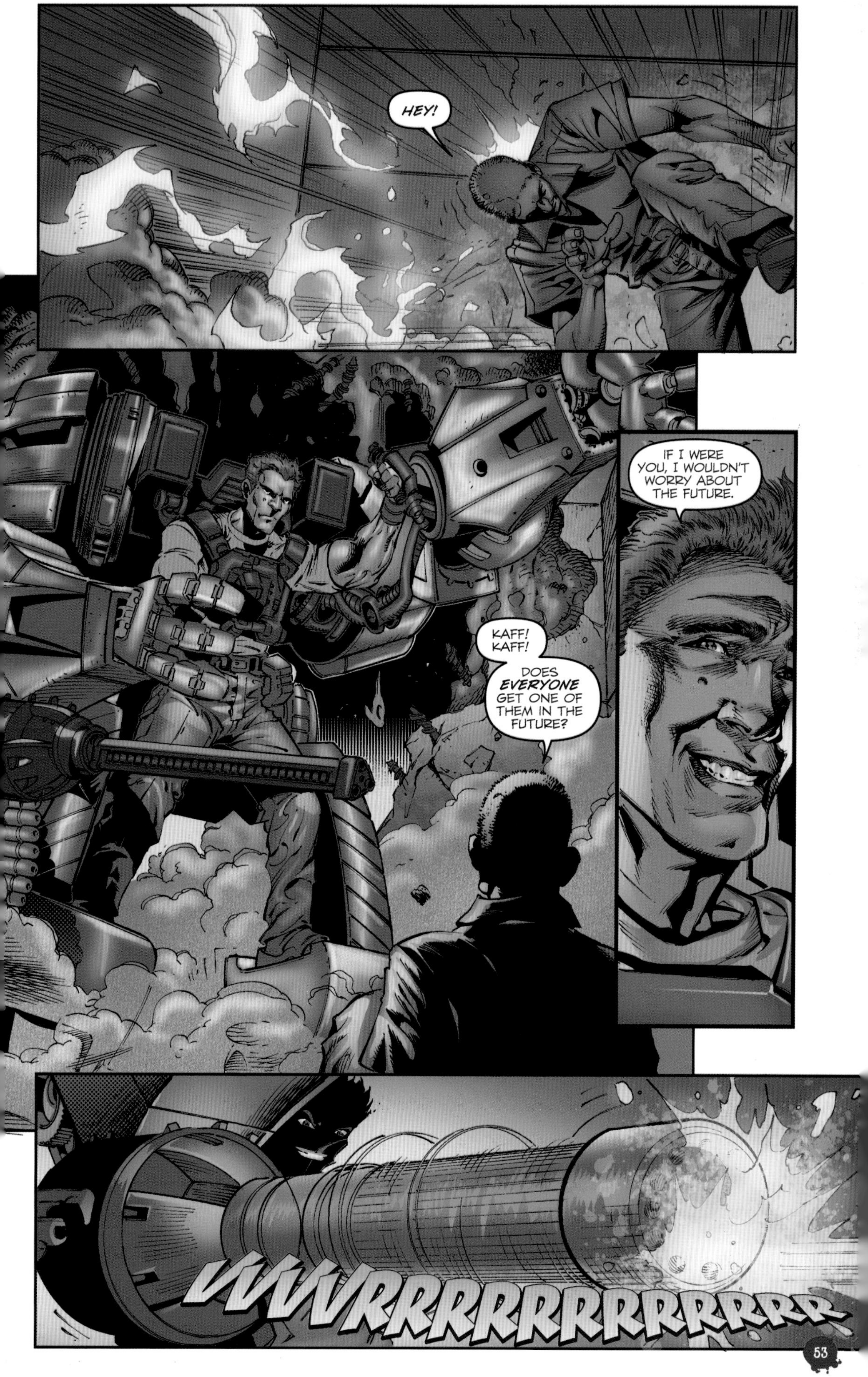
HEY!
IF I WERE YOU, I WOULDN'T WORRY ABOUT THE FUTURE.
KAFF! KAFF!
DOES EVERYONE GET ONE OF THEM IN THE FUTURE?
VVVRRRRRRRRRRRRR

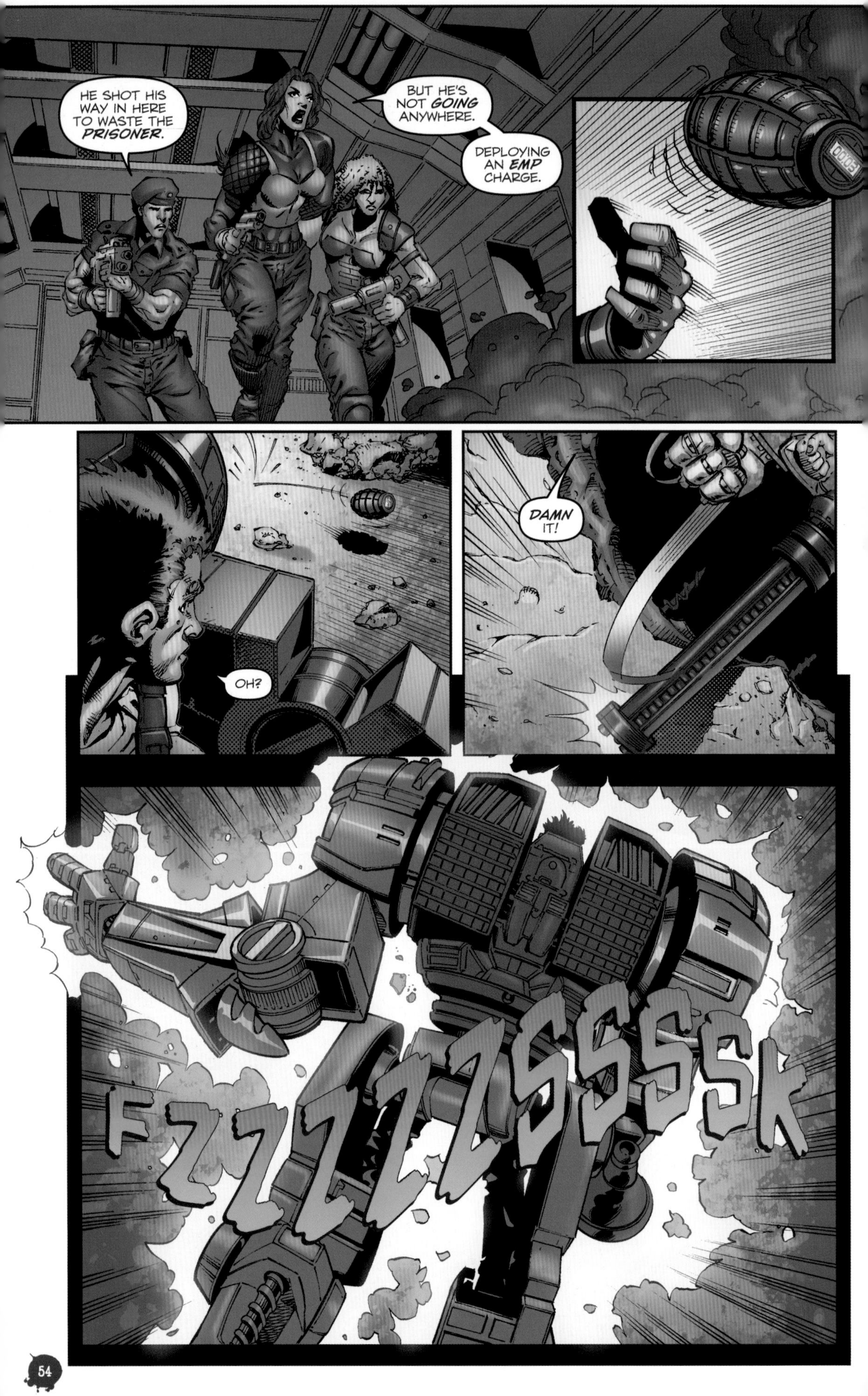
HE SHOT HIS WAY IN HERE TO WASTE THE PRISONER.
BUT HE'S NOT GOING ANYWHERE.
DEPLOYING AN EMP CHARGE.
OH?
DAMN IT!
FZZZZZSSSSSK

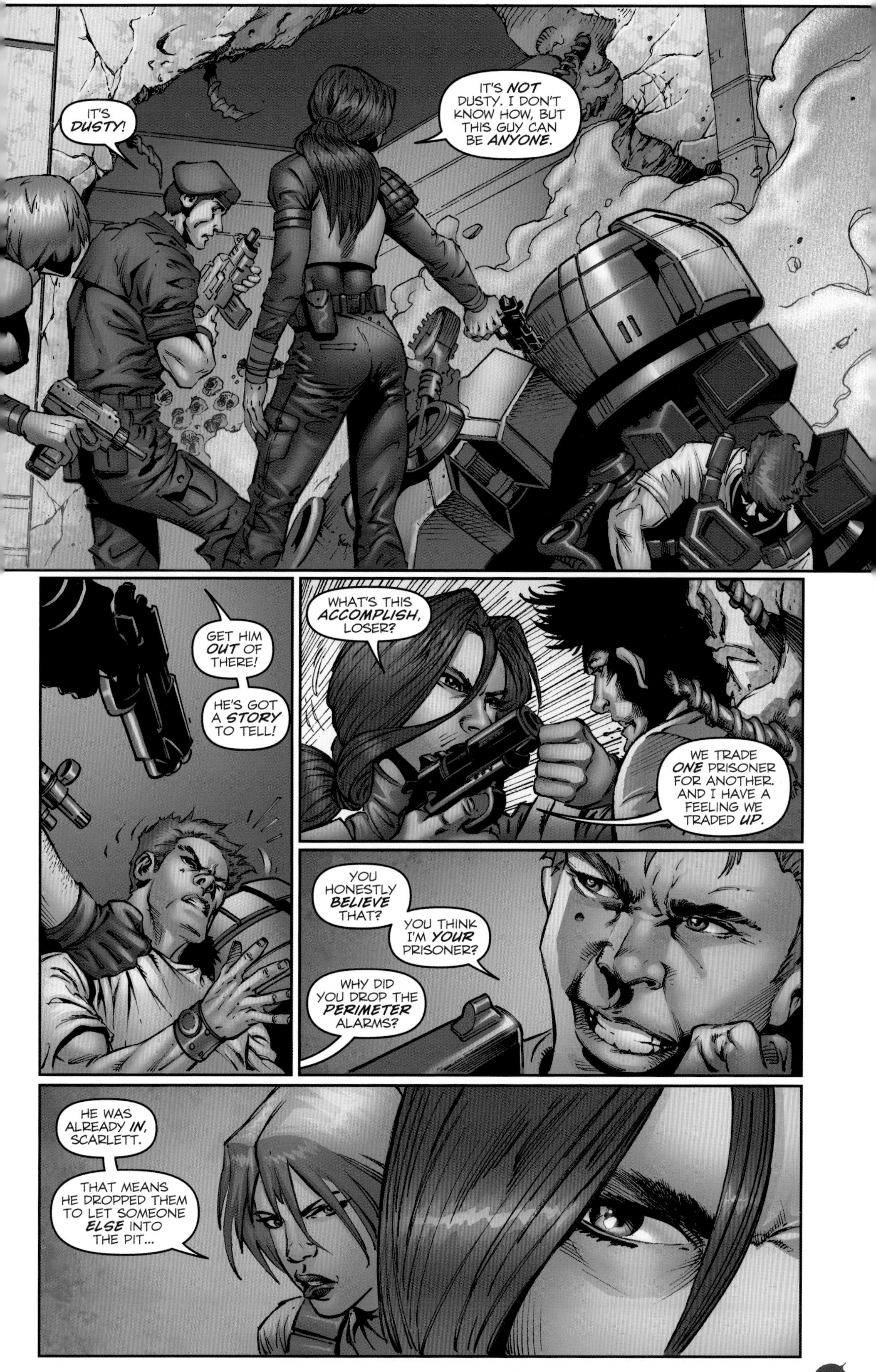

IT'S DUSTY!
IT'S NOT DUSTY. I DON'T KNOW HOW, BUT THIS GUY CAN BE ANYONE.
GET HIM OUT OF THERE!
HE'S GOT A STORY TO TELL!
WHAT'S THIS ACCOMPLISH, LOSER?
WE TRADE ONE PRISONER FOR ANOTHER. AND I HAVE A FEELING WE TRADED UP.
YOU HONESTLY BELIEVE THAT?
YOU THINK I'M YOUR PRISONER?
WHY DID YOU DROP THE PERIMETER ALARMS?
HE WAS ALREADY IN, SCARLETT.
THAT MEANS HE DROPPED THEM TO LET SOMEONE ELSE INTO THE PIT...

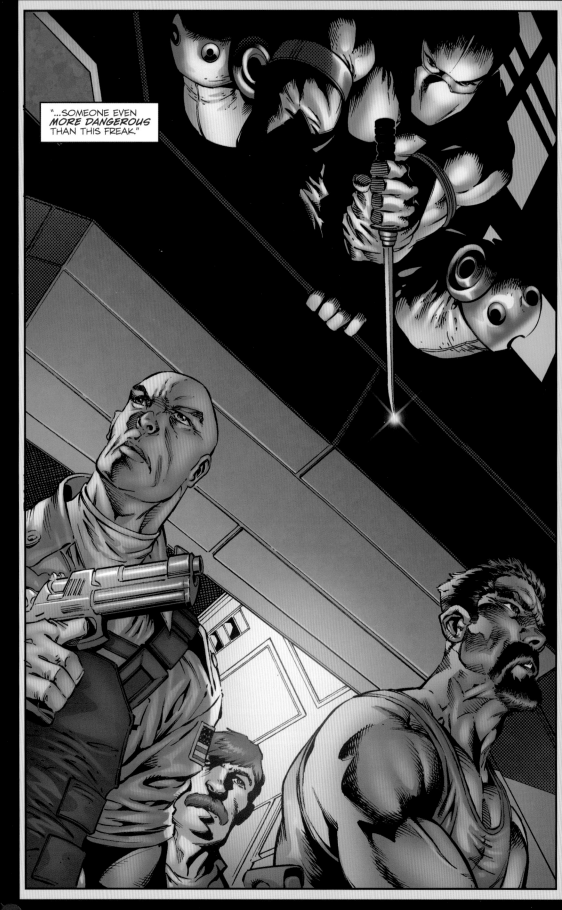

"...SOMEONE EVEN *MORE DANGEROUS* THAN THIS FREAK."

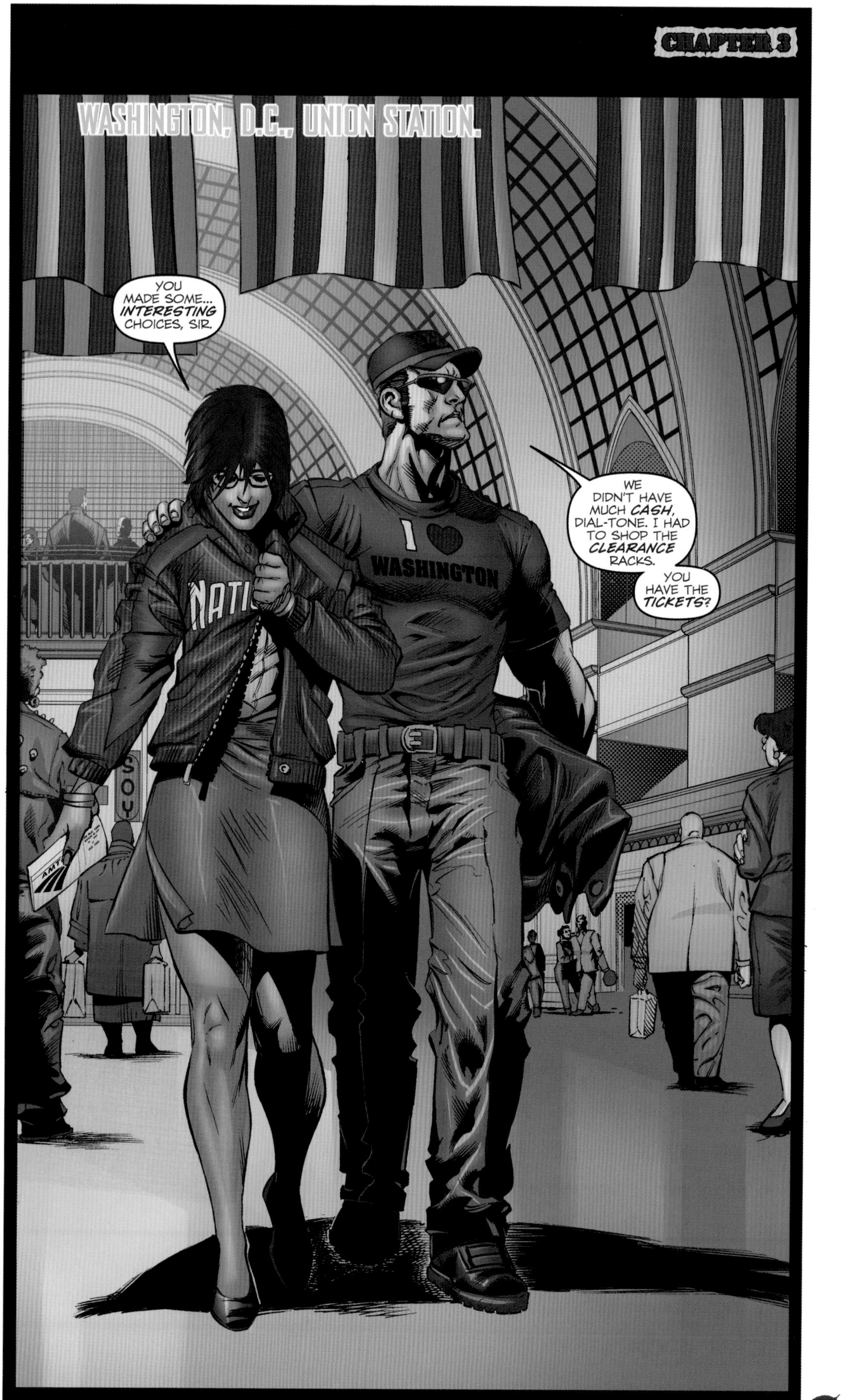
CHAPTER 3
WASHINGTON, D.C., UNION STATION.
YOU MADE SOME... INTERESTING CHOICES, SIR.
WE DIDN'T HAVE MUCH CASH, DIAL-TONE. I HAD TO SHOP THE CLEARANCE RACKS.
YOU HAVE THE TICKETS?
I ♥ WASHINGTON

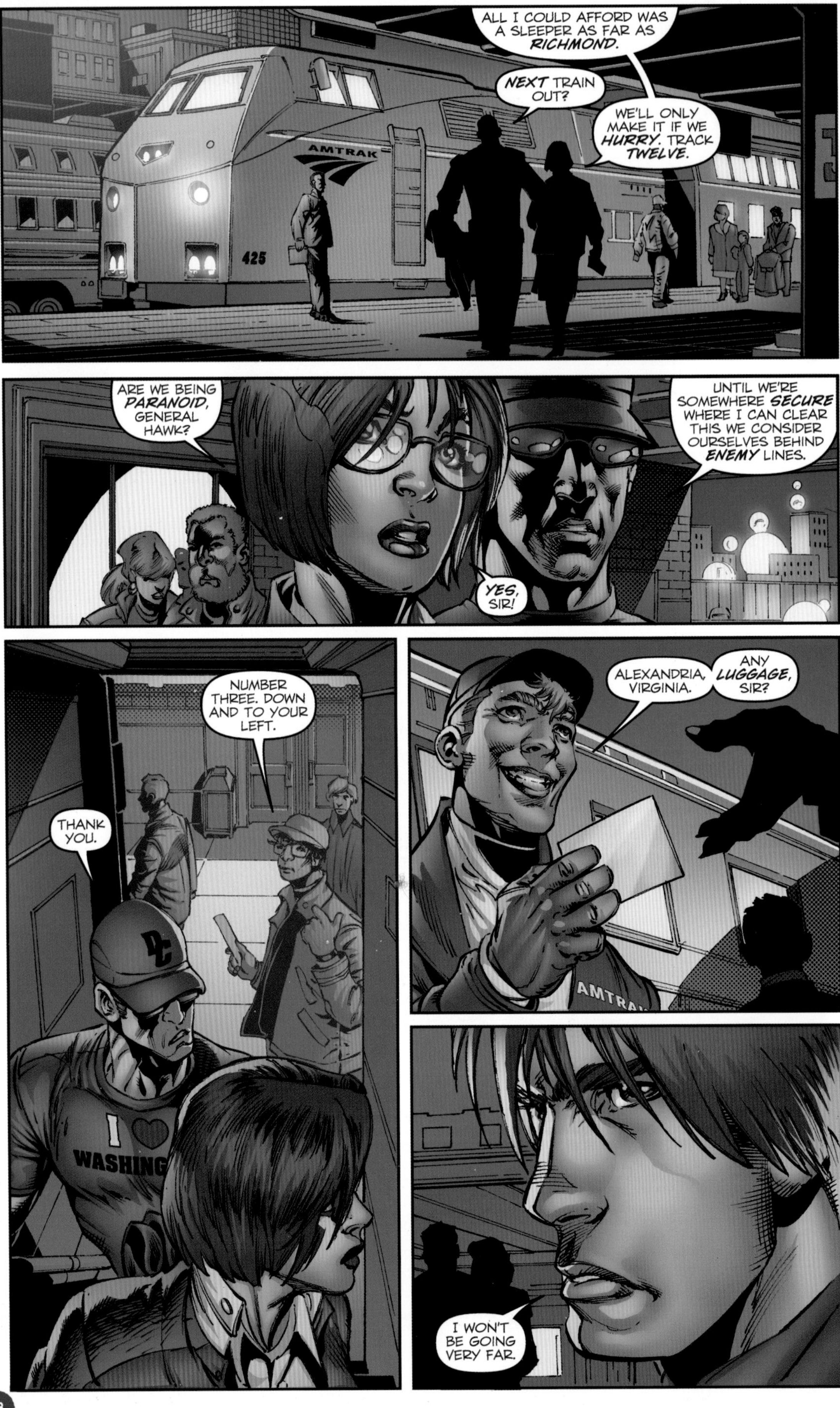
ALL I COULD AFFORD WAS A SLEEPER AS FAR AS RICHMOND.
NEXT TRAIN OUT?
WE'LL ONLY MAKE IT IF WE HURRY. TRACK TWELVE.
AMTRAK
425
ARE WE BEING PARANOID, GENERAL HAWK?
UNTIL WE'RE SOMEWHERE SECURE WHERE I CAN CLEAR THIS WE CONSIDER OURSELVES BEHIND ENEMY LINES.
YES, SIR!
NUMBER THREE. DOWN AND TO YOUR LEFT.
THANK YOU.
DC
I WASHING
ALEXANDRIA, VIRGINIA.
ANY LUGGAGE, SIR?
AMTRAK
I WON'T BE GOING VERY FAR.

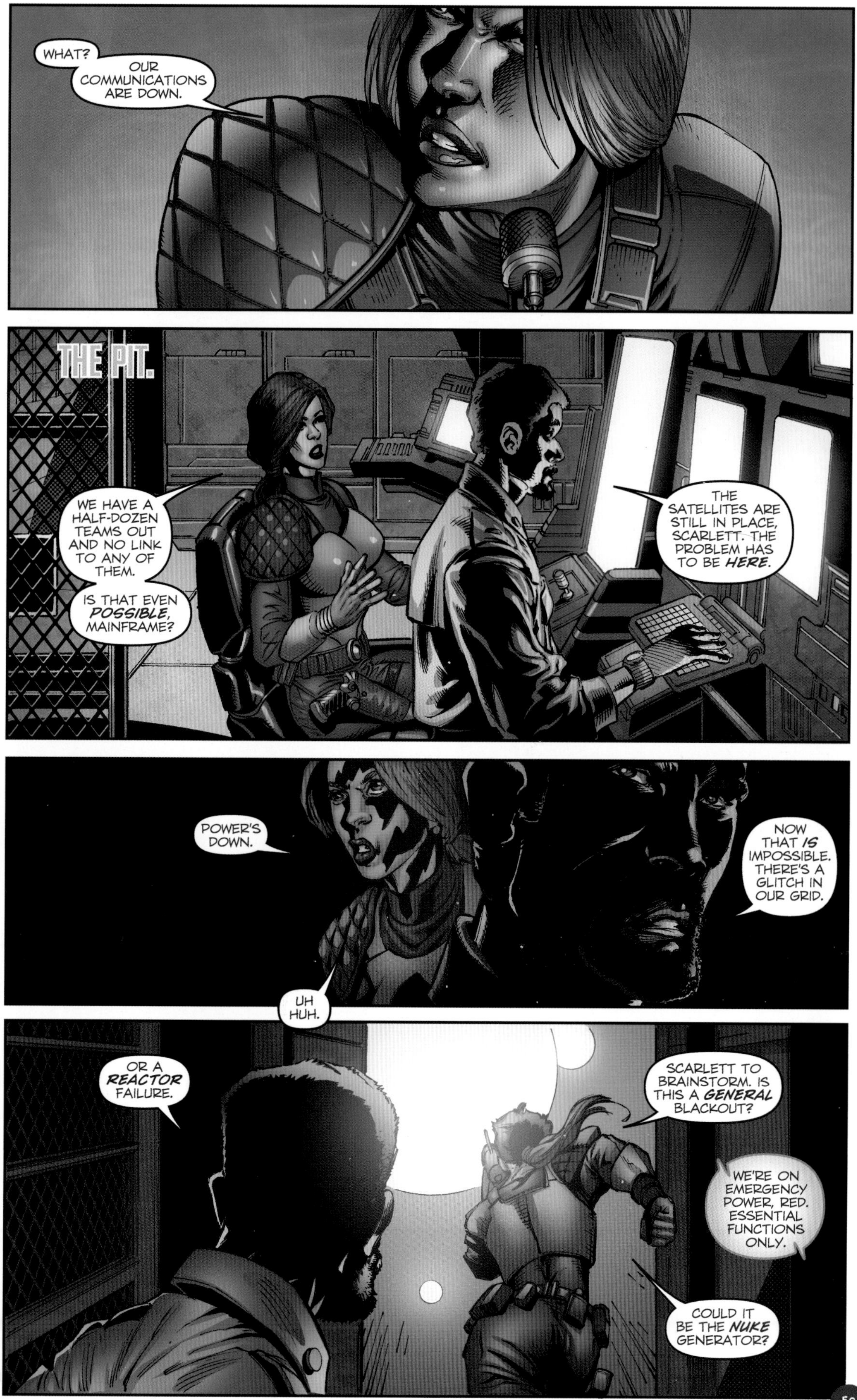
WHAT?
OUR COMMUNICATIONS ARE DOWN.
THE PIT.
WE HAVE A HALF-DOZEN TEAMS OUT AND NO LINK TO ANY OF THEM.
IS THAT EVEN POSSIBLE, MAINFRAME?
THE SATELLITES ARE STILL IN PLACE, SCARLETT. THE PROBLEM HAS TO BE HERE.
POWER'S DOWN.
NOW THAT IS IMPOSSIBLE. THERE'S A GLITCH IN OUR GRID.
UH HUH.
OR A REACTOR FAILURE.
SCARLETT TO BRAINSTORM. IS THIS A GENERAL BLACKOUT?
WE'RE ON EMERGENCY POWER, RED. ESSENTIAL FUNCTIONS ONLY.
COULD IT BE THE NUKE GENERATOR?

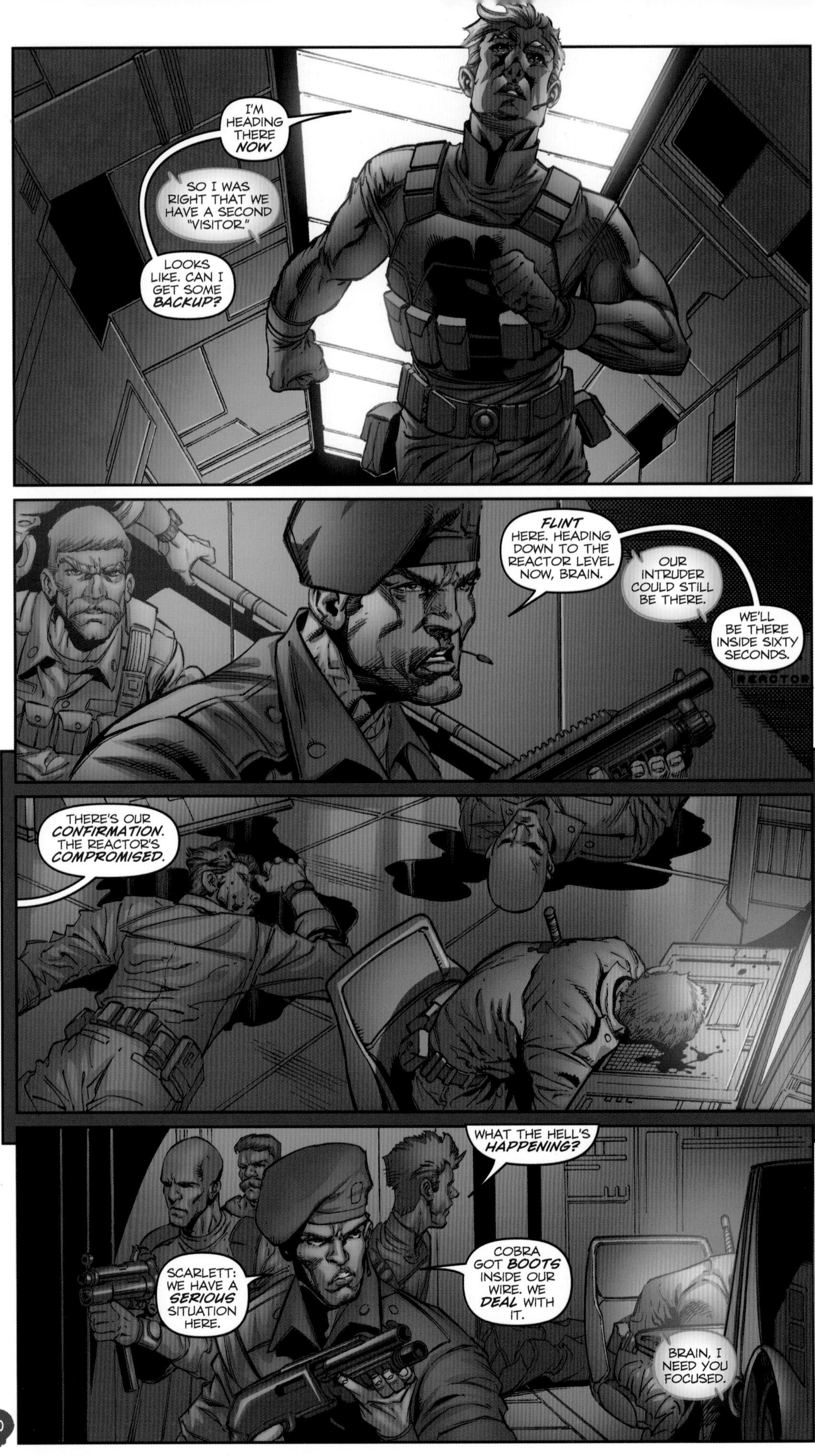
I'M HEADING THERE NOW.
SO I WAS RIGHT THAT WE HAVE A SECOND "VISITOR."
LOOKS LIKE. CAN I GET SOME BACKUP?
FLINT HERE. HEADING DOWN TO THE REACTOR LEVEL NOW, BRAIN.
OUR INTRUDER COULD STILL BE THERE.
WE'LL BE THERE INSIDE SIXTY SECONDS.
REACTOR
THERE'S OUR CONFIRMATION. THE REACTOR'S COMPROMISED.
WHAT THE HELL'S HAPPENING?
SCARLETT: WE HAVE A SERIOUS SITUATION HERE.
COBRA GOT BOOTS INSIDE OUR WIRE. WE DEAL WITH IT.
BRAIN, I NEED YOU FOCUSED.

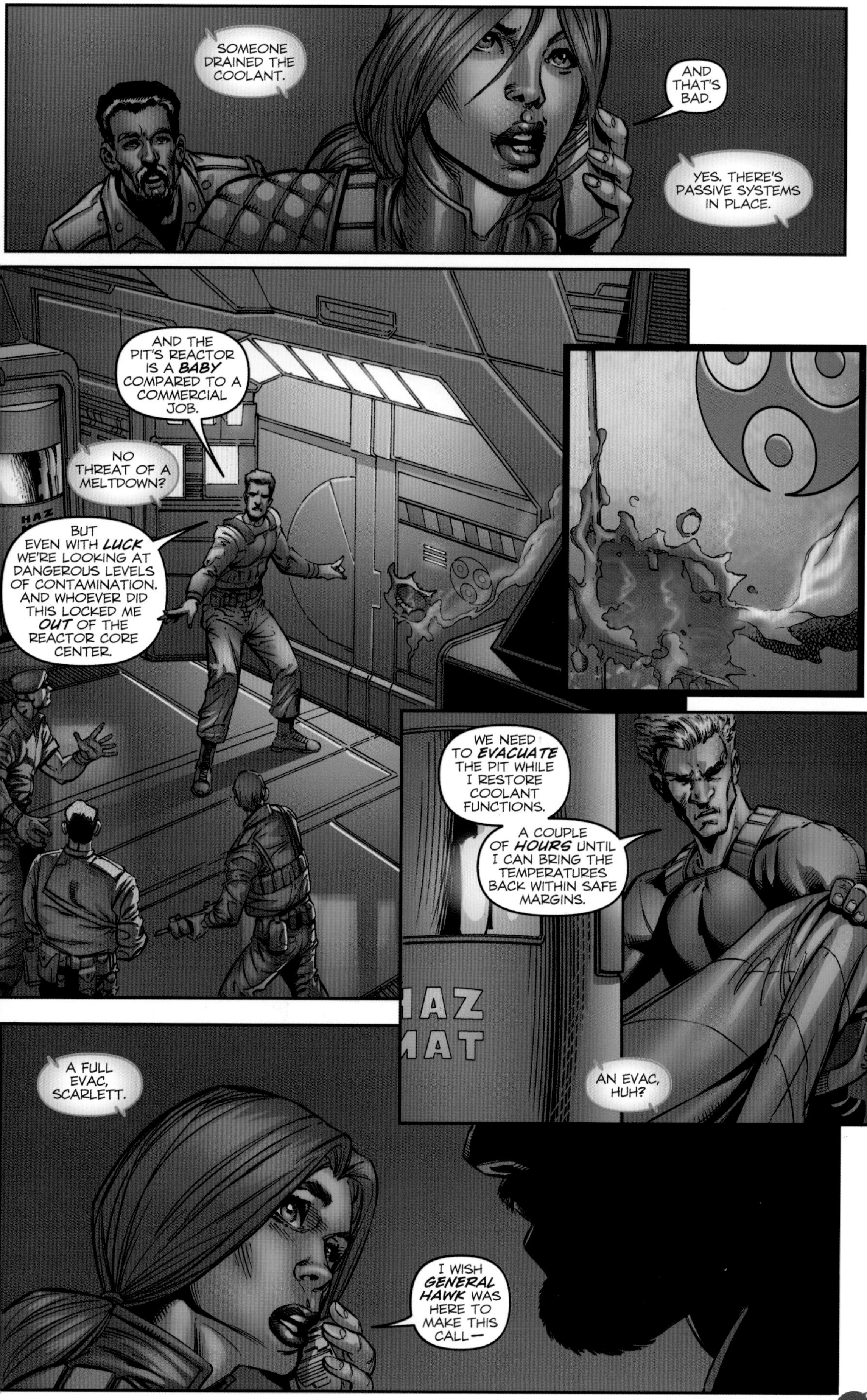
SOMEONE DRAINED THE COOLANT.
AND THAT'S BAD.
YES. THERE'S PASSIVE SYSTEMS IN PLACE.
AND THE PIT'S REACTOR IS A BABY COMPARED TO A COMMERCIAL JOB.
NO THREAT OF A MELTDOWN?
BUT EVEN WITH LUCK WE'RE LOOKING AT DANGEROUS LEVELS OF CONTAMINATION. AND WHOEVER DID THIS LOCKED ME OUT OF THE REACTOR CORE CENTER.
HAZ
WE NEED TO EVACUATE THE PIT WHILE I RESTORE COOLANT FUNCTIONS.
A COUPLE OF HOURS UNTIL I CAN BRING THE TEMPERATURES BACK WITHIN SAFE MARGINS.
HAZ MAT
AN EVAC, HUH?
A FULL EVAC, SCARLETT.
I WISH GENERAL HAWK WAS HERE TO MAKE THIS CALL—

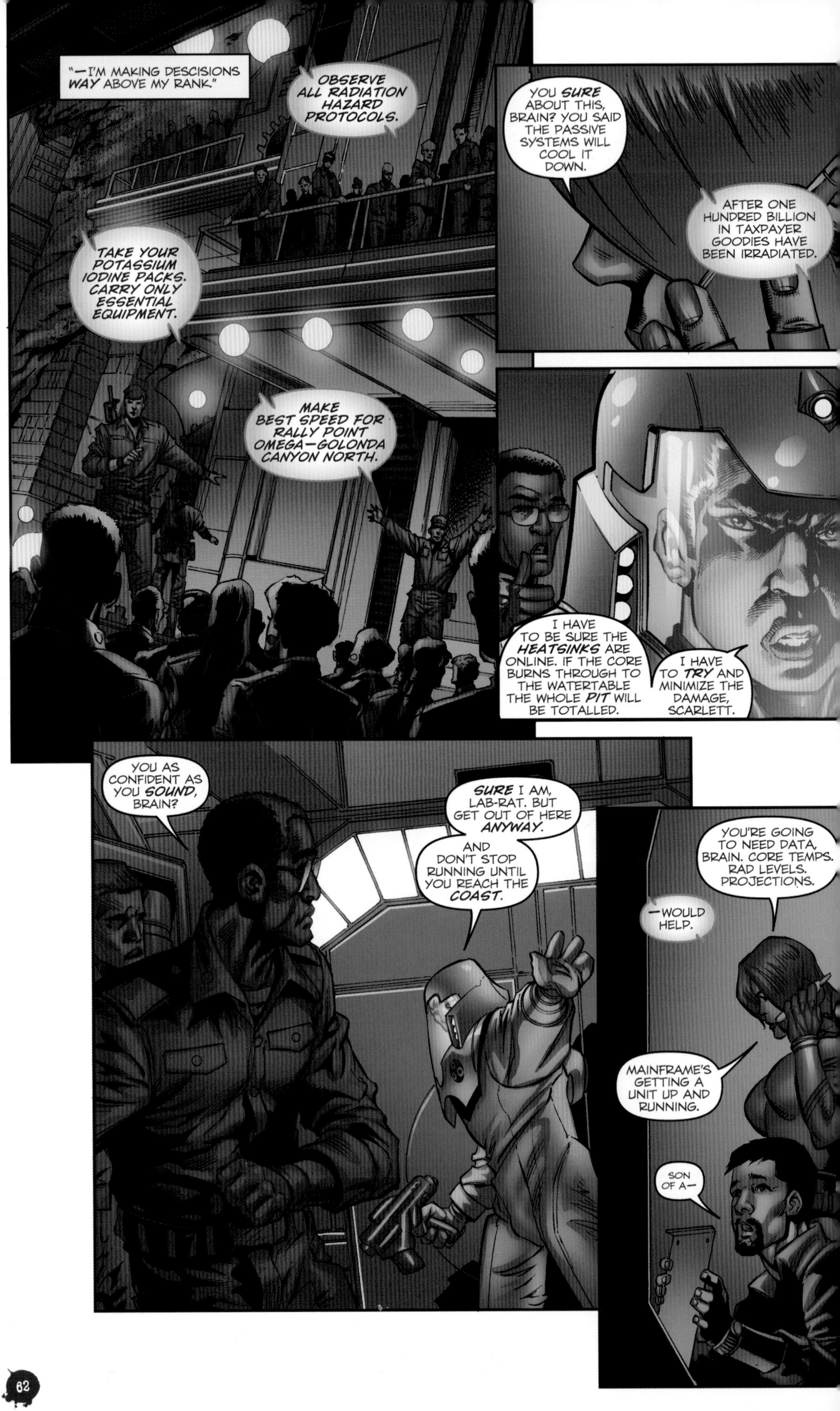

"—I'M MAKING DESCISIONS WAY ABOVE MY RANK."
OBSERVE ALL RADIATION HAZARD PROTOCOLS.
TAKE YOUR POTASSIUM IODINE PACKS. CARRY ONLY ESSENTIAL EQUIPMENT.
MAKE BEST SPEED FOR RALLY POINT OMEGA—GOLONDA CANYON NORTH.
YOU SURE ABOUT THIS, BRAIN? YOU SAID THE PASSIVE SYSTEMS WILL COOL IT DOWN.
AFTER ONE HUNDRED BILLION IN TAXPAYER GOODIES HAVE BEEN IRRADIATED.
I HAVE TO BE SURE THE HEATSINKS ARE ONLINE. IF THE CORE BURNS THROUGH TO THE WATERTABLE THE WHOLE PIT WILL BE TOTALLED.
I HAVE TO TRY AND MINIMIZE THE DAMAGE, SCARLETT.
YOU AS CONFIDENT AS YOU SOUND, BRAIN?
SURE I AM, LAB-RAT. BUT GET OUT OF HERE ANYWAY.
AND DON'T STOP RUNNING UNTIL YOU REACH THE COAST.
YOU'RE GOING TO NEED DATA, BRAIN. CORE TEMPS. RAD LEVELS. PROJECTIONS.
—WOULD HELP.
MAINFRAME'S GETTING A UNIT UP AND RUNNING.
SON OF A—

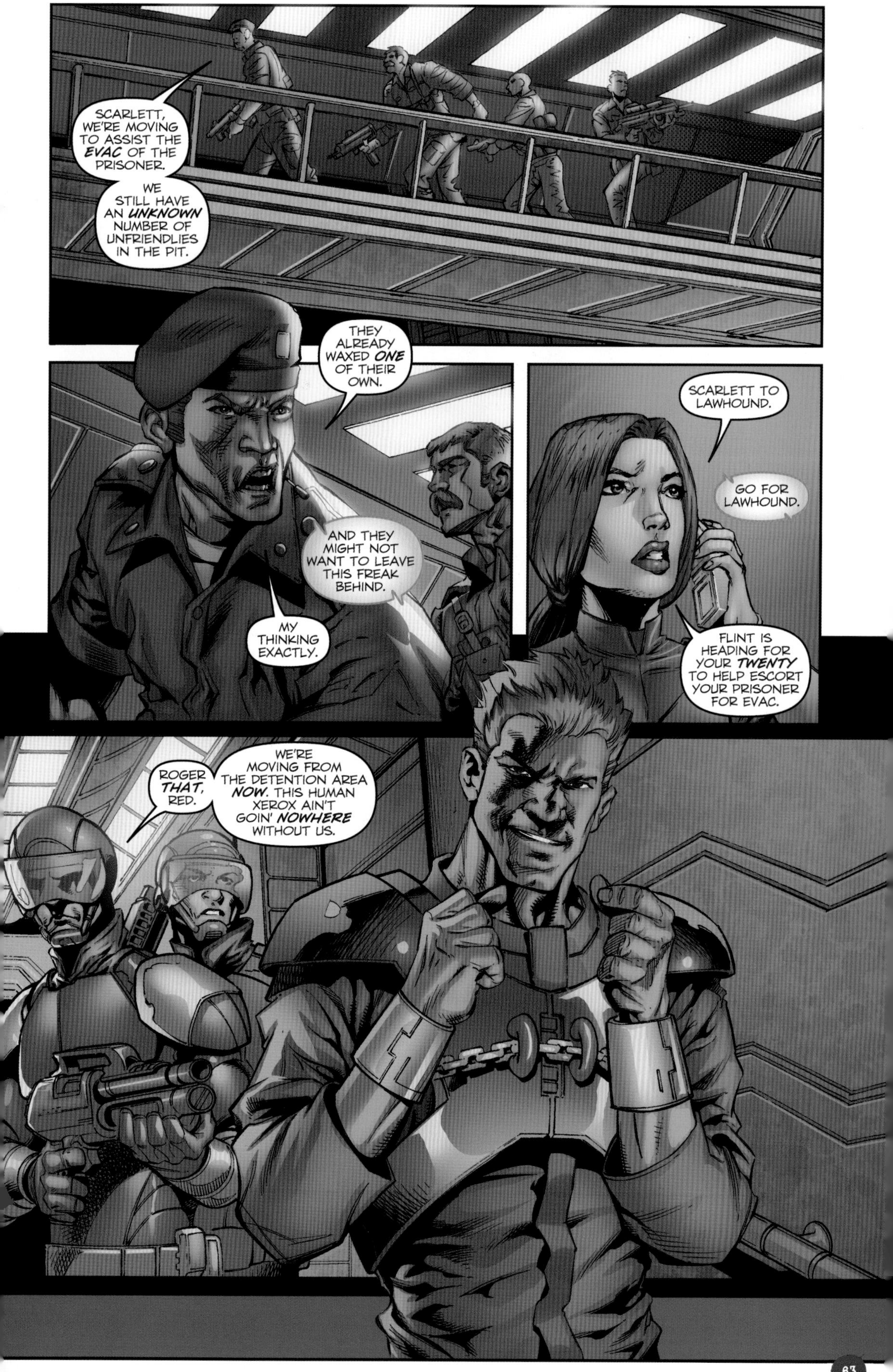
SCARLETT, WE'RE MOVING TO ASSIST THE EVAC OF THE PRISONER.
WE STILL HAVE AN UNKNOWN NUMBER OF UNFRIENDLIES IN THE PIT.
THEY ALREADY WAXED ONE OF THEIR OWN.
AND THEY MIGHT NOT WANT TO LEAVE THIS FREAK BEHIND.
MY THINKING EXACTLY.
SCARLETT TO LAWHOUND.
GO FOR LAWHOUND.
FLINT IS HEADING FOR YOUR TWENTY TO HELP ESCORT YOUR PRISONER FOR EVAC.
ROGER THAT, RED.
WE'RE MOVING FROM THE DETENTION AREA NOW. THIS HUMAN XEROX AIN'T GOIN' NOWHERE WITHOUT US.

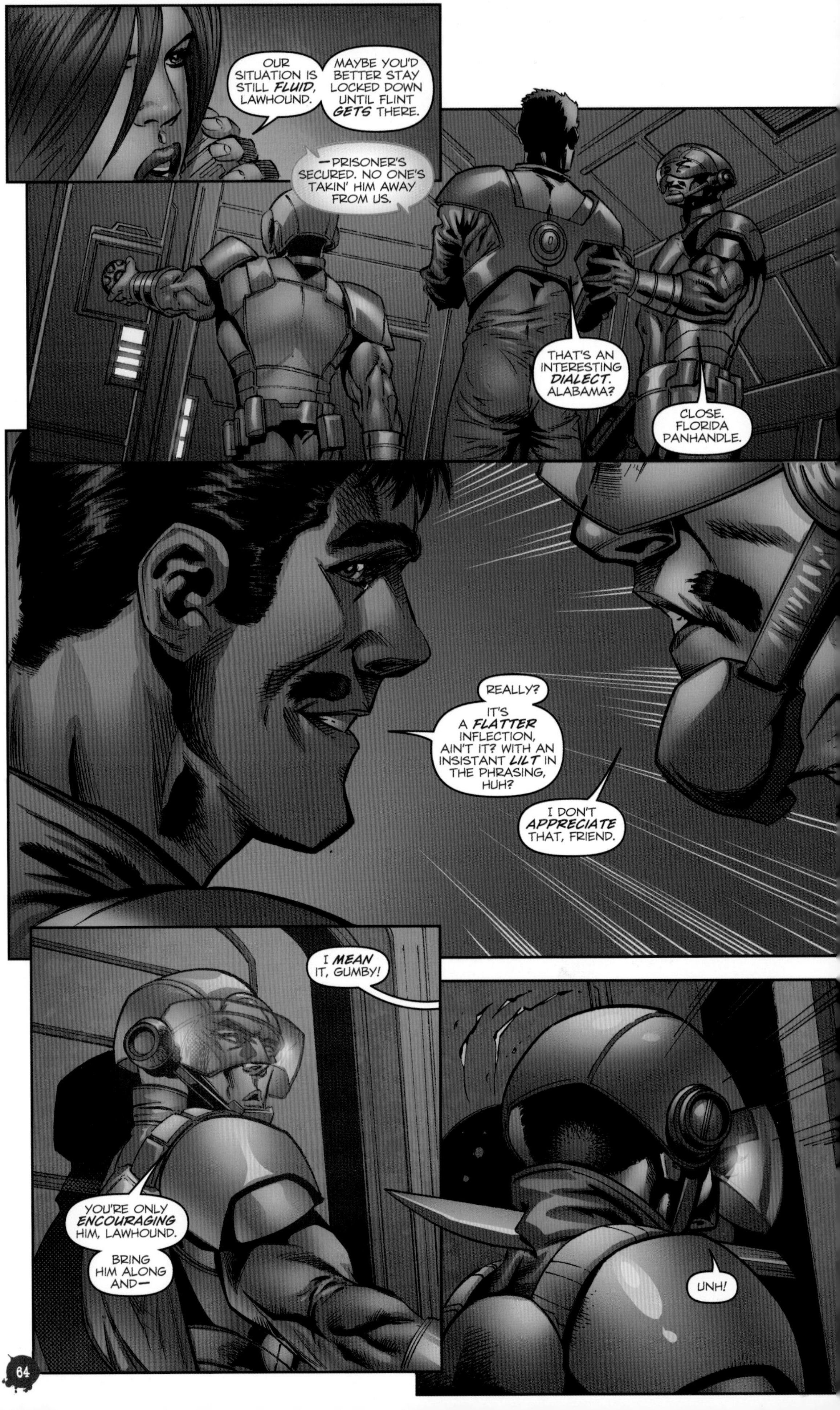
OUR SITUATION IS STILL FLUID, LAWHOUND.
MAYBE YOU'D BETTER STAY LOCKED DOWN UNTIL FLINT GETS THERE.
—PRISONER'S SECURED. NO ONE'S TAKIN' HIM AWAY FROM US.
THAT'S AN INTERESTING DIALECT. ALABAMA?
CLOSE. FLORIDA PANHANDLE.
REALLY? IT'S A FLATTER INFLECTION, AIN'T IT? WITH AN INSISTANT LILT IN THE PHRASING, HUH?
I DON'T APPRECIATE THAT, FRIEND.
I MEAN IT, GUMBY!
YOU'RE ONLY ENCOURAGING HIM, LAWHOUND.
BRING HIM ALONG AND—
UNH!

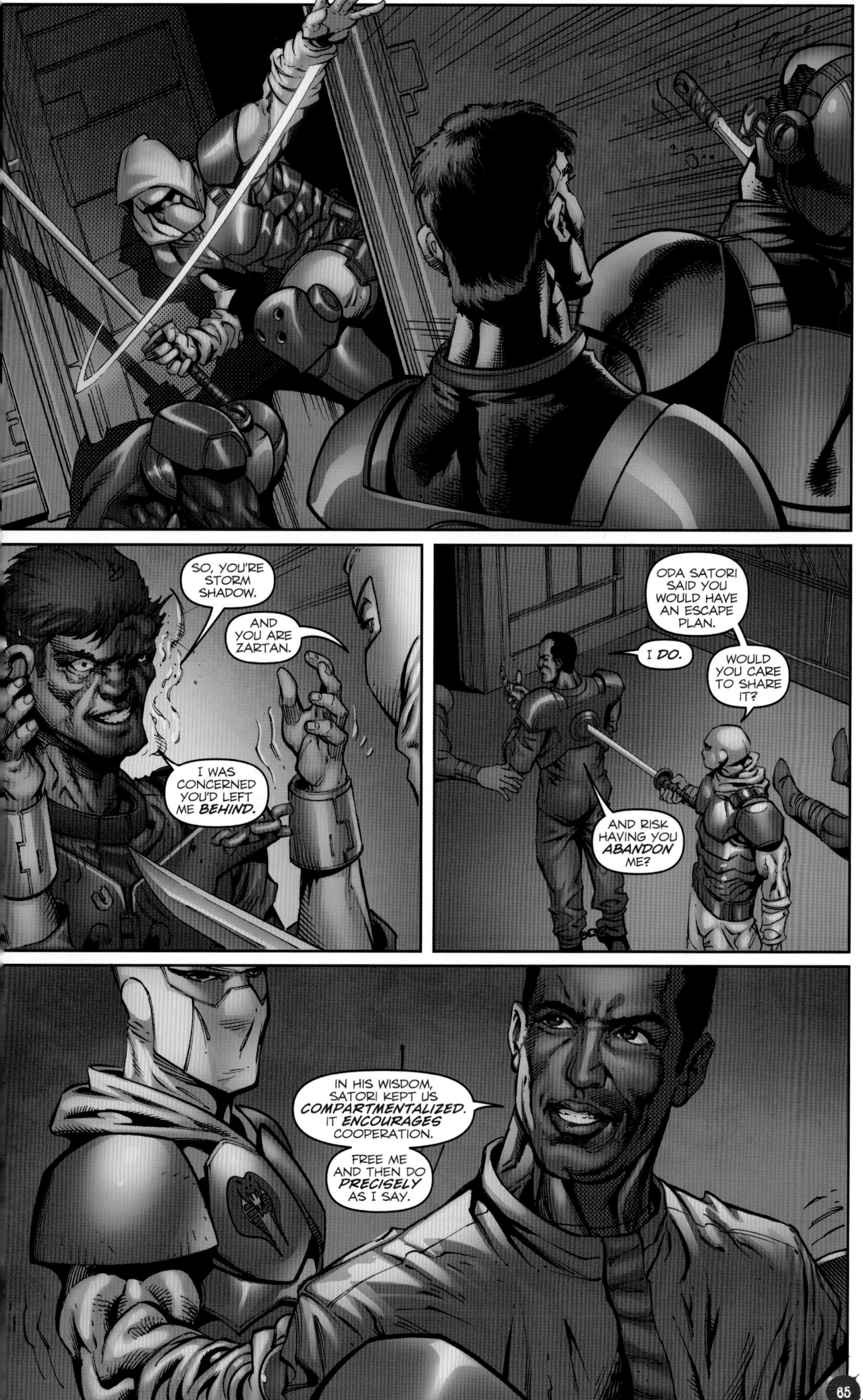
SO, YOU'RE STORM SHADOW.
AND YOU ARE ZARTAN.
I WAS CONCERNED YOU'D LEFT ME BEHIND.
ODA SATORI SAID YOU WOULD HAVE AN ESCAPE PLAN.
I DO.
WOULD YOU CARE TO SHARE IT?
AND RISK HAVING YOU ABANDON ME?
IN HIS WISDOM, SATORI KEPT US COMPARTMENTALIZED. IT ENCOURAGES COOPERATION.
FREE ME AND THEN DO PRECISELY AS I SAY.

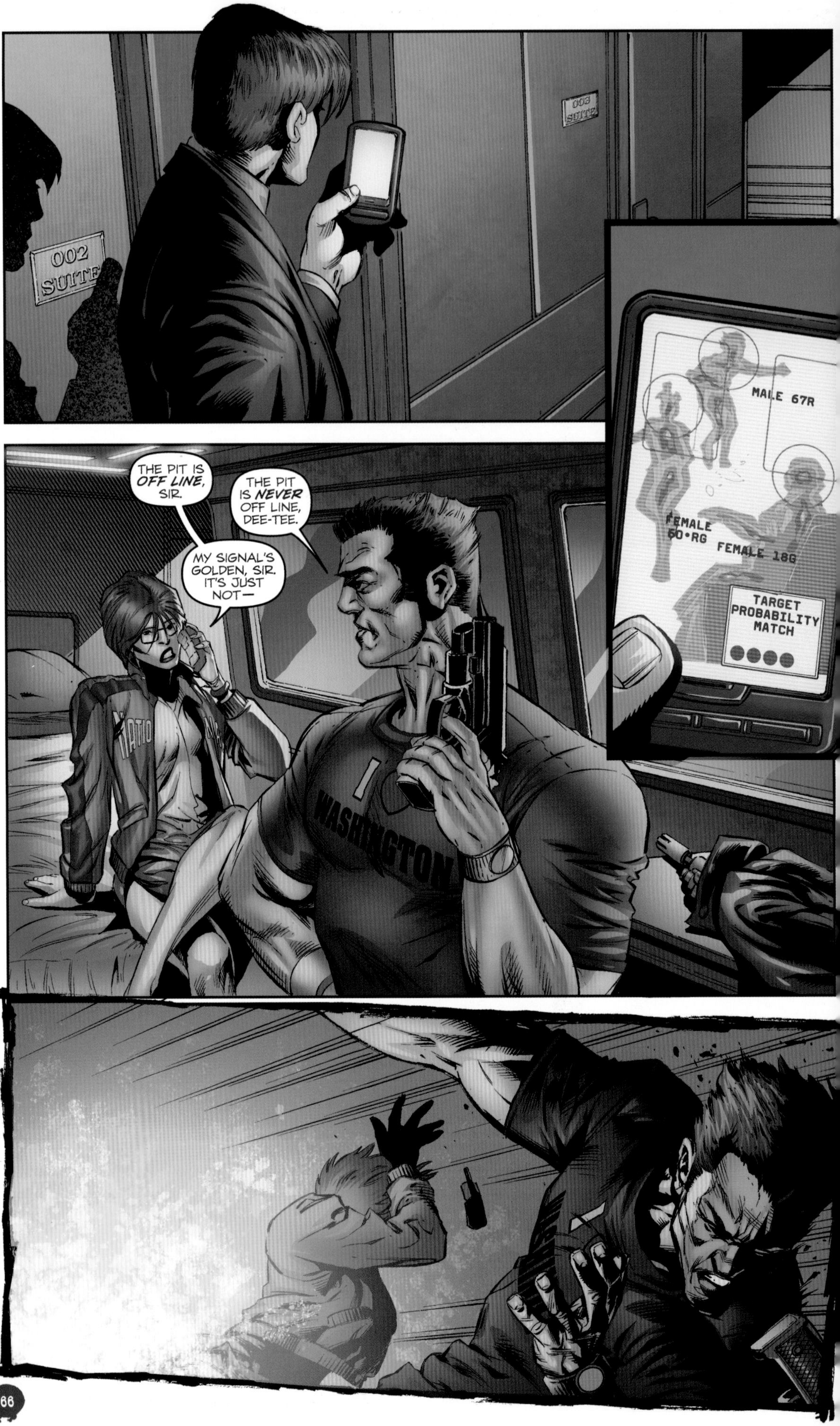
002
SUITE
003
SUITE
MALE 67R
FEMALE
60•RG
FEMALE 18G
TARGET
PROBABILITY
MATCH
THE PIT IS *OFF LINE*, SIR.
THE PIT IS *NEVER* OFF LINE, DEE-TEE.
MY SIGNAL'S GOLDEN, SIR. IT'S JUST NOT—
WASHINGTON

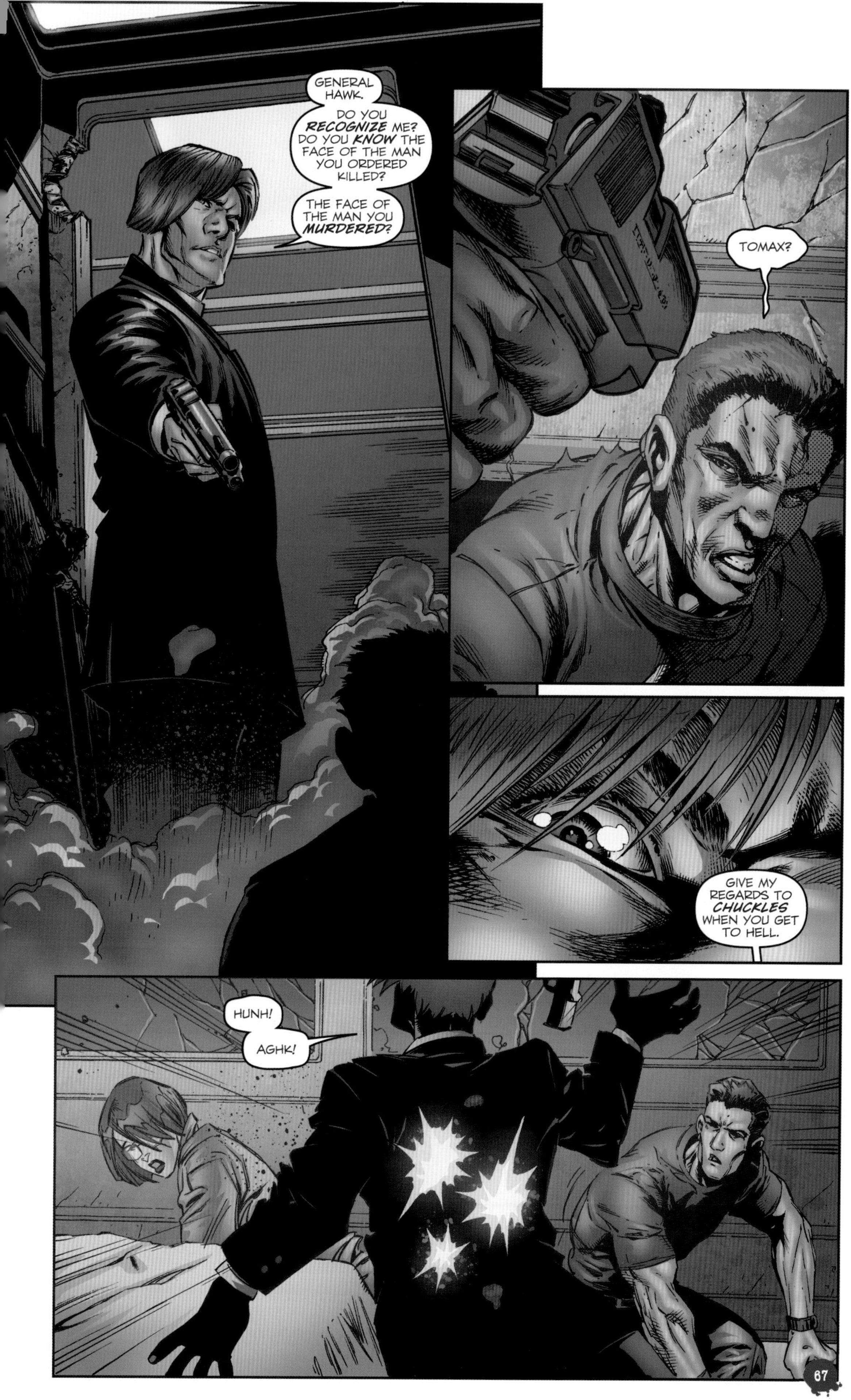
GENERAL HAWK.
DO YOU **RECOGNIZE** ME? DO YOU **KNOW** THE FACE OF THE MAN YOU ORDERED KILLED?
THE FACE OF THE MAN YOU **MURDERED?**
TOMAX?
GIVE MY REGARDS TO **CHUCKLES** WHEN YOU GET TO HELL.
HUNH!
AGHK!

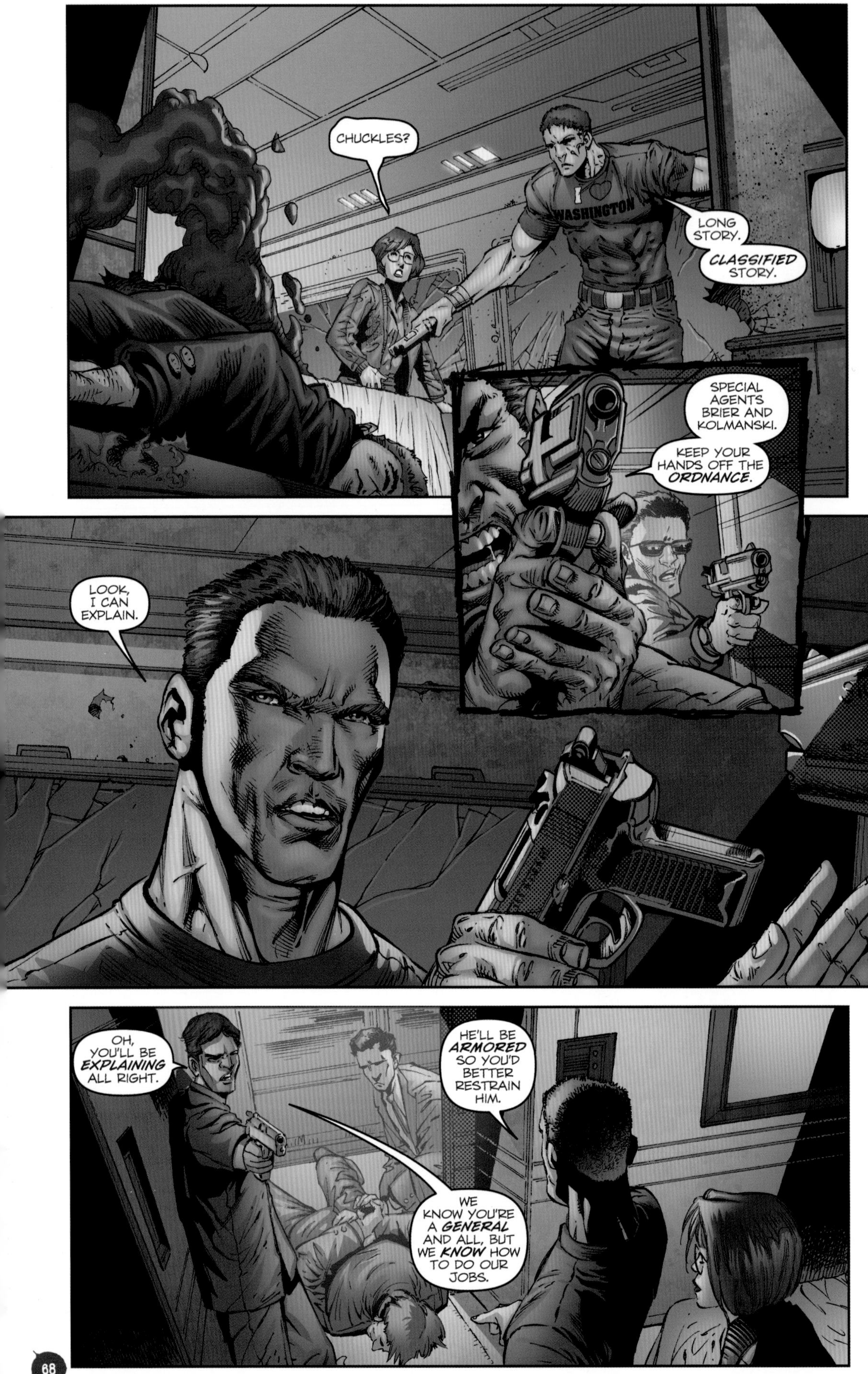
CHUCKLES?
LONG STORY.
CLASSIFIED STORY.
SPECIAL AGENTS BRIER AND KOLMANSKI.
KEEP YOUR HANDS OFF THE ORDNANCE.
LOOK, I CAN EXPLAIN.
OH, YOU'LL BE EXPLAINING ALL RIGHT.
HE'LL BE ARMORED SO YOU'D BETTER RESTRAIN HIM.
WE KNOW YOU'RE A GENERAL AND ALL, BUT WE KNOW HOW TO DO OUR JOBS.

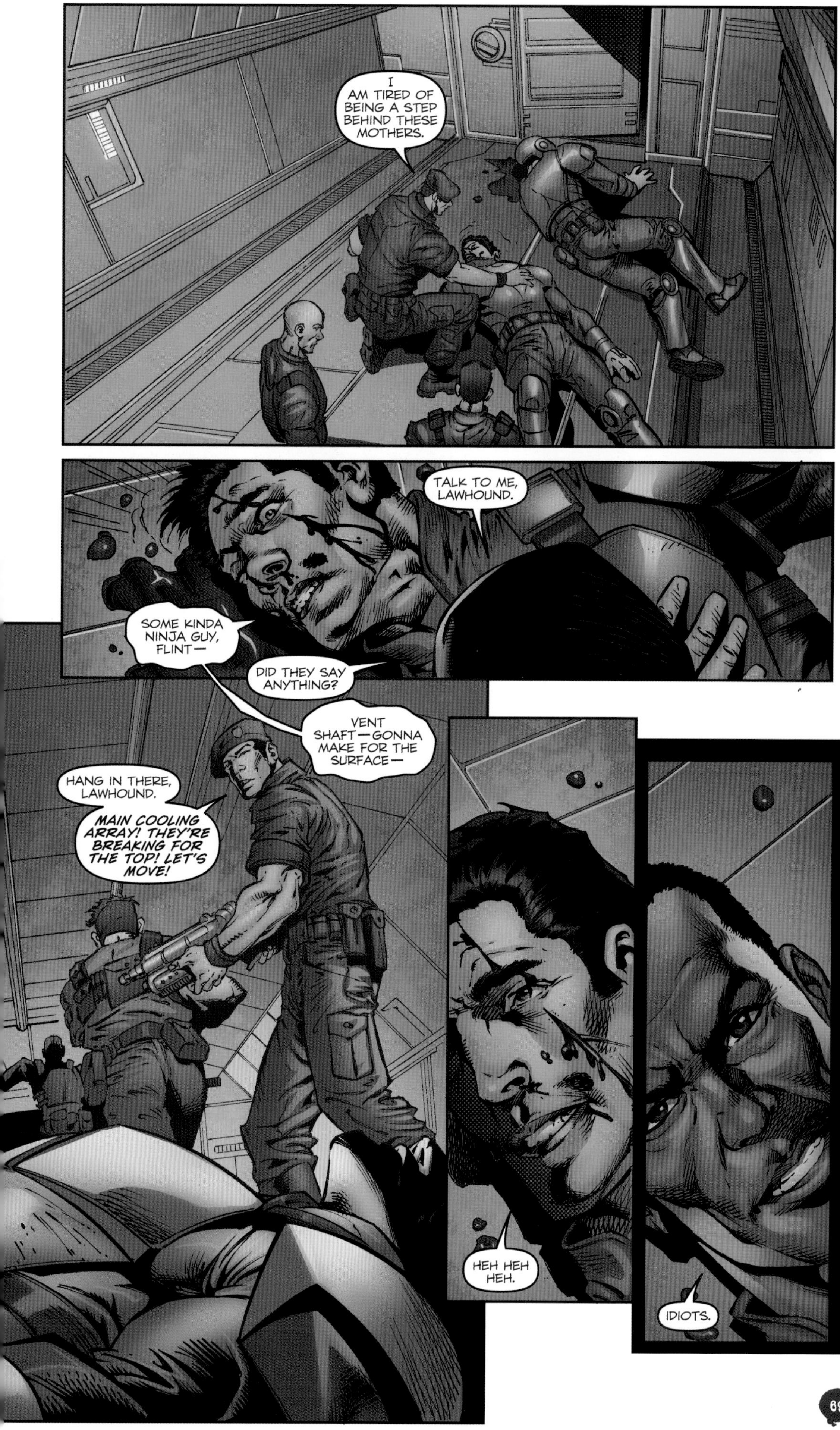

I AM TIRED OF BEING A STEP BEHIND THESE MOTHERS.
TALK TO ME, LAWHOUND.
SOME KINDA NINJA GUY, FLINT—
DID THEY SAY ANYTHING?
VENT SHAFT—GONNA MAKE FOR THE SURFACE—
HANG IN THERE, LAWHOUND.
MAIN COOLING ARRAY! THEY'RE BREAKING FOR THE TOP! LET'S MOVE!
HEH HEH HEH.
IDIOTS.

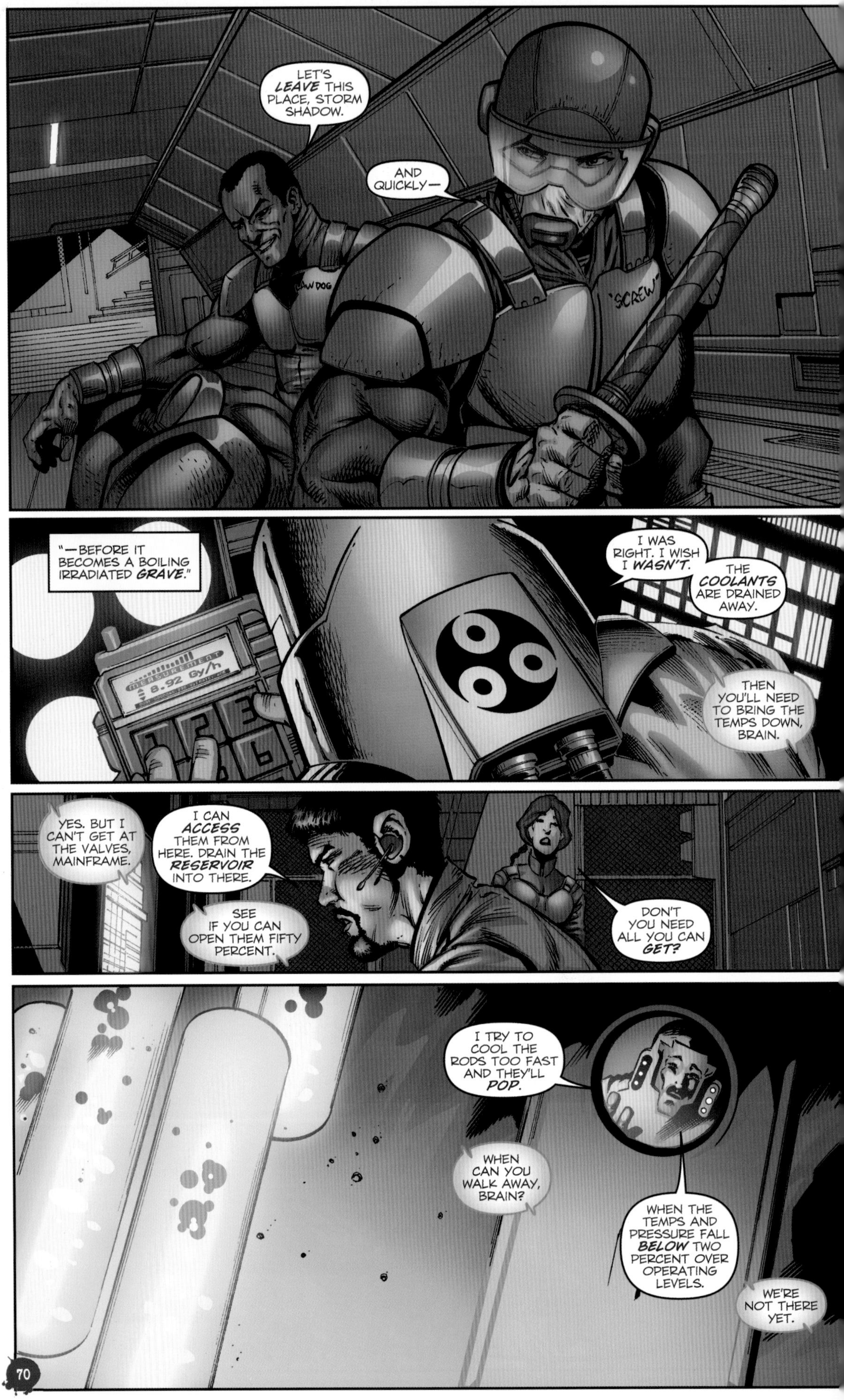

LET'S **LEAVE** THIS PLACE, STORM SHADOW.
AND QUICKLY—
"SCREW"
"—BEFORE IT BECOMES A BOILING IRRADIATED **GRAVE**."
I WAS RIGHT. I WISH I **WASN'T**.
THE **COOLANTS** ARE DRAINED AWAY.
MEASUREMENT
8.92 Gy/h
THEN YOU'LL NEED TO BRING THE TEMPS DOWN, BRAIN.
YES. BUT I CAN'T GET AT THE VALVES, MAINFRAME.
I CAN **ACCESS** THEM FROM HERE. DRAIN THE **RESERVOIR** INTO THERE.
SEE IF YOU CAN OPEN THEM FIFTY PERCENT.
DON'T YOU NEED ALL YOU CAN **GET?**
I TRY TO COOL THE RODS TOO FAST AND THEY'LL **POP**.
WHEN CAN YOU WALK AWAY, BRAIN?
WHEN THE TEMPS AND PRESSURE FALL **BELOW** TWO PERCENT OVER OPERATING LEVELS.
WE'RE NOT THERE YET.

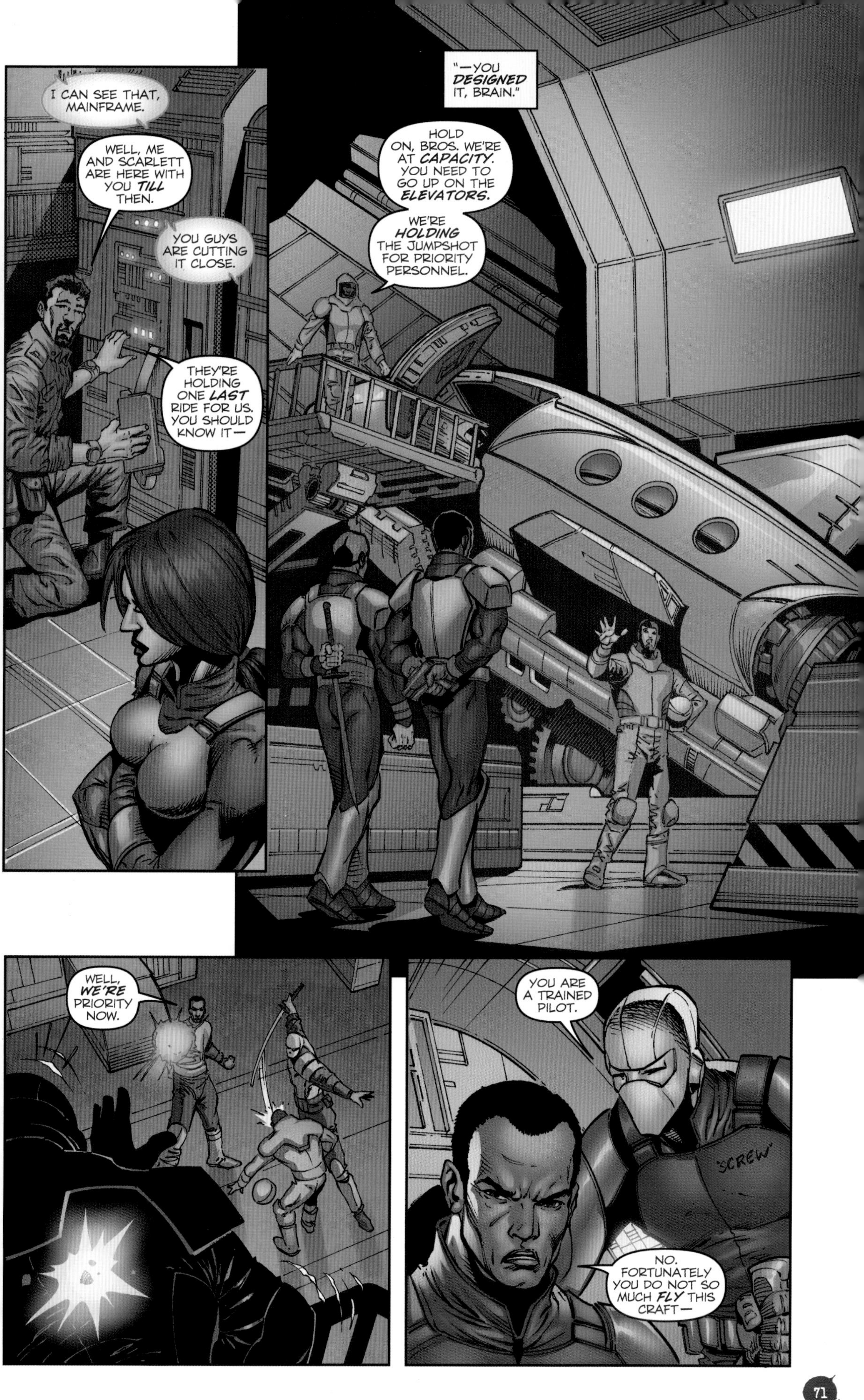
I CAN SEE THAT, MAINFRAME.
WELL, ME AND SCARLETT ARE HERE WITH YOU TILL THEN.
YOU GUYS ARE CUTTING IT CLOSE.
THEY'RE HOLDING ONE LAST RIDE FOR US. YOU SHOULD KNOW IT—
"—YOU DESIGNED IT, BRAIN."
HOLD ON, BROS. WE'RE AT CAPACITY. YOU NEED TO GO UP ON THE ELEVATORS.
WE'RE HOLDING THE JUMPSHOT FOR PRIORITY PERSONNEL.
WELL, WE'RE PRIORITY NOW.
YOU ARE A TRAINED PILOT.
SCREW
NO. FORTUNATELY YOU DO NOT SO MUCH FLY THIS CRAFT—

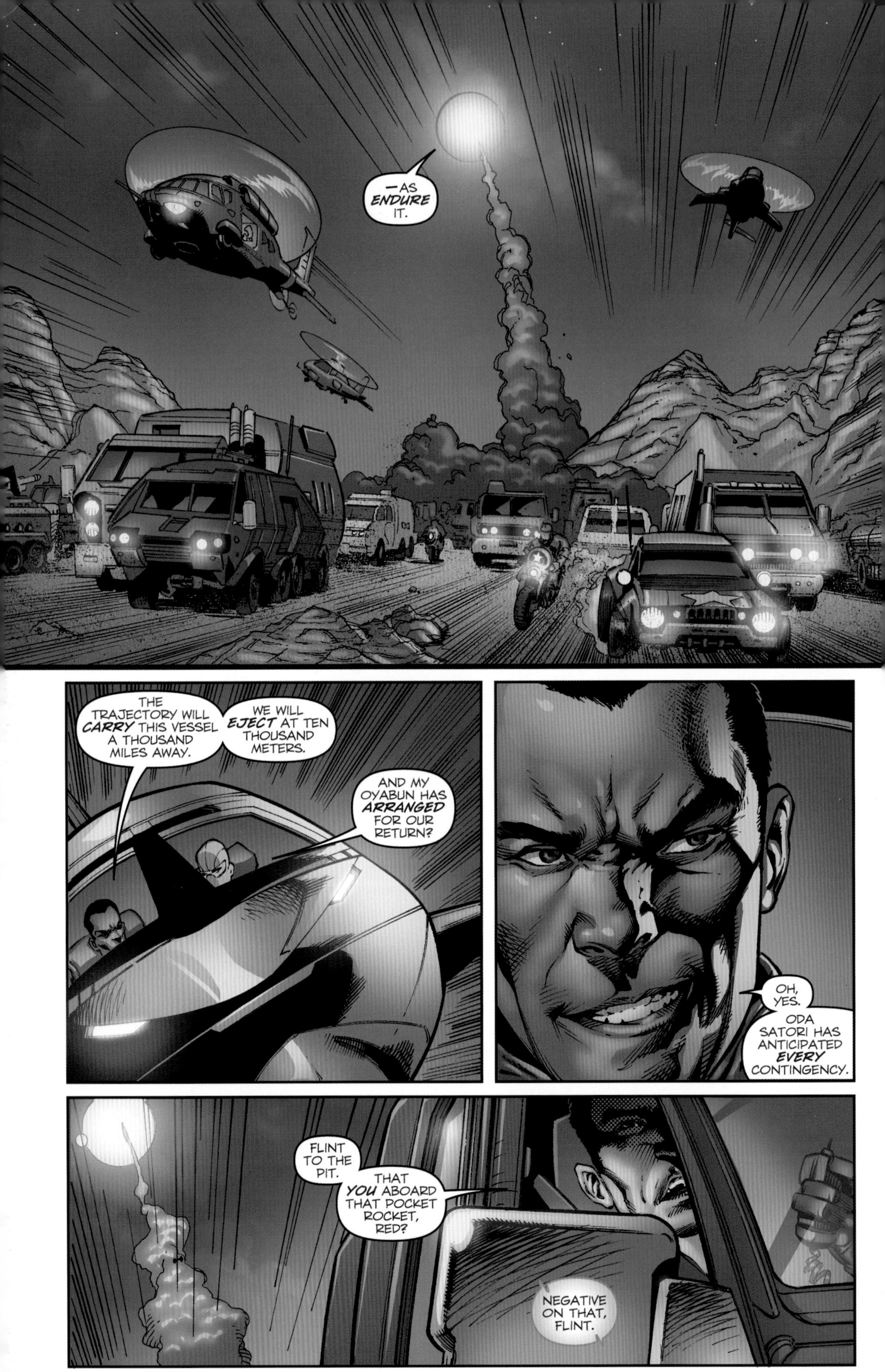
—AS ENDURE IT.
THE TRAJECTORY WILL CARRY THIS VESSEL A THOUSAND MILES AWAY.
WE WILL EJECT AT TEN THOUSAND METERS.
AND MY OYABUN HAS ARRANGED FOR OUR RETURN?
OH, YES.
ODA SATORI HAS ANTICIPATED EVERY CONTINGENCY.
FLINT TO THE PIT.
THAT YOU ABOARD THAT POCKET ROCKET, RED?
NEGATIVE ON THAT, FLINT.

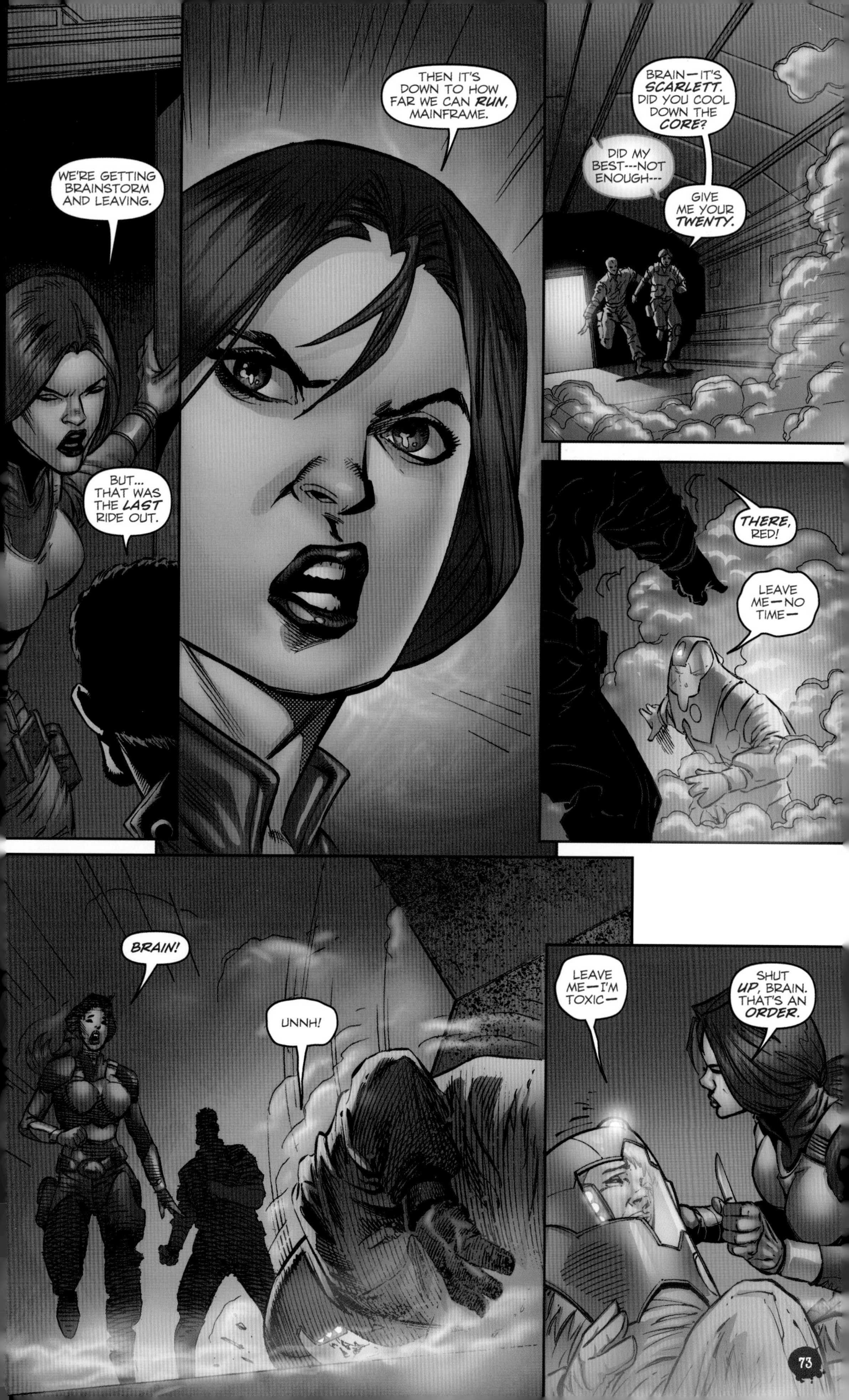
WE'RE GETTING BRAINSTORM AND LEAVING.
BUT... THAT WAS THE LAST RIDE OUT.
THEN IT'S DOWN TO HOW FAR WE CAN RUN, MAINFRAME.
BRAIN—IT'S SCARLETT. DID YOU COOL DOWN THE CORE?
DID MY BEST---NOT ENOUGH---
GIVE ME YOUR TWENTY.
THERE, RED!
LEAVE ME—NO TIME—
BRAIN!
UNNH!
LEAVE ME—I'M TOXIC—
SHUT UP, BRAIN. THAT'S AN ORDER.

HE CAN'T WALK.

WE *CARRY* HIM. AFTER I GET SOME *IODINE* IN HIM.

NO TIME... NO TIME...

WHAT ARE WE *LOOKING* AT HERE? FIRE? NUKE BLAST?

WHEN THE CORE MELTS THROUGH TO THE WATERTABLE IT'LL SUPERHEAT THE AQUIFER FOR A MILE AROUND.

MILLIONS OF CUBIC FEET OF INSTANT STEAM LOOKING FOR A WAY *OUT.*

SO WE DIE LIKE *LOBSTERS.*

NO. LOBSTERS GO INTO THE POT *ALIVE.*

THE CONCUSSIVE WAVE WILL SQUASH US FLAT *LONG* BEFORE THEN.

SWEET.

STAY CLEAR OF TRANSPORT

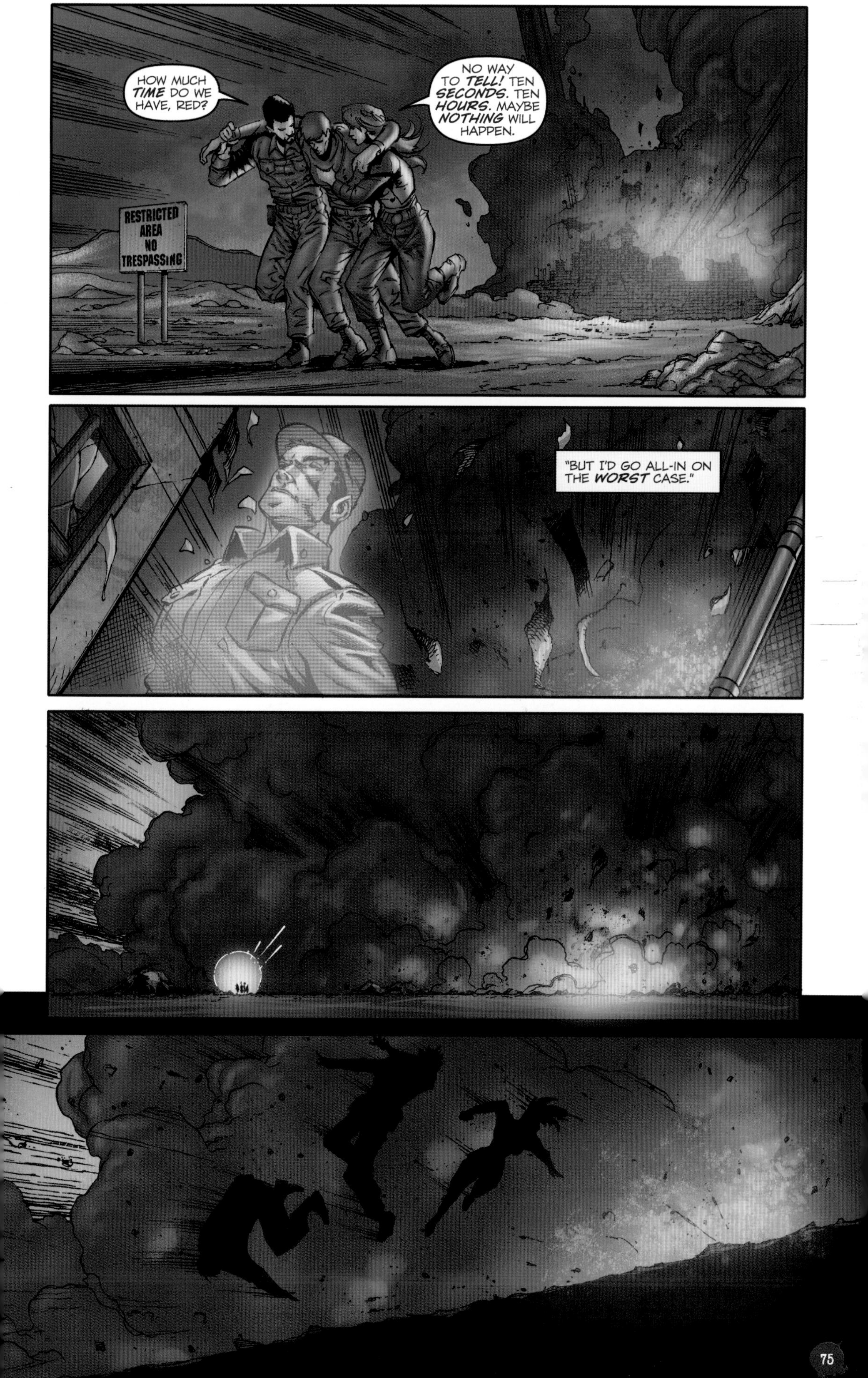
HOW MUCH TIME DO WE HAVE, RED?
NO WAY TO TELL! TEN SECONDS. TEN HOURS. MAYBE NOTHING WILL HAPPEN.
RESTRICTED AREA NO TRESPASSING
"BUT I'D GO ALL-IN ON THE WORST CASE."

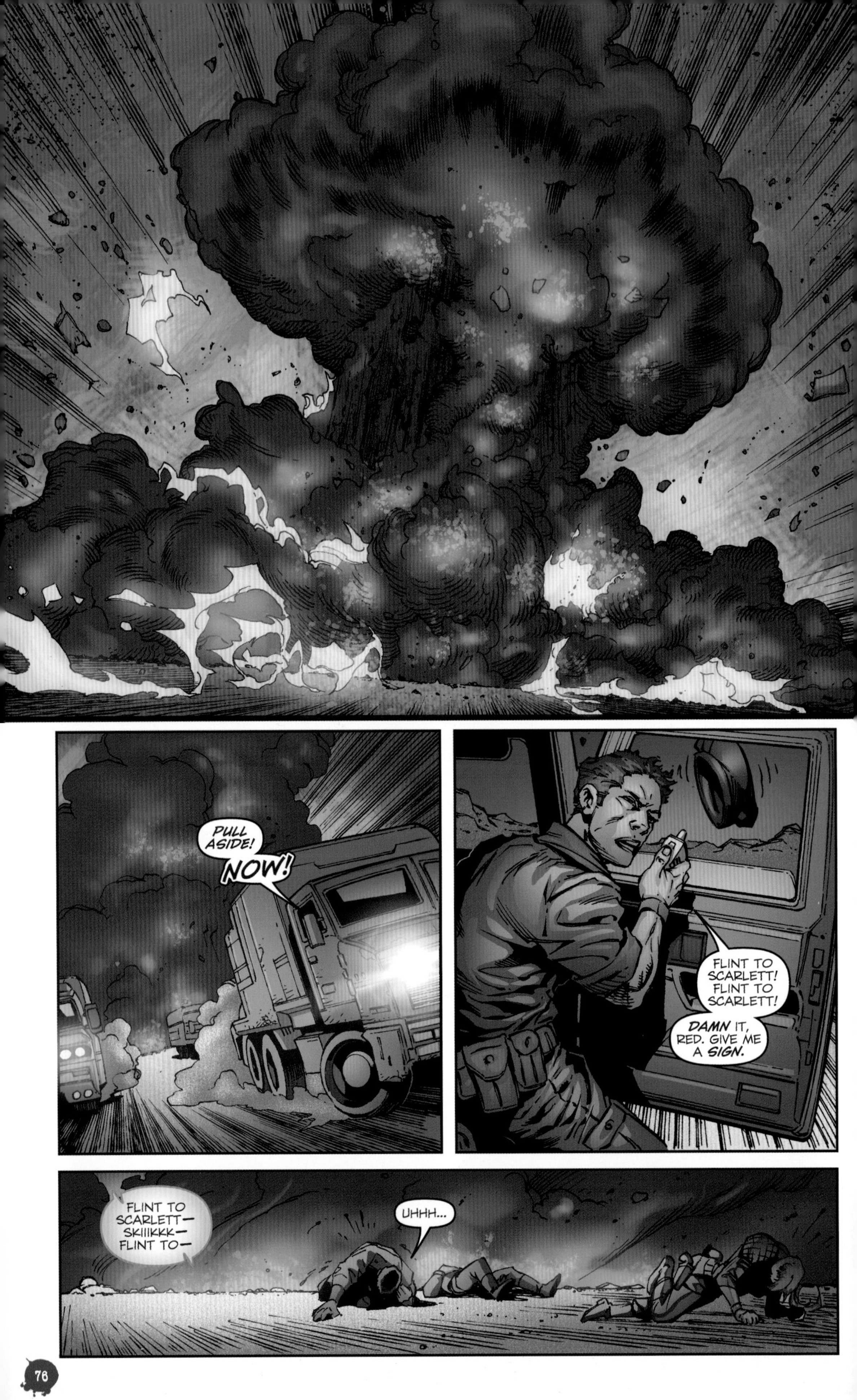
PULL ASIDE!
NOW!
FLINT TO SCARLETT! FLINT TO SCARLETT!
DAMN IT, RED. GIVE ME A SIGN.
FLINT TO SCARLETT— SKIIIKKK— FLINT TO—
UHHH...

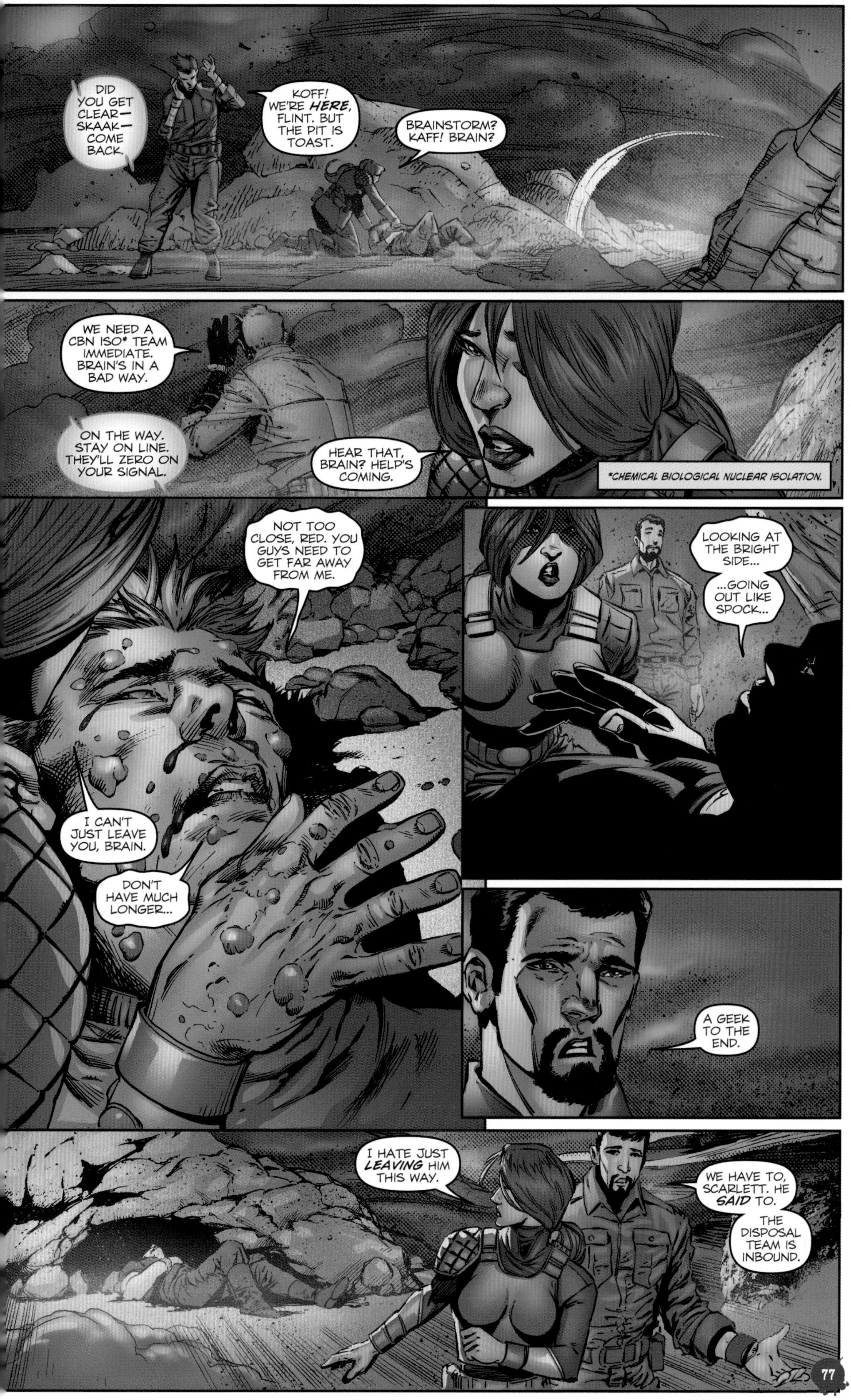
DID YOU GET CLEAR— SKAAK— COME BACK.
KOFF! WE'RE *HERE*, FLINT. BUT THE PIT IS TOAST.
BRAINSTORM? KAFF! BRAIN?
WE NEED A CBN ISO* TEAM IMMEDIATE. BRAIN'S IN A BAD WAY.
ON THE WAY. STAY ON LINE. THEY'LL ZERO ON YOUR SIGNAL.
HEAR THAT, BRAIN? HELP'S COMING.
*CHEMICAL BIOLOGICAL NUCLEAR ISOLATION.
NOT TOO CLOSE, RED. YOU GUYS NEED TO GET FAR AWAY FROM ME.
I CAN'T JUST LEAVE YOU, BRAIN.
DON'T HAVE MUCH LONGER...
LOOKING AT THE BRIGHT SIDE...
...GOING OUT LIKE SPOCK...
A GEEK TO THE END.
I HATE JUST *LEAVING* HIM THIS WAY.
WE HAVE TO, SCARLETT. HE *SAID* TO.
THE DISPOSAL TEAM IS INBOUND.

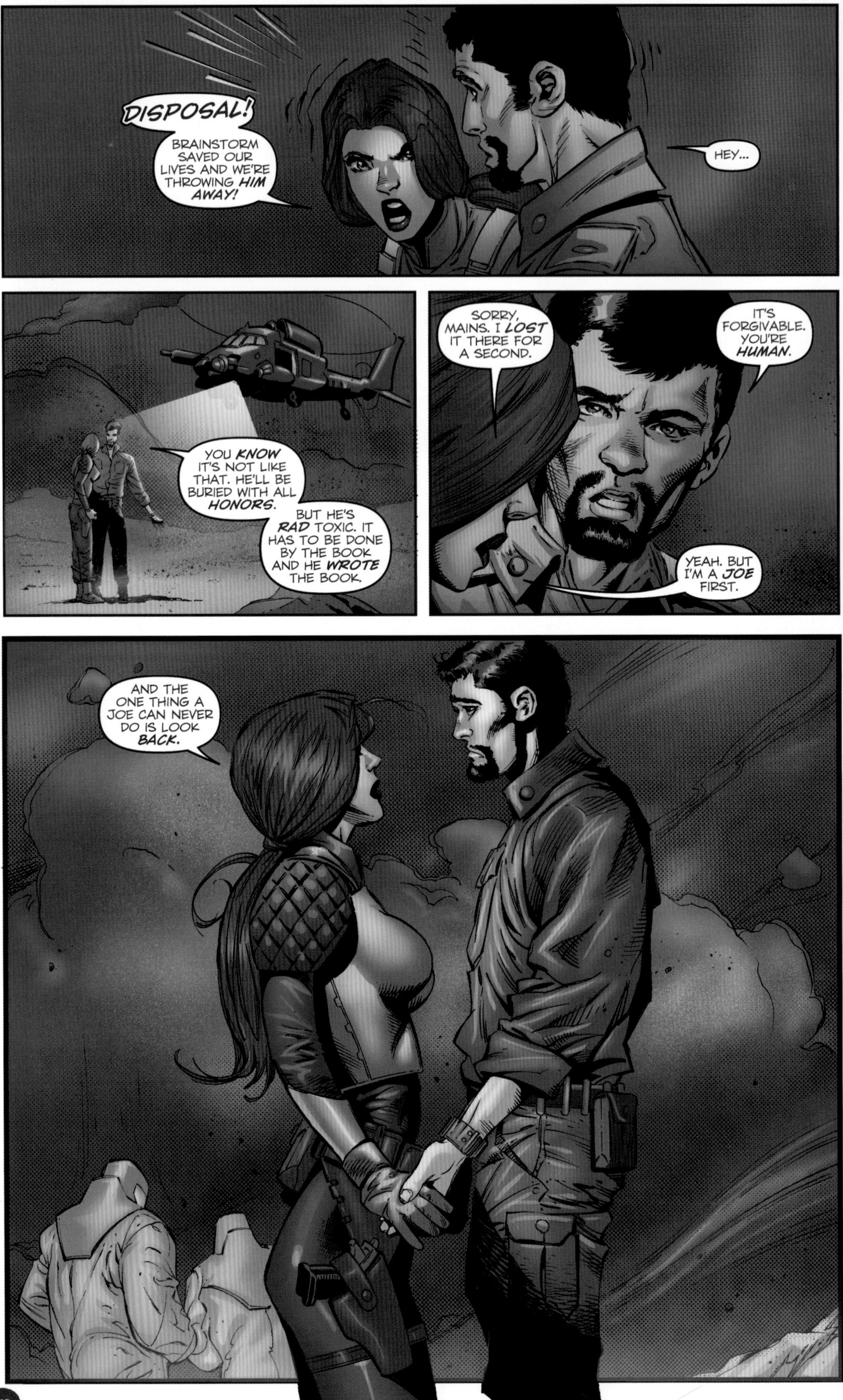
DISPOSAL!
BRAINSTORM SAVED OUR LIVES AND WE'RE THROWING HIM AWAY!
HEY...
YOU KNOW IT'S NOT LIKE THAT. HE'LL BE BURIED WITH ALL HONORS.
BUT HE'S RAD TOXIC. IT HAS TO BE DONE BY THE BOOK AND HE WROTE THE BOOK.
SORRY, MAINS. I LOST IT THERE FOR A SECOND.
IT'S FORGIVABLE. YOU'RE HUMAN.
YEAH. BUT I'M A JOE FIRST.
AND THE ONE THING A JOE CAN NEVER DO IS LOOK BACK.

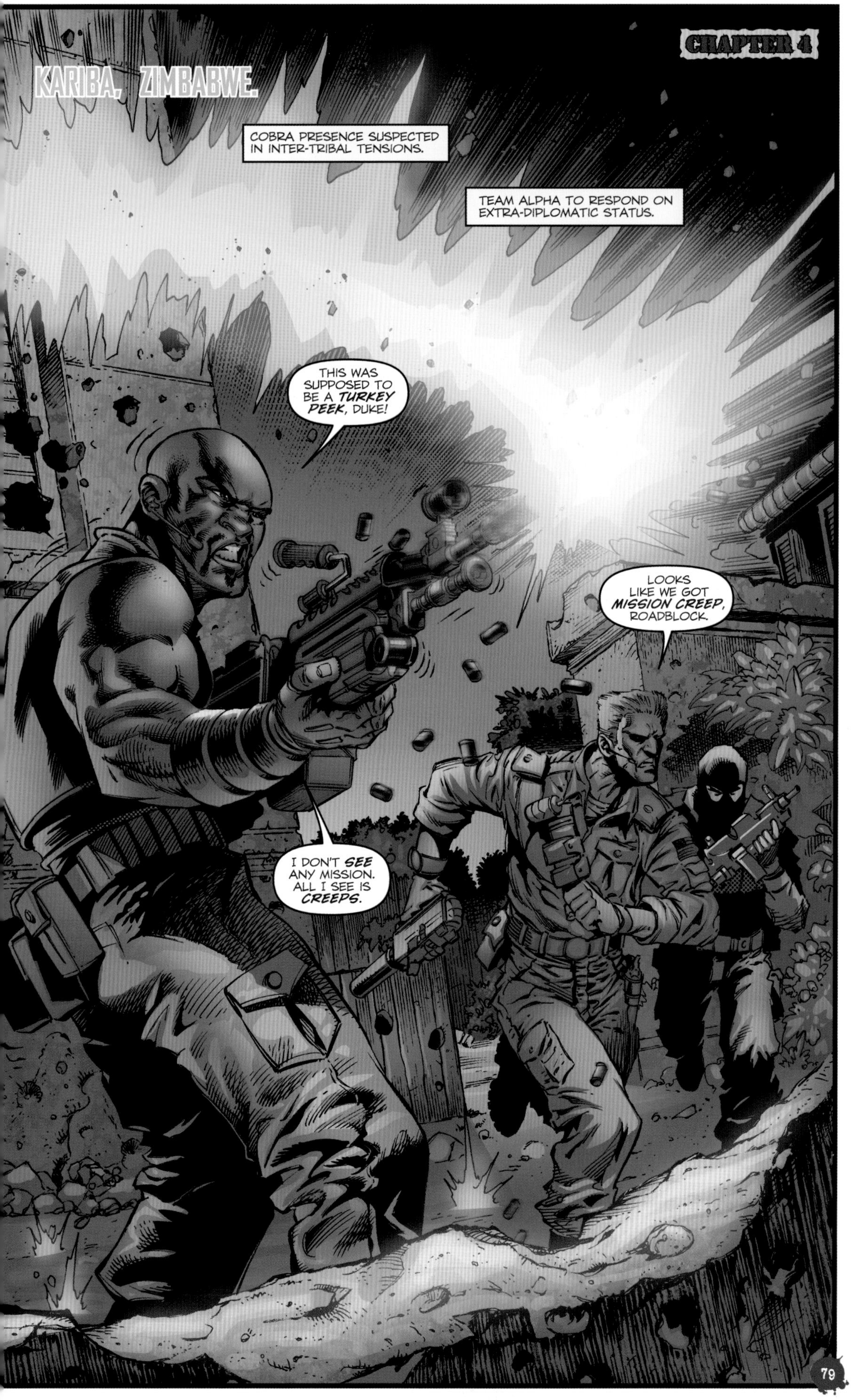
CHAPTER 4
KARIBA, ZIMBABWE.
COBRA PRESENCE SUSPECTED IN INTER-TRIBAL TENSIONS.
TEAM ALPHA TO RESPOND ON EXTRA-DIPLOMATIC STATUS.
THIS WAS SUPPOSED TO BE A TURKEY PEEK, DUKE!
LOOKS LIKE WE GOT MISSION CREEP, ROADBLOCK.
I DON'T SEE ANY MISSION. ALL I SEE IS CREEPS.

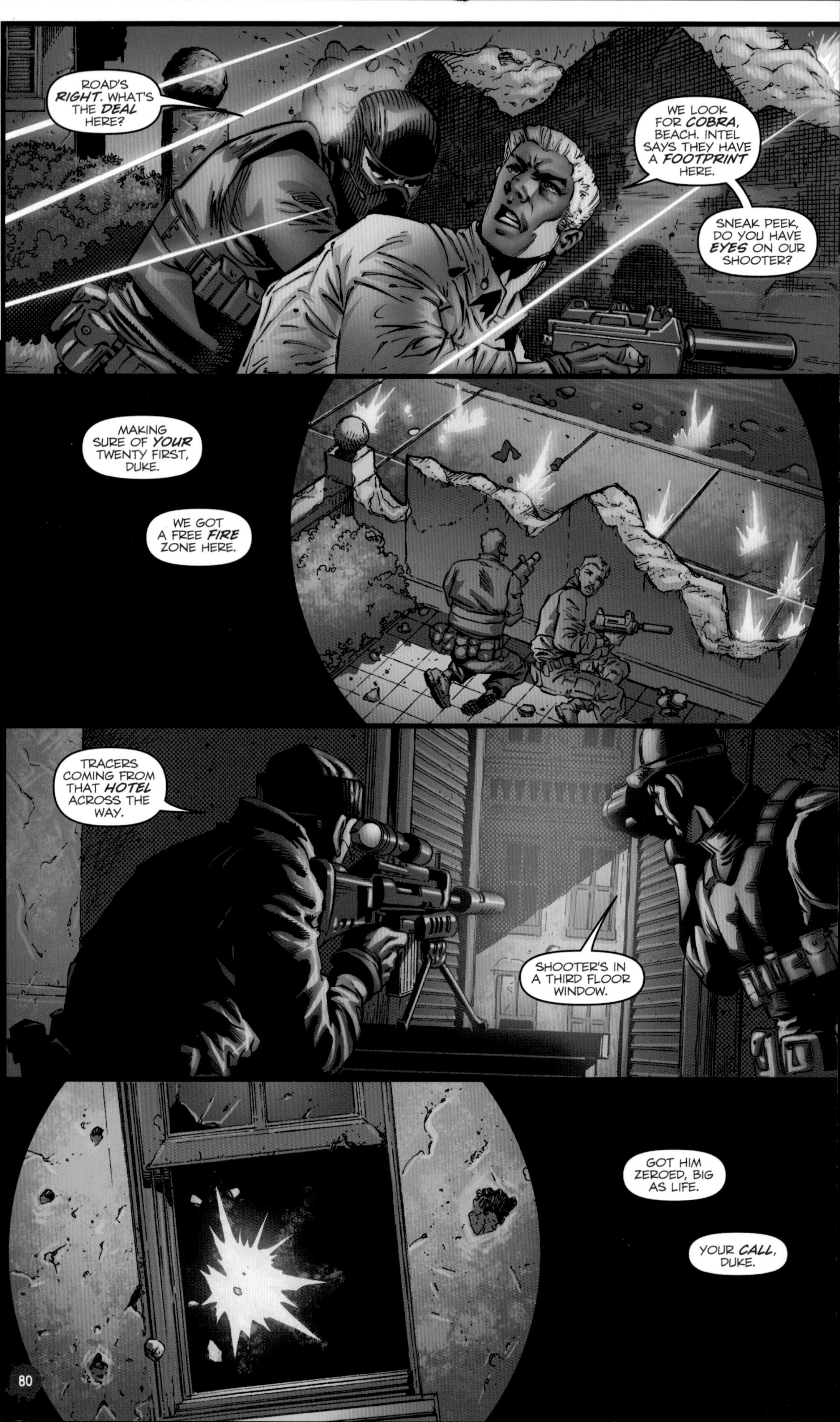
ROAD'S RIGHT. WHAT'S THE DEAL HERE?
WE LOOK FOR COBRA, BEACH. INTEL SAYS THEY HAVE A FOOTPRINT HERE.
SNEAK PEEK, DO YOU HAVE EYES ON OUR SHOOTER?
MAKING SURE OF YOUR TWENTY FIRST, DUKE.
WE GOT A FREE FIRE ZONE HERE.
TRACERS COMING FROM THAT HOTEL ACROSS THE WAY.
SHOOTER'S IN A THIRD FLOOR WINDOW.
GOT HIM ZEROED, BIG AS LIFE.
YOUR CALL, DUKE.

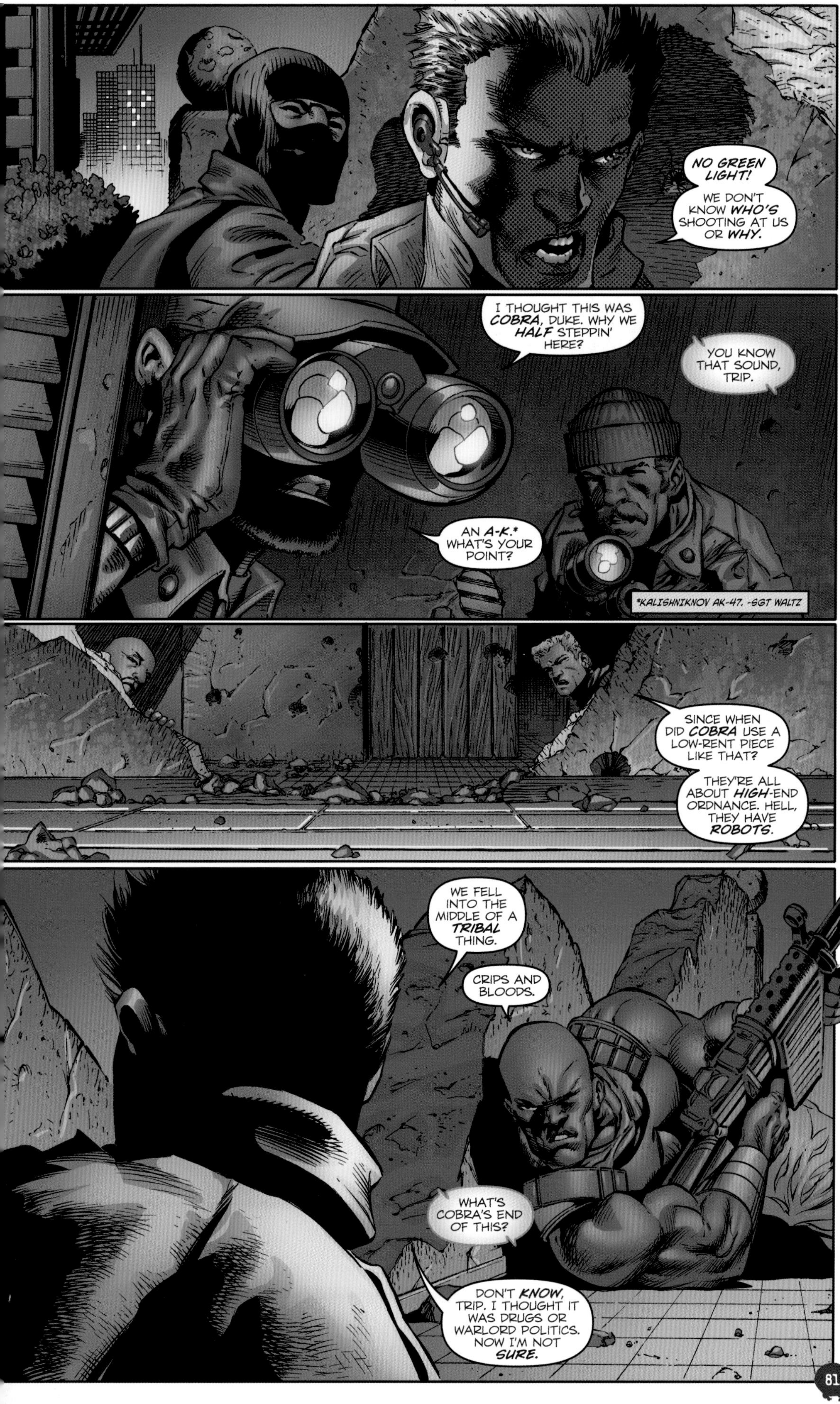
NO GREEN LIGHT!
WE DON'T KNOW WHO'S SHOOTING AT US OR WHY.
I THOUGHT THIS WAS COBRA, DUKE. WHY WE HALF STEPPIN' HERE?
YOU KNOW THAT SOUND, TRIP.
AN A-K.* WHAT'S YOUR POINT?
*KALISHNIKNOV AK-47. -SGT WALTZ
SINCE WHEN DID COBRA USE A LOW-RENT PIECE LIKE THAT?
THEY'RE ALL ABOUT HIGH-END ORDNANCE. HELL, THEY HAVE ROBOTS.
WE FELL INTO THE MIDDLE OF A TRIBAL THING.
CRIPS AND BLOODS.
WHAT'S COBRA'S END OF THIS?
DON'T KNOW, TRIP. I THOUGHT IT WAS DRUGS OR WARLORD POLITICS. NOW I'M NOT SURE.

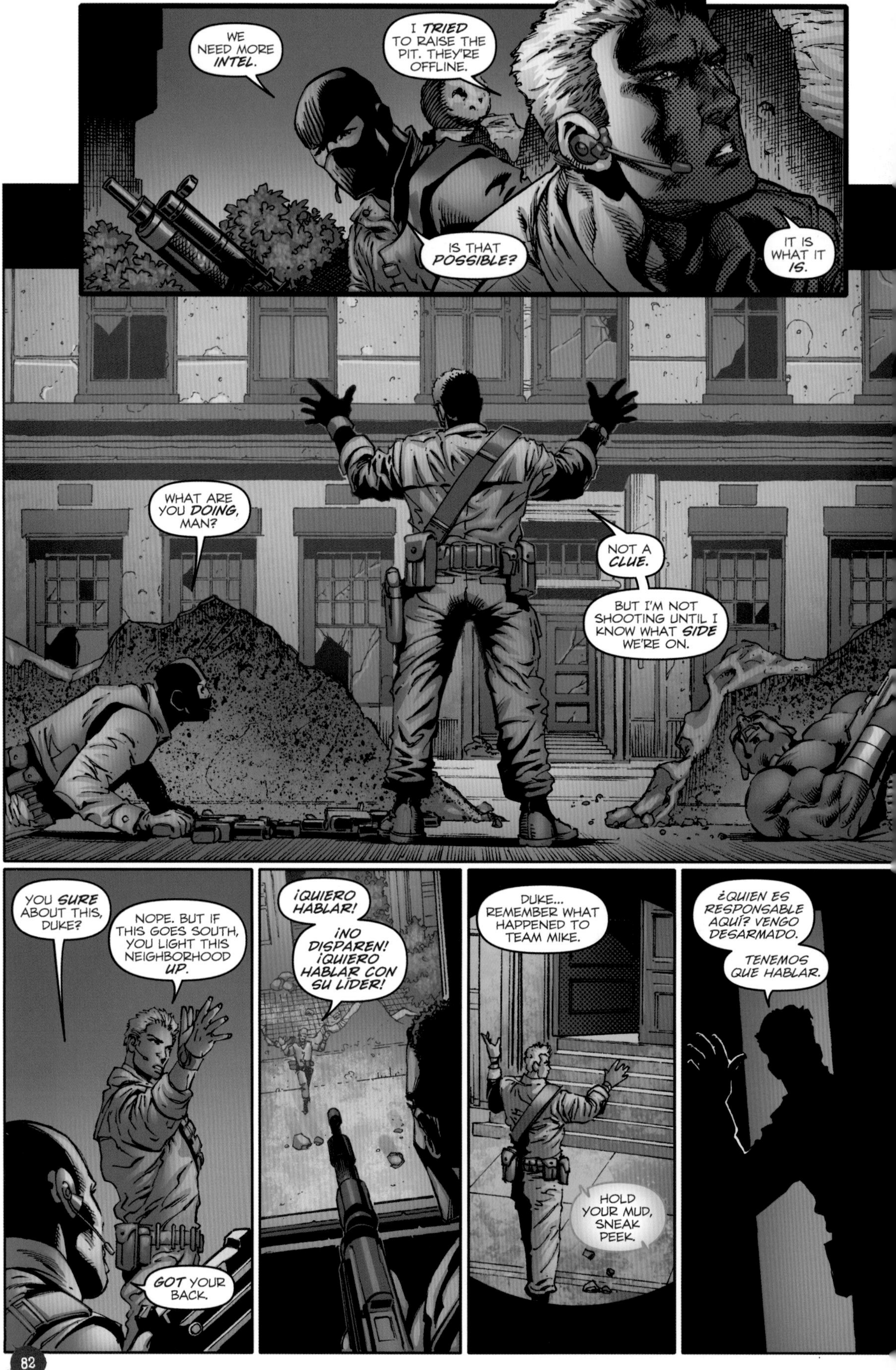

WE NEED MORE INTEL.
I TRIED TO RAISE THE PIT. THEY'RE OFFLINE.
IS THAT POSSIBLE?
IT IS WHAT IT IS.
WHAT ARE YOU DOING, MAN?
NOT A CLUE.
BUT I'M NOT SHOOTING UNTIL I KNOW WHAT SIDE WE'RE ON.
YOU SURE ABOUT THIS, DUKE?
NOPE. BUT IF THIS GOES SOUTH, YOU LIGHT THIS NEIGHBORHOOD UP.
GOT YOUR BACK.
¡QUIERO HABLAR!
¡NO DISPAREN! ¡QUIERO HABLAR CON SU LÍDER!
DUKE... REMEMBER WHAT HAPPENED TO TEAM MIKE.
HOLD YOUR MUD, SNEAK PEEK.
¿QUIEN ES RESPONSABLE AQUÍ? VENGO DESARMADO.
TENEMOS QUE HABLAR.

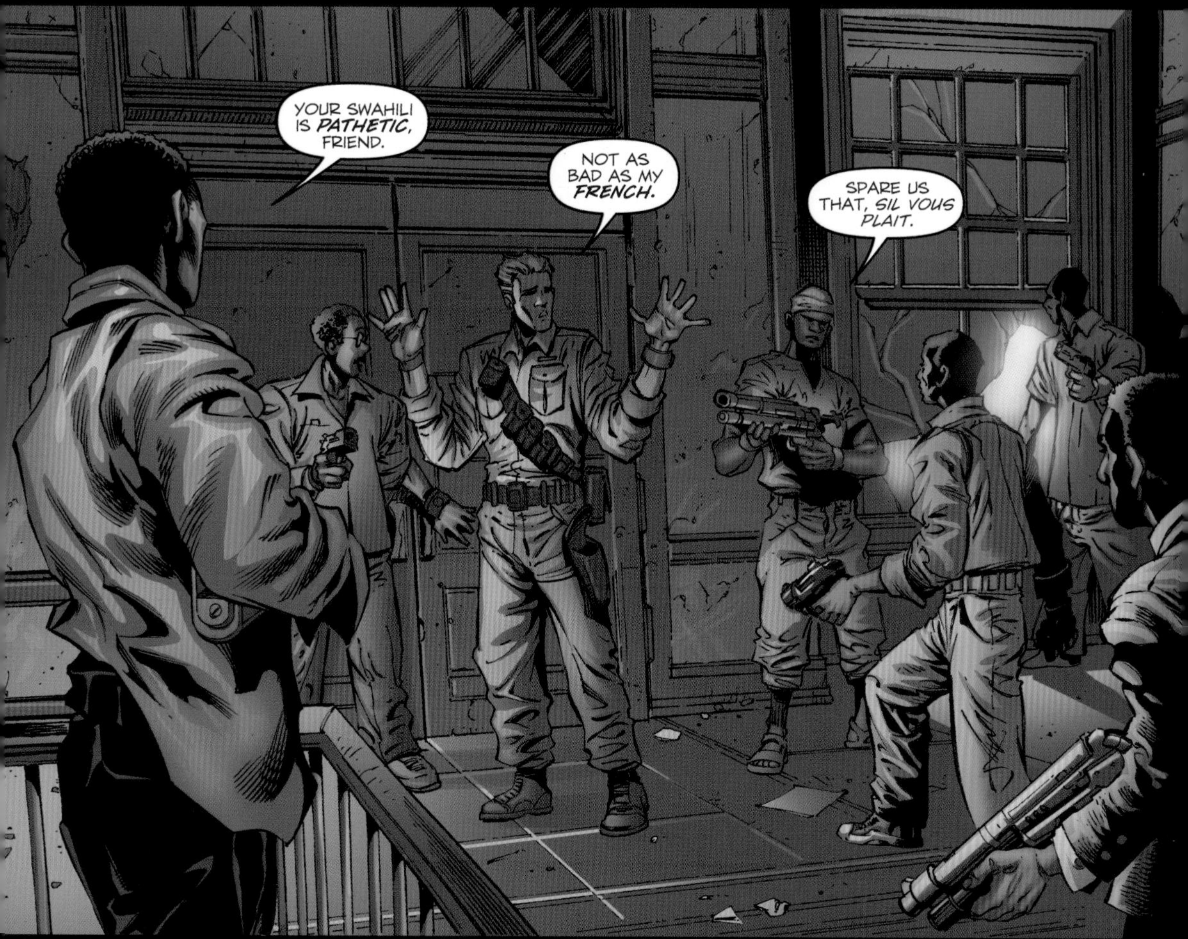
YOUR SWAHILI IS PATHETIC, FRIEND.
NOT AS BAD AS MY FRENCH.
SPARE US THAT, SIL VOUS PLAIT.

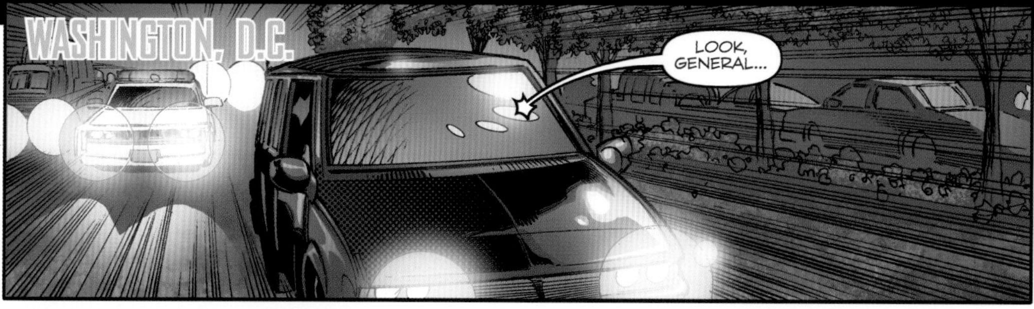
WASHINGTON, D.C.
LOOK, GENERAL...

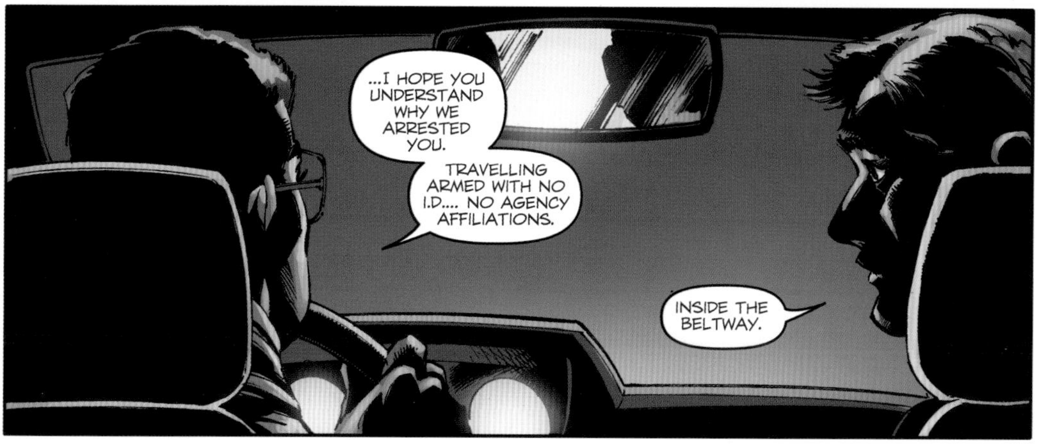
...I HOPE YOU UNDERSTAND WHY WE ARRESTED YOU.
TRAVELLING ARMED WITH NO I.D.... NO AGENCY AFFILIATIONS.
INSIDE THE BELTWAY.

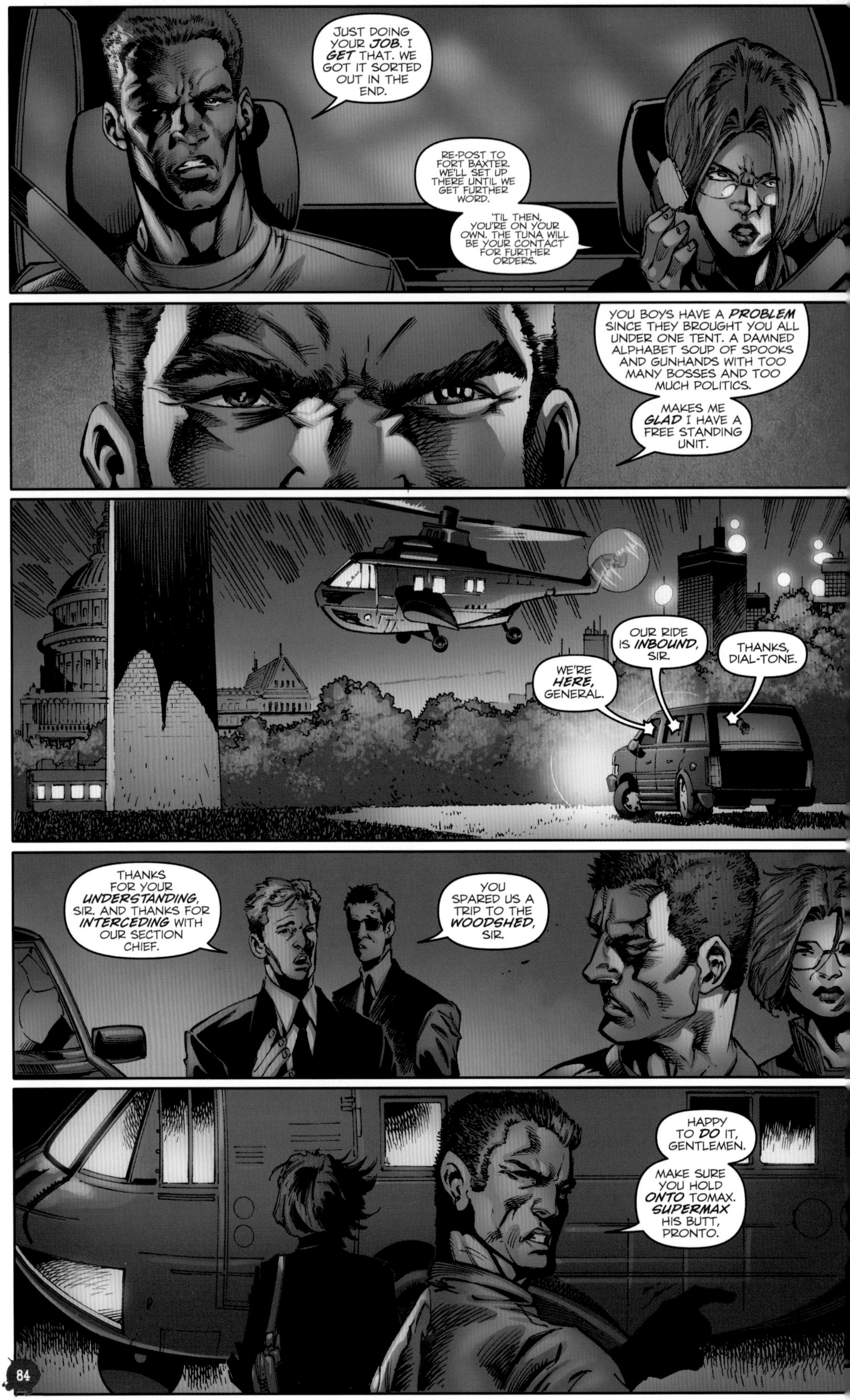
JUST DOING YOUR JOB. I GET THAT. WE GOT IT SORTED OUT IN THE END.
RE-POST TO FORT BAXTER. WE'LL SET UP THERE UNTIL WE GET FURTHER WORD.
'TIL THEN, YOU'RE ON YOUR OWN. THE TUNA WILL BE YOUR CONTACT FOR FURTHER ORDERS.
YOU BOYS HAVE A PROBLEM SINCE THEY BROUGHT YOU ALL UNDER ONE TENT. A DAMNED ALPHABET SOUP OF SPOOKS AND GUNHANDS WITH TOO MANY BOSSES AND TOO MUCH POLITICS.
MAKES ME GLAD I HAVE A FREE STANDING UNIT.
WE'RE HERE, GENERAL.
OUR RIDE IS INBOUND, SIR.
THANKS, DIAL-TONE.
THANKS FOR YOUR UNDERSTANDING, SIR. AND THANKS FOR INTERCEDING WITH OUR SECTION CHIEF.
YOU SPARED US A TRIP TO THE WOODSHED, SIR.
HAPPY TO DO IT, GENTLEMEN.
MAKE SURE YOU HOLD ONTO TOMAX. SUPERMAX HIS BUTT, PRONTO.

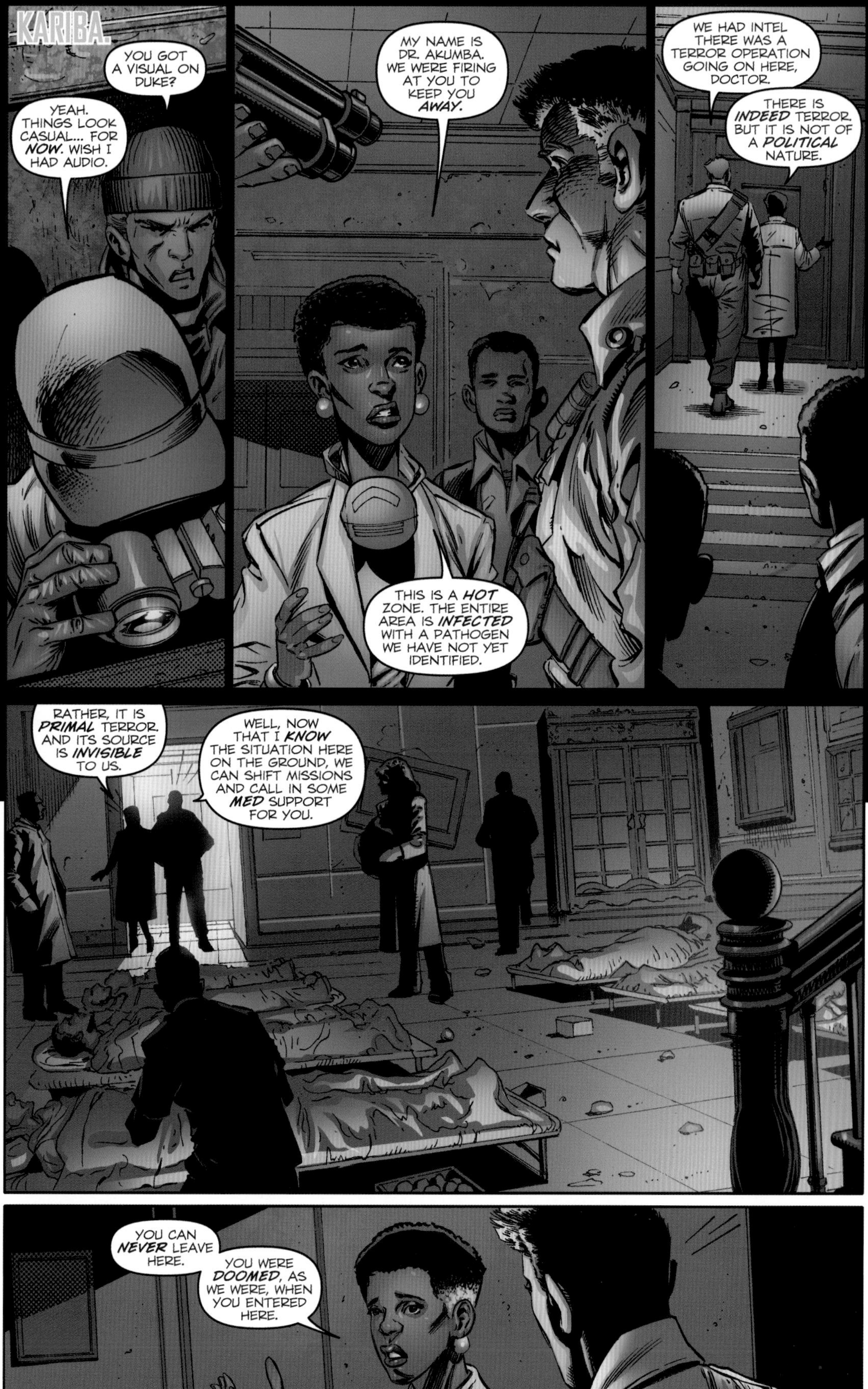
KARIBA.
YOU GOT A VISUAL ON DUKE?
YEAH. THINGS LOOK CASUAL... FOR NOW. WISH I HAD AUDIO.
MY NAME IS DR. AKUMBA. WE WERE FIRING AT YOU TO KEEP YOU AWAY.
THIS IS A HOT ZONE. THE ENTIRE AREA IS INFECTED WITH A PATHOGEN WE HAVE NOT YET IDENTIFIED.
WE HAD INTEL THERE WAS A TERROR OPERATION GOING ON HERE, DOCTOR.
THERE IS INDEED TERROR. BUT IT IS NOT OF A POLITICAL NATURE.
RATHER, IT IS PRIMAL TERROR. AND ITS SOURCE IS INVISIBLE TO US.
WELL, NOW THAT I KNOW THE SITUATION HERE ON THE GROUND, WE CAN SHIFT MISSIONS AND CALL IN SOME MED SUPPORT FOR YOU.
YOU CAN NEVER LEAVE HERE.
YOU WERE DOOMED, AS WE WERE, WHEN YOU ENTERED HERE.

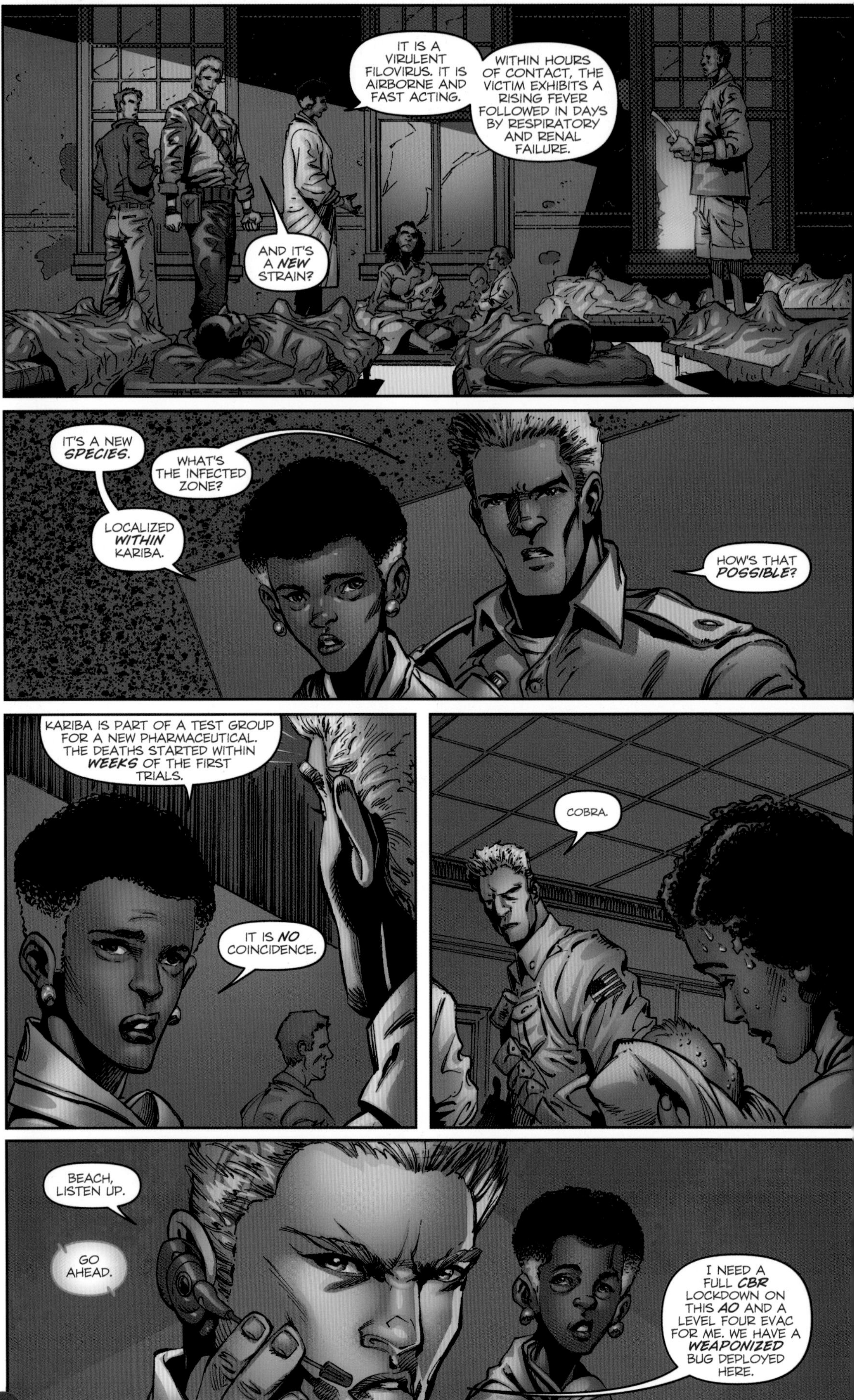
IT IS A VIRULENT FILOVIRUS. IT IS AIRBORNE AND FAST ACTING.
WITHIN HOURS OF CONTACT, THE VICTIM EXHIBITS A RISING FEVER FOLLOWED IN DAYS BY RESPIRATORY AND RENAL FAILURE.
AND IT'S A *NEW* STRAIN?
IT'S A NEW *SPECIES*.
WHAT'S THE INFECTED ZONE?
LOCALIZED *WITHIN* KARIBA.
HOW'S THAT *POSSIBLE*?
KARIBA IS PART OF A TEST GROUP FOR A NEW PHARMACEUTICAL. THE DEATHS STARTED WITHIN *WEEKS* OF THE FIRST TRIALS.
IT IS *NO* COINCIDENCE.
COBRA.
BEACH, LISTEN UP.
GO AHEAD.
I NEED A FULL *CBR* LOCKDOWN ON THIS *AO* AND A LEVEL FOUR EVAC FOR ME. WE HAVE A *WEAPONIZED* BUG DEPLOYED HERE.

ELKO COUNTY, NEVADA.

MOVE, MOVE, MOVE, JOES!

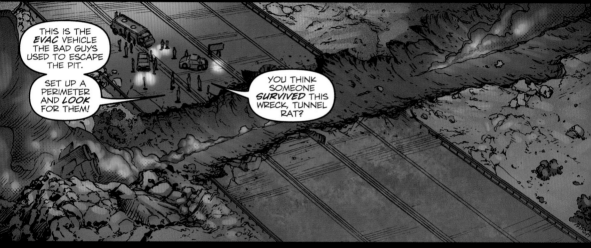

THIS IS THE *EVAC* VEHICLE THE BAD GUYS USED TO ESCAPE THE PIT.

SET UP A PERIMETER AND *LOOK* FOR THEM!

YOU THINK SOMEONE *SURVIVED* THIS WRECK, TUNNEL RAT?

YO. WE GOT ANY HELOS IN THE AREA?

THAT'S NOT ONE OF *OURS.*

ANY OF *YOU* GUYS EVER SEEN A CHOPPER LIKE THAT?

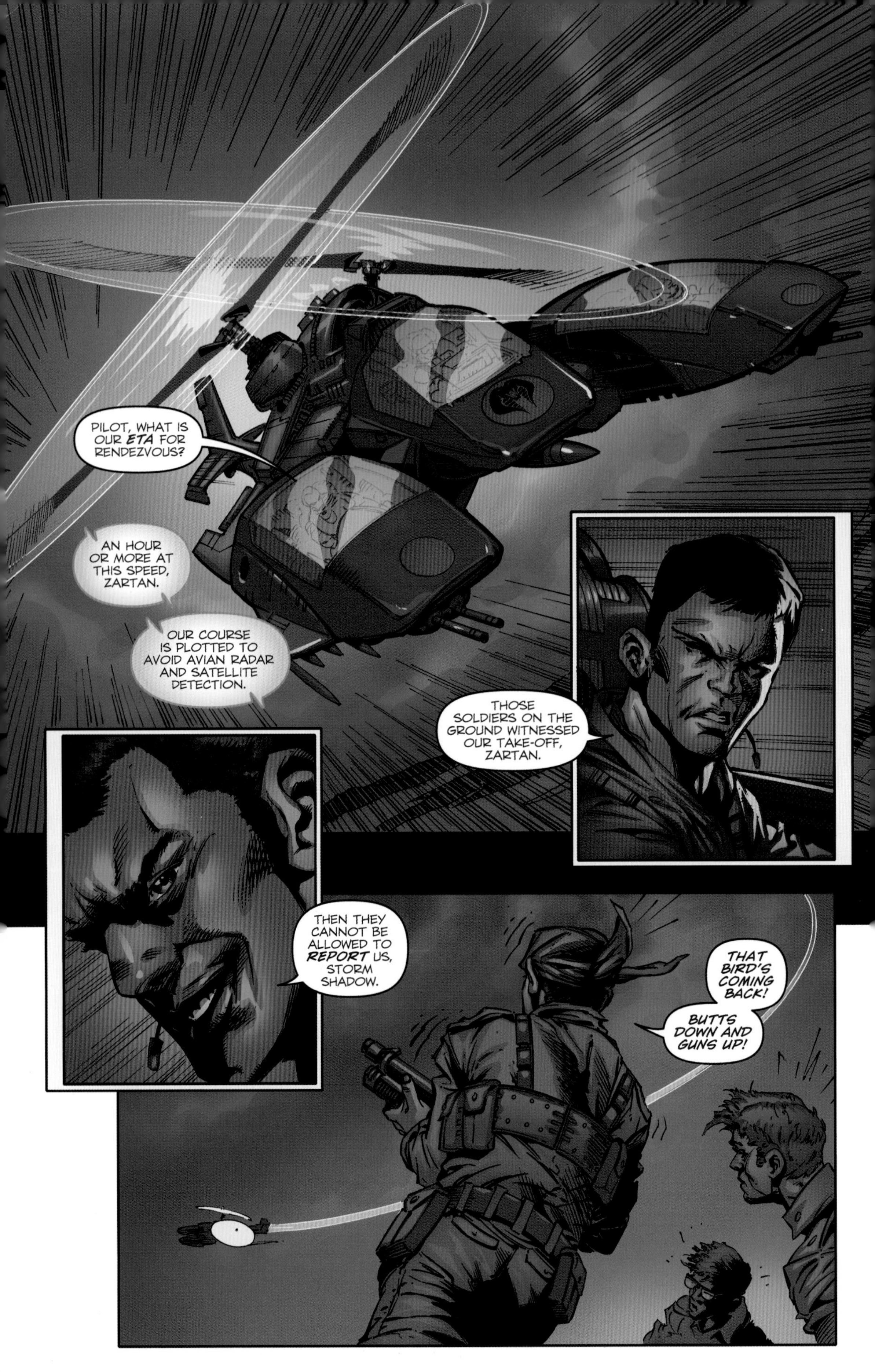
PILOT, WHAT IS OUR ETA FOR RENDEZVOUS?
AN HOUR OR MORE AT THIS SPEED, ZARTAN.
OUR COURSE IS PLOTTED TO AVOID AVIAN RADAR AND SATELLITE DETECTION.
THOSE SOLDIERS ON THE GROUND WITNESSED OUR TAKE-OFF, ZARTAN.
THEN THEY CANNOT BE ALLOWED TO REPORT US, STORM SHADOW.
THAT BIRD'S COMING BACK!
BUTTS DOWN AND GUNS UP!

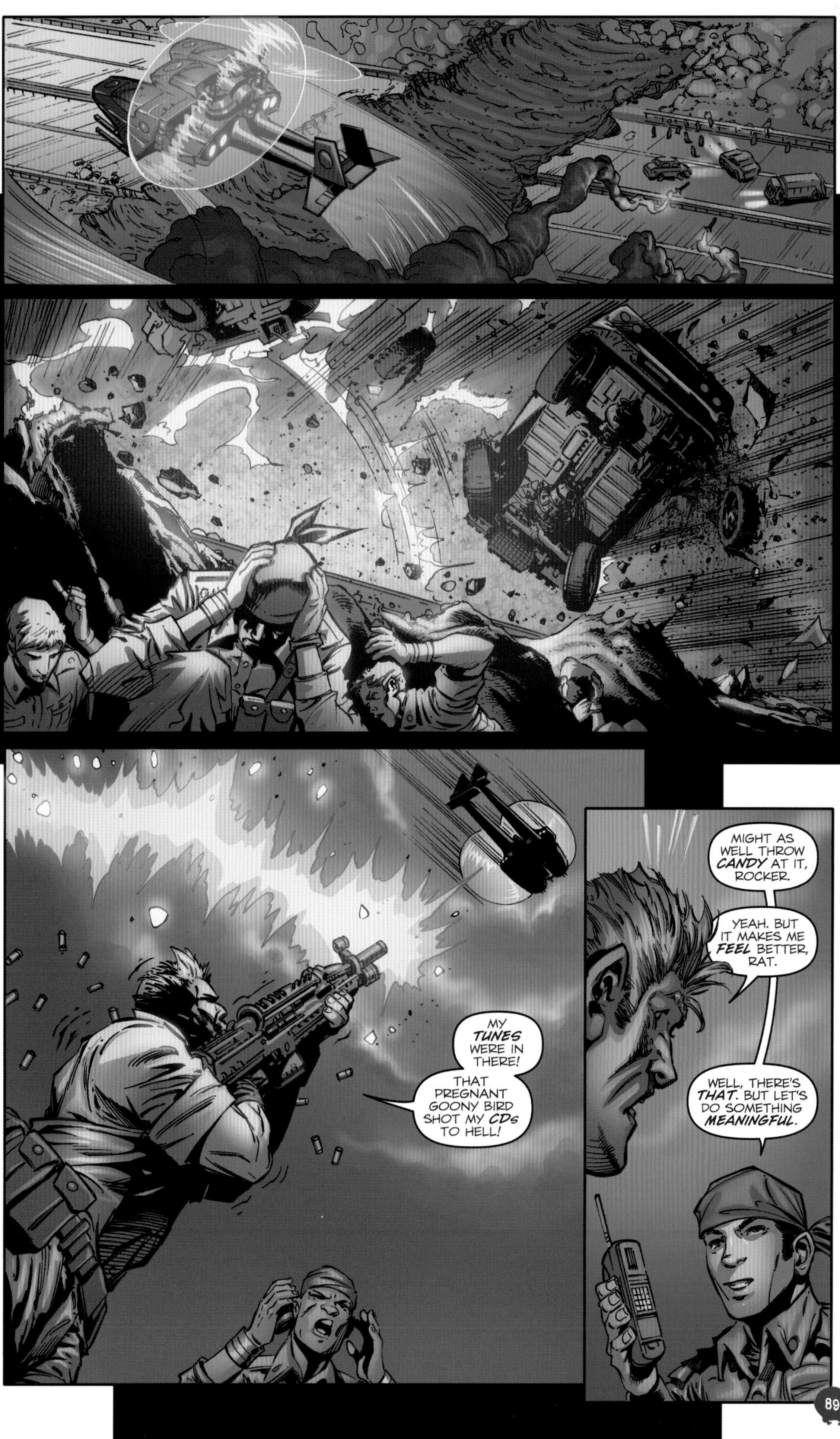
MY TUNES WERE IN THERE!
THAT PREGNANT GOONY BIRD SHOT MY CDs TO HELL!
MIGHT AS WELL THROW CANDY AT IT, ROCKER.
YEAH. BUT IT MAKES ME FEEL BETTER, RAT.
WELL, THERE'S THAT. BUT LET'S DO SOMETHING MEANINGFUL.

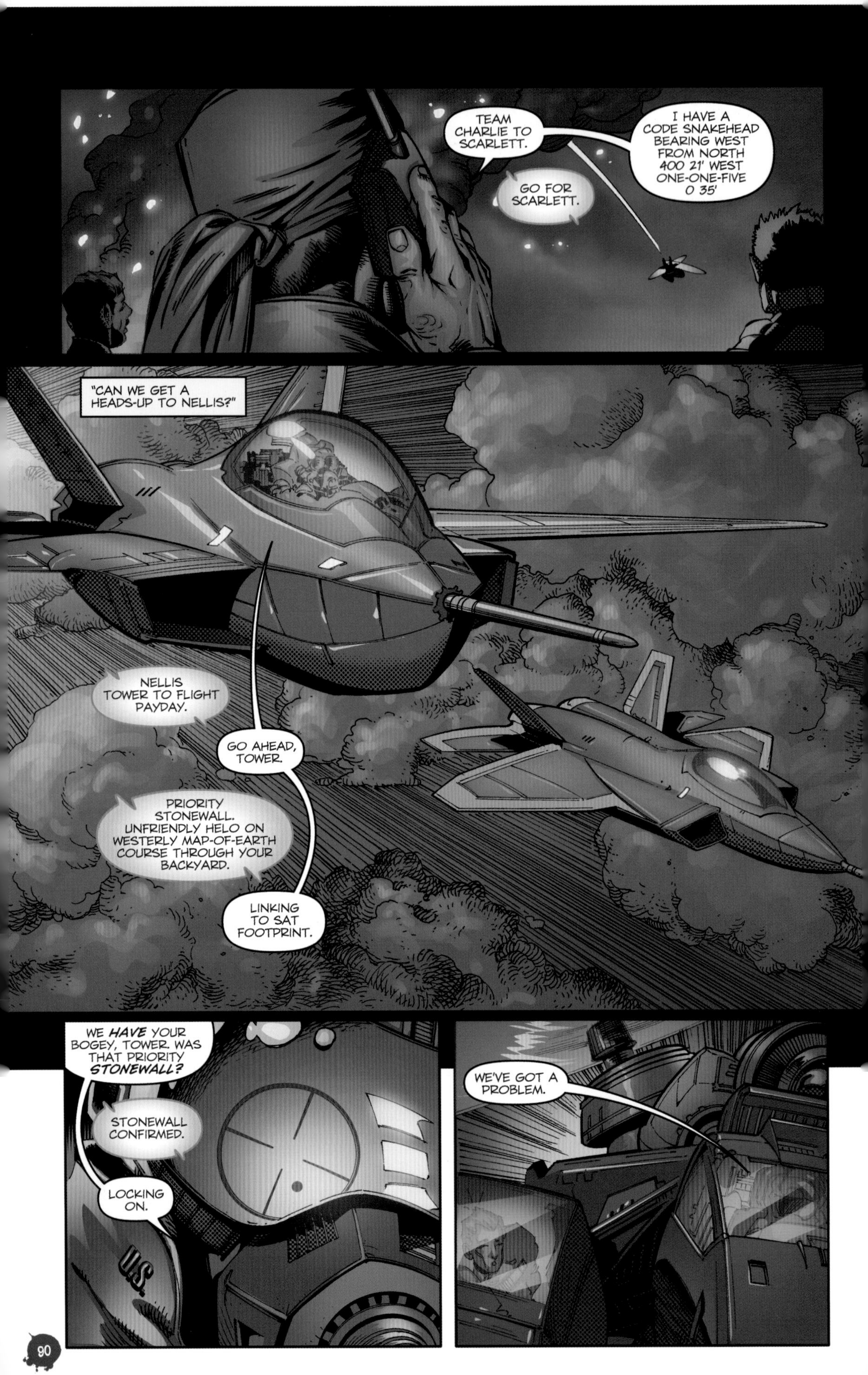
TEAM CHARLIE TO SCARLETT.
GO FOR SCARLETT.
I HAVE A CODE SNAKEHEAD BEARING WEST FROM NORTH 400 21' WEST ONE-ONE-FIVE 0 35'
"CAN WE GET A HEADS-UP TO NELLIS?"
NELLIS TOWER TO FLIGHT PAYDAY.
GO AHEAD, TOWER.
PRIORITY STONEWALL. UNFRIENDLY HELO ON WESTERLY MAP-OF-EARTH COURSE THROUGH YOUR BACKYARD.
LINKING TO SAT FOOTPRINT.
WE *HAVE* YOUR BOGEY, TOWER. WAS THAT PRIORITY *STONEWALL?*
STONEWALL CONFIRMED.
LOCKING ON.
U.S.
WE'VE GOT A PROBLEM.

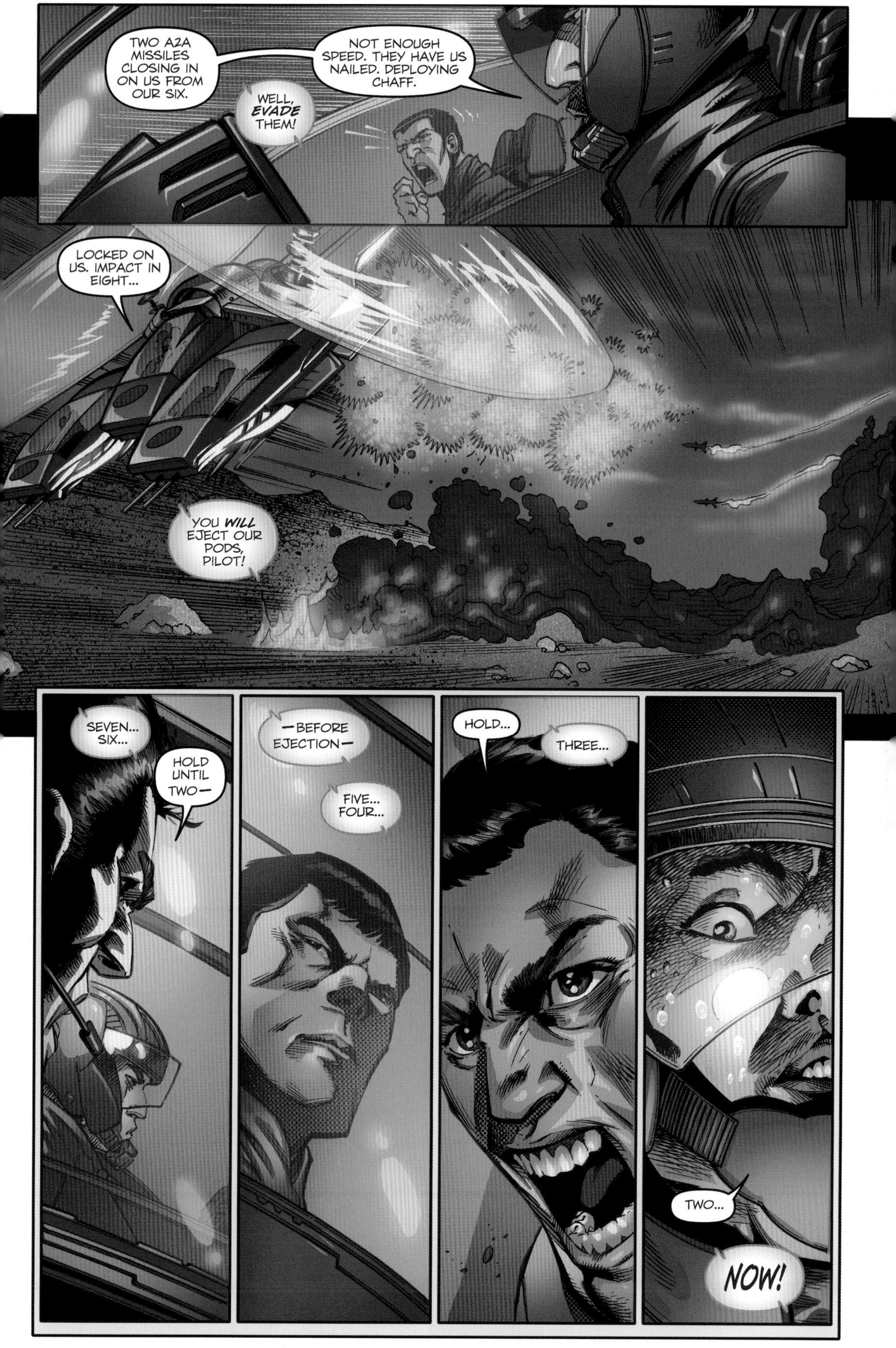
TWO A2A MISSILES CLOSING IN ON US FROM OUR SIX.
NOT ENOUGH SPEED. THEY HAVE US NAILED. DEPLOYING CHAFF.
WELL, EVADE THEM!
LOCKED ON US. IMPACT IN EIGHT...
YOU WILL EJECT OUR PODS, PILOT!
SEVEN... SIX...
HOLD UNTIL TWO—
—BEFORE EJECTION—
FIVE... FOUR...
HOLD...
THREE...
TWO...
NOW!

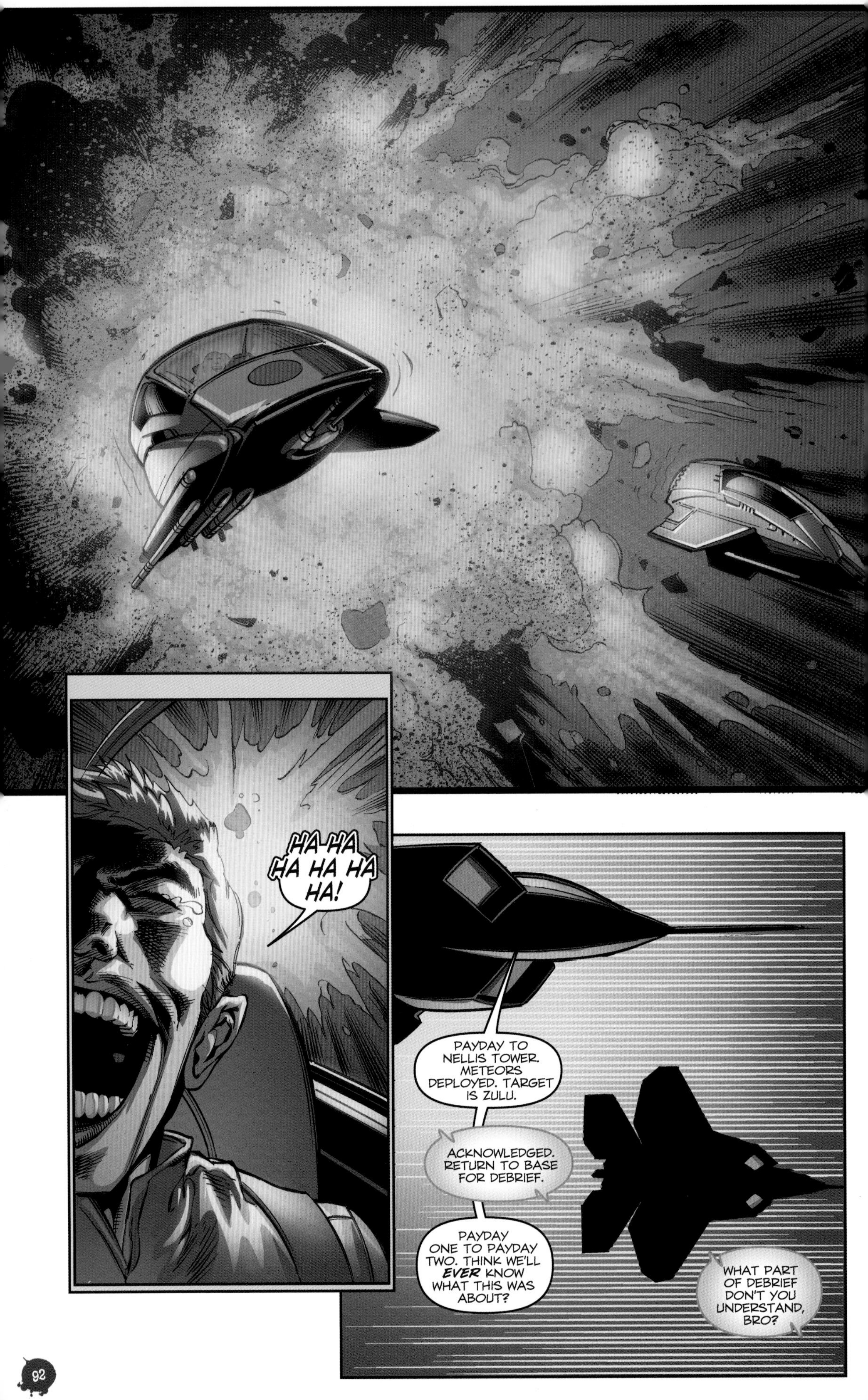
HA-HA HA HA HA HA!
PAYDAY TO NELLIS TOWER. METEORS DEPLOYED. TARGET IS ZULU.
ACKNOWLEDGED. RETURN TO BASE FOR DEBRIEF.
PAYDAY ONE TO PAYDAY TWO. THINK WE'LL *EVER* KNOW WHAT THIS WAS ABOUT?
WHAT PART OF DEBRIEF DON'T YOU UNDERSTAND, BRO?

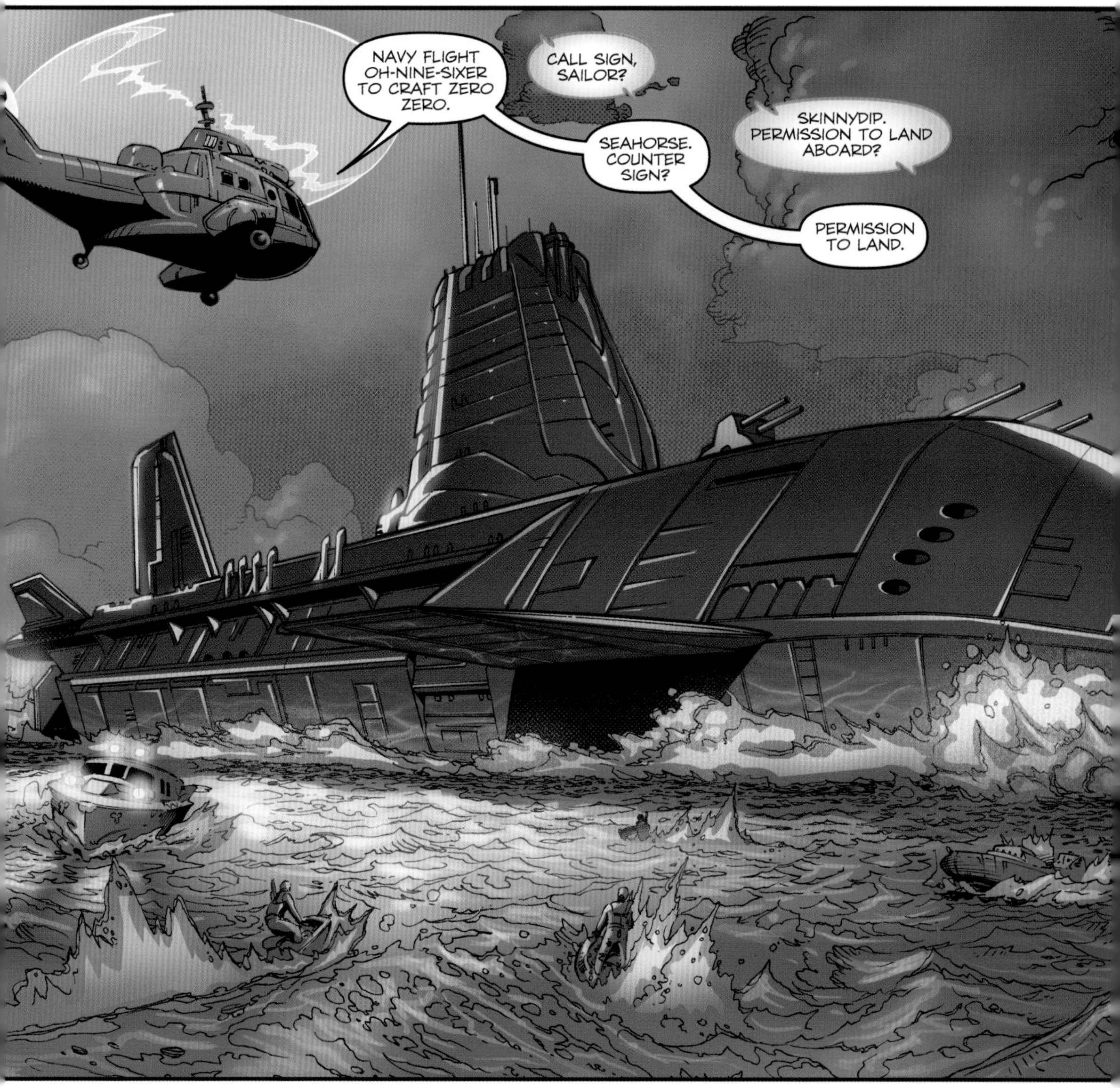
NAVY FLIGHT OH-NINE-SIXER TO CRAFT ZERO ZERO.
CALL SIGN, SAILOR?
SEAHORSE. COUNTER SIGN?
SKINNYDIP. PERMISSION TO LAND ABOARD?
PERMISSION TO LAND.

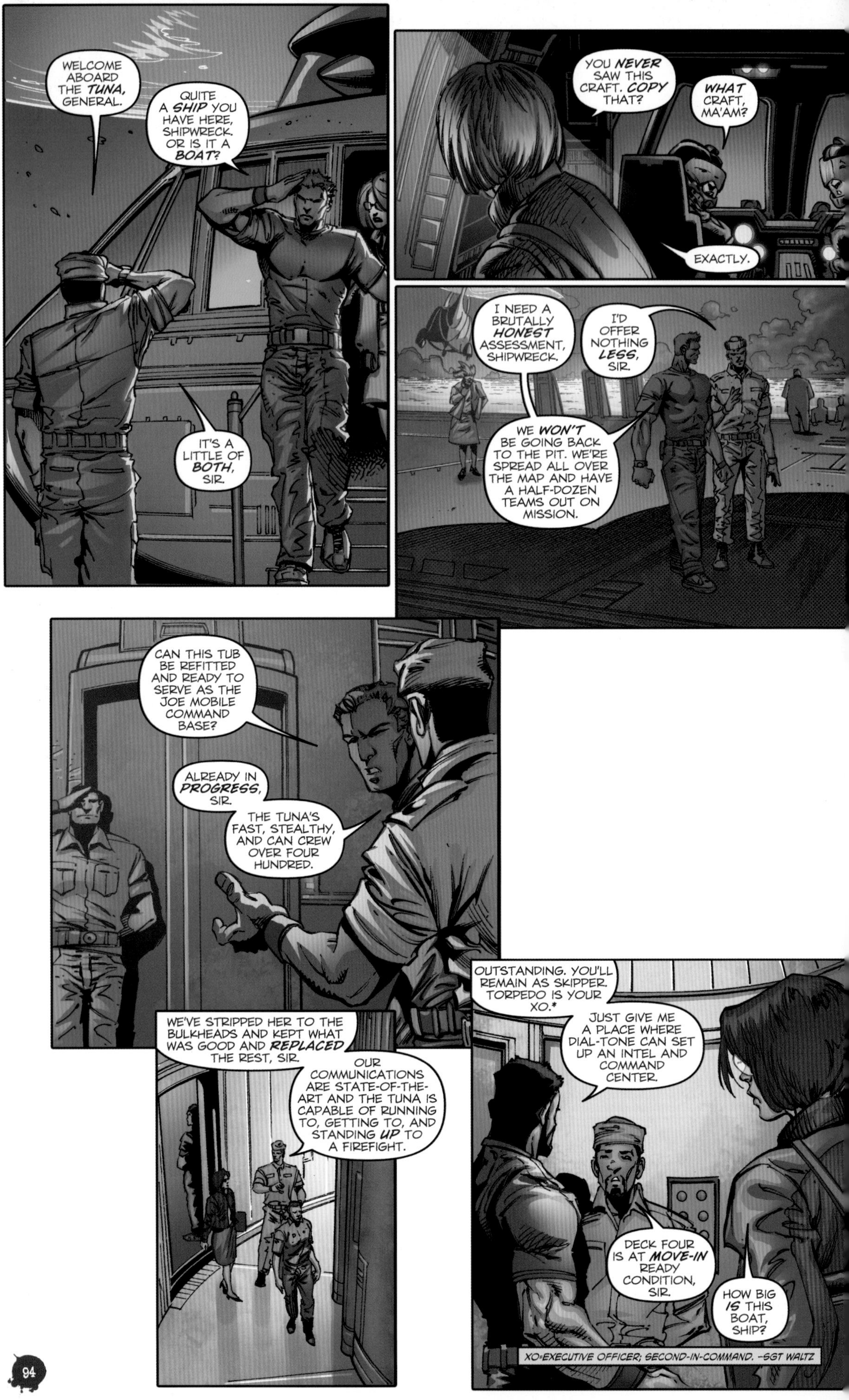
WELCOME ABOARD THE TUNA, GENERAL.
QUITE A SHIP YOU HAVE HERE, SHIPWRECK. OR IS IT A BOAT?
IT'S A LITTLE OF BOTH, SIR.
YOU NEVER SAW THIS CRAFT. COPY THAT?
WHAT CRAFT, MA'AM?
EXACTLY.
I NEED A BRUTALLY HONEST ASSESSMENT, SHIPWRECK.
I'D OFFER NOTHING LESS, SIR.
WE WON'T BE GOING BACK TO THE PIT. WE'RE SPREAD ALL OVER THE MAP AND HAVE A HALF-DOZEN TEAMS OUT ON MISSION.
CAN THIS TUB BE REFITTED AND READY TO SERVE AS THE JOE MOBILE COMMAND BASE?
ALREADY IN PROGRESS, SIR.
THE TUNA'S FAST, STEALTHY, AND CAN CREW OVER FOUR HUNDRED.
WE'VE STRIPPED HER TO THE BULKHEADS AND KEPT WHAT WAS GOOD AND REPLACED THE REST, SIR.
OUR COMMUNICATIONS ARE STATE-OF-THE-ART AND THE TUNA IS CAPABLE OF RUNNING TO, GETTING TO, AND STANDING UP TO A FIREFIGHT.
OUTSTANDING. YOU'LL REMAIN AS SKIPPER. TORPEDO IS YOUR XO.*
JUST GIVE ME A PLACE WHERE DIAL-TONE CAN SET UP AN INTEL AND COMMAND CENTER.
DECK FOUR IS AT MOVE-IN READY CONDITION, SIR.
HOW BIG IS THIS BOAT, SHIP?
XO=EXECUTIVE OFFICER; SECOND-IN-COMMAND. –SGT WALTZ

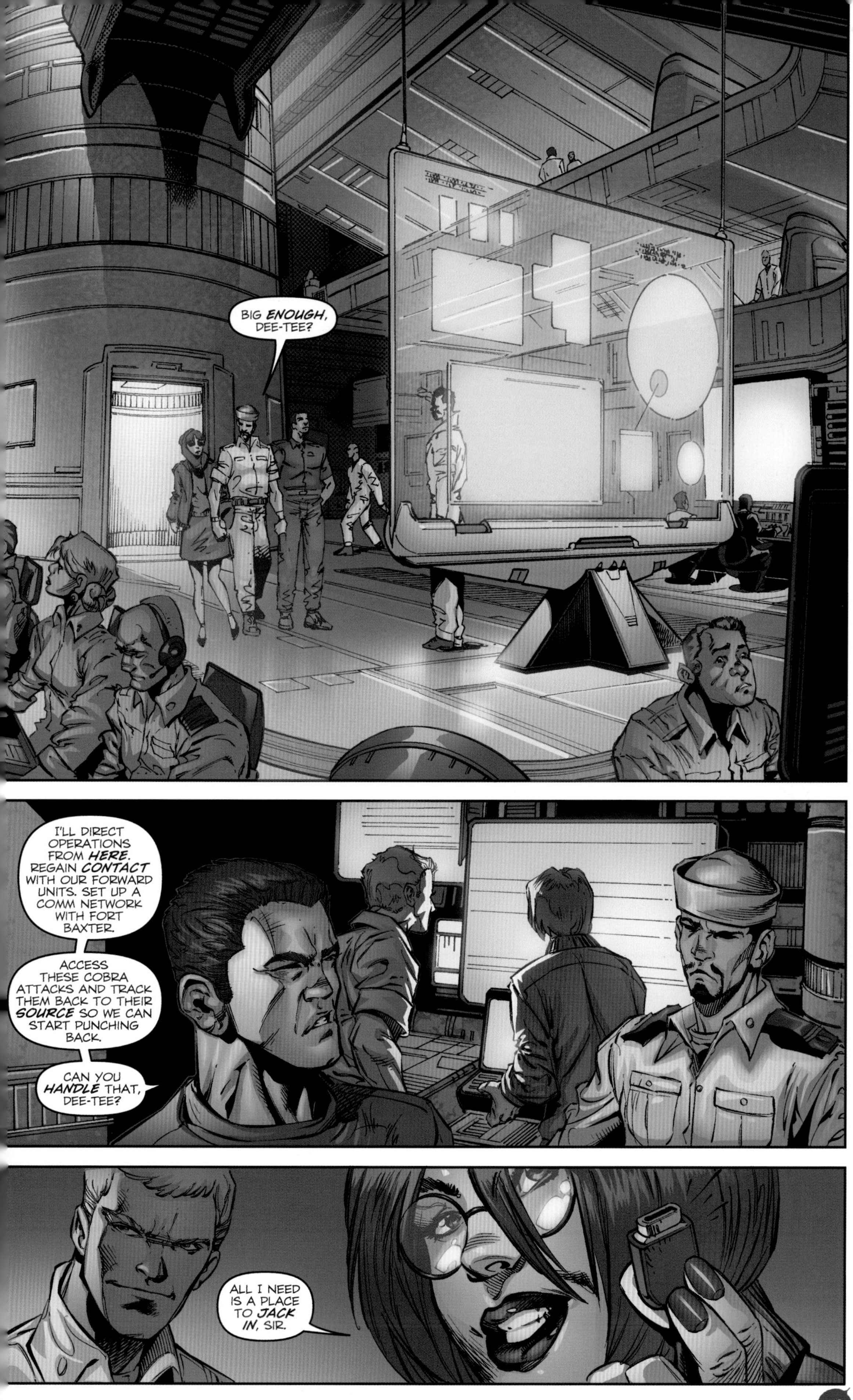
BIG ENOUGH, DEE-TEE?
I'LL DIRECT OPERATIONS FROM HERE. REGAIN CONTACT WITH OUR FORWARD UNITS. SET UP A COMM NETWORK WITH FORT BAXTER.
ACCESS THESE COBRA ATTACKS AND TRACK THEM BACK TO THEIR SOURCE SO WE CAN START PUNCHING BACK.
CAN YOU HANDLE THAT, DEE-TEE?
ALL I NEED IS A PLACE TO JACK IN, SIR.

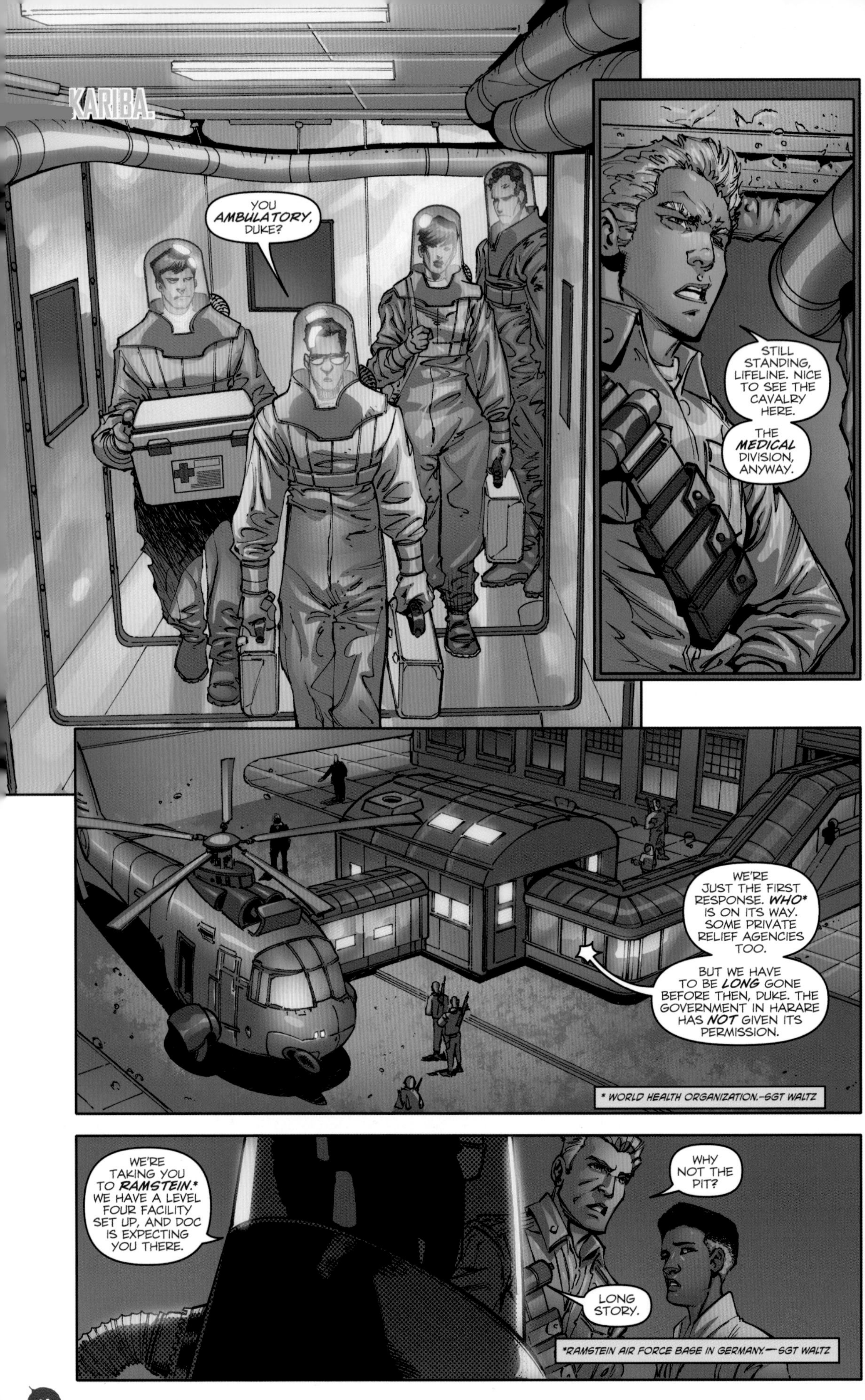
KARIBA.
YOU AMBULATORY, DUKE?
STILL STANDING, LIFELINE. NICE TO SEE THE CAVALRY HERE.
THE MEDICAL DIVISION, ANYWAY.
WE'RE JUST THE FIRST RESPONSE. WHO* IS ON ITS WAY. SOME PRIVATE RELIEF AGENCIES TOO.
BUT WE HAVE TO BE LONG GONE BEFORE THEN, DUKE. THE GOVERNMENT IN HARARE HAS NOT GIVEN ITS PERMISSION.
* WORLD HEALTH ORGANIZATION.—SGT WALTZ
WE'RE TAKING YOU TO RAMSTEIN.* WE HAVE A LEVEL FOUR FACILITY SET UP, AND DOC IS EXPECTING YOU THERE.
WHY NOT THE PIT?
LONG STORY.
*RAMSTEIN AIR FORCE BASE IN GERMANY.—SGT WALTZ

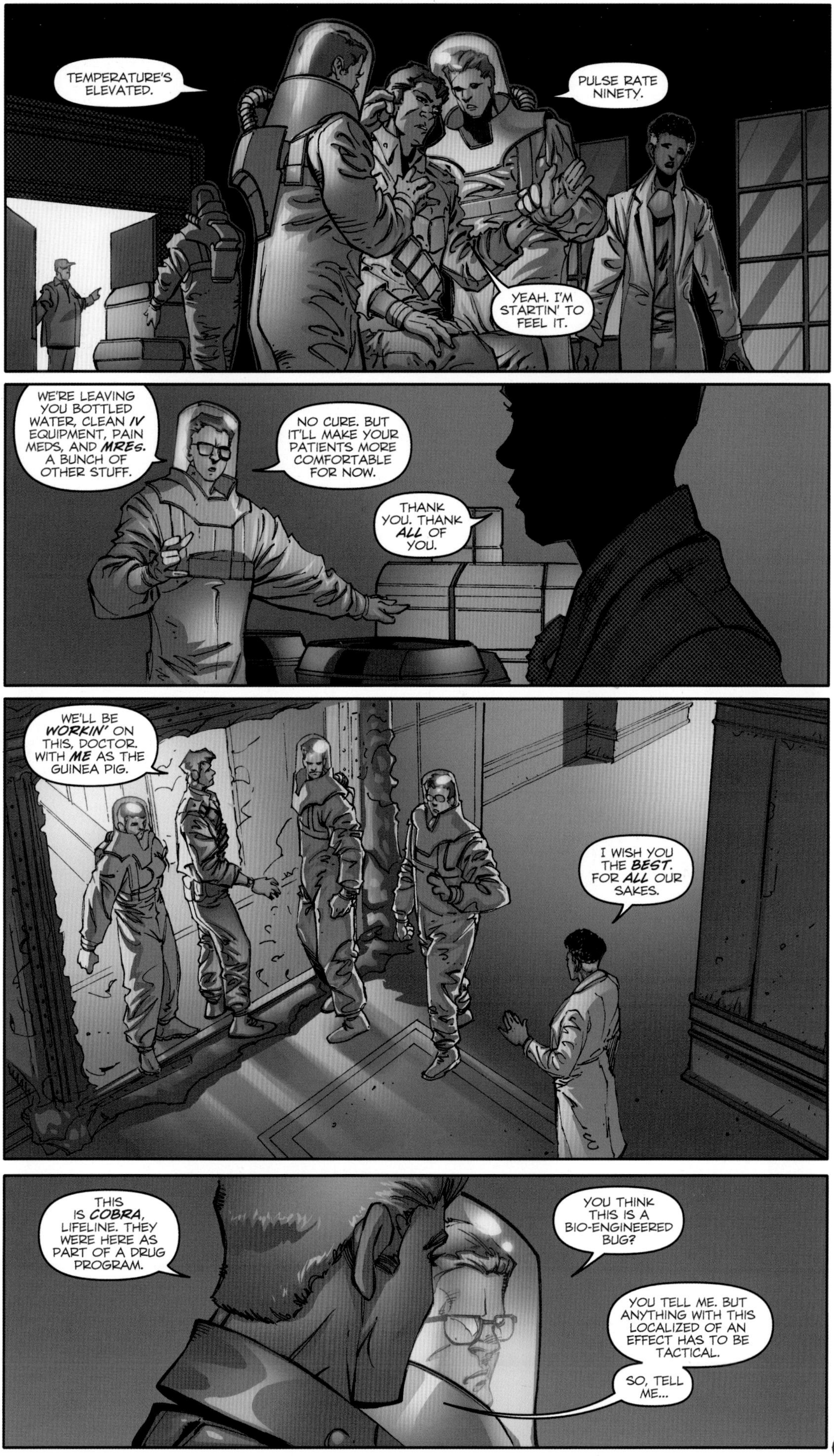
TEMPERATURE'S ELEVATED.
PULSE RATE NINETY.
YEAH. I'M STARTIN' TO FEEL IT.
WE'RE LEAVING YOU BOTTLED WATER, CLEAN IV EQUIPMENT, PAIN MEDS, AND MREs. A BUNCH OF OTHER STUFF.
NO CURE. BUT IT'LL MAKE YOUR PATIENTS MORE COMFORTABLE FOR NOW.
THANK YOU. THANK ALL OF YOU.
WE'LL BE WORKIN' ON THIS, DOCTOR. WITH ME AS THE GUINEA PIG.
I WISH YOU THE BEST. FOR ALL OUR SAKES.
THIS IS COBRA, LIFELINE. THEY WERE HERE AS PART OF A DRUG PROGRAM.
YOU THINK THIS IS A BIO-ENGINEERED BUG?
YOU TELL ME. BUT ANYTHING WITH THIS LOCALIZED OF AN EFFECT HAS TO BE TACTICAL.
SO, TELL ME...

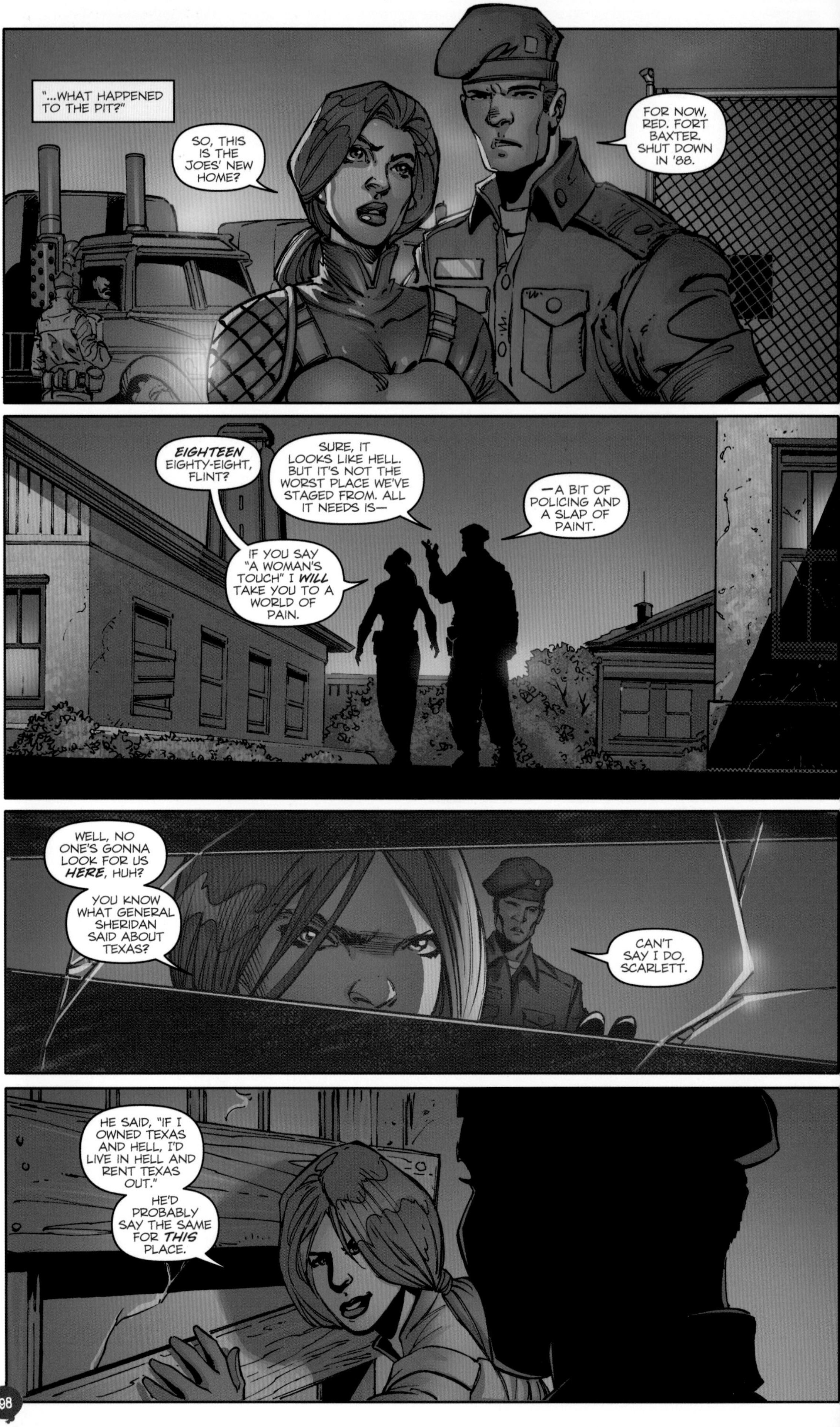
"...WHAT HAPPENED TO THE PIT?"
SO, THIS IS THE JOES' NEW HOME?
FOR NOW, RED. FORT BAXTER. SHUT DOWN IN '88.
EIGHTEEN EIGHTY-EIGHT, FLINT?
SURE, IT LOOKS LIKE HELL. BUT IT'S NOT THE WORST PLACE WE'VE STAGED FROM. ALL IT NEEDS IS—
—A BIT OF POLICING AND A SLAP OF PAINT.
IF YOU SAY "A WOMAN'S TOUCH" I WILL TAKE YOU TO A WORLD OF PAIN.
WELL, NO ONE'S GONNA LOOK FOR US HERE, HUH?
YOU KNOW WHAT GENERAL SHERIDAN SAID ABOUT TEXAS?
CAN'T SAY I DO, SCARLETT.
HE SAID, "IF I OWNED TEXAS AND HELL, I'D LIVE IN HELL AND RENT TEXAS OUT."
HE'D PROBABLY SAY THE SAME FOR THIS PLACE.

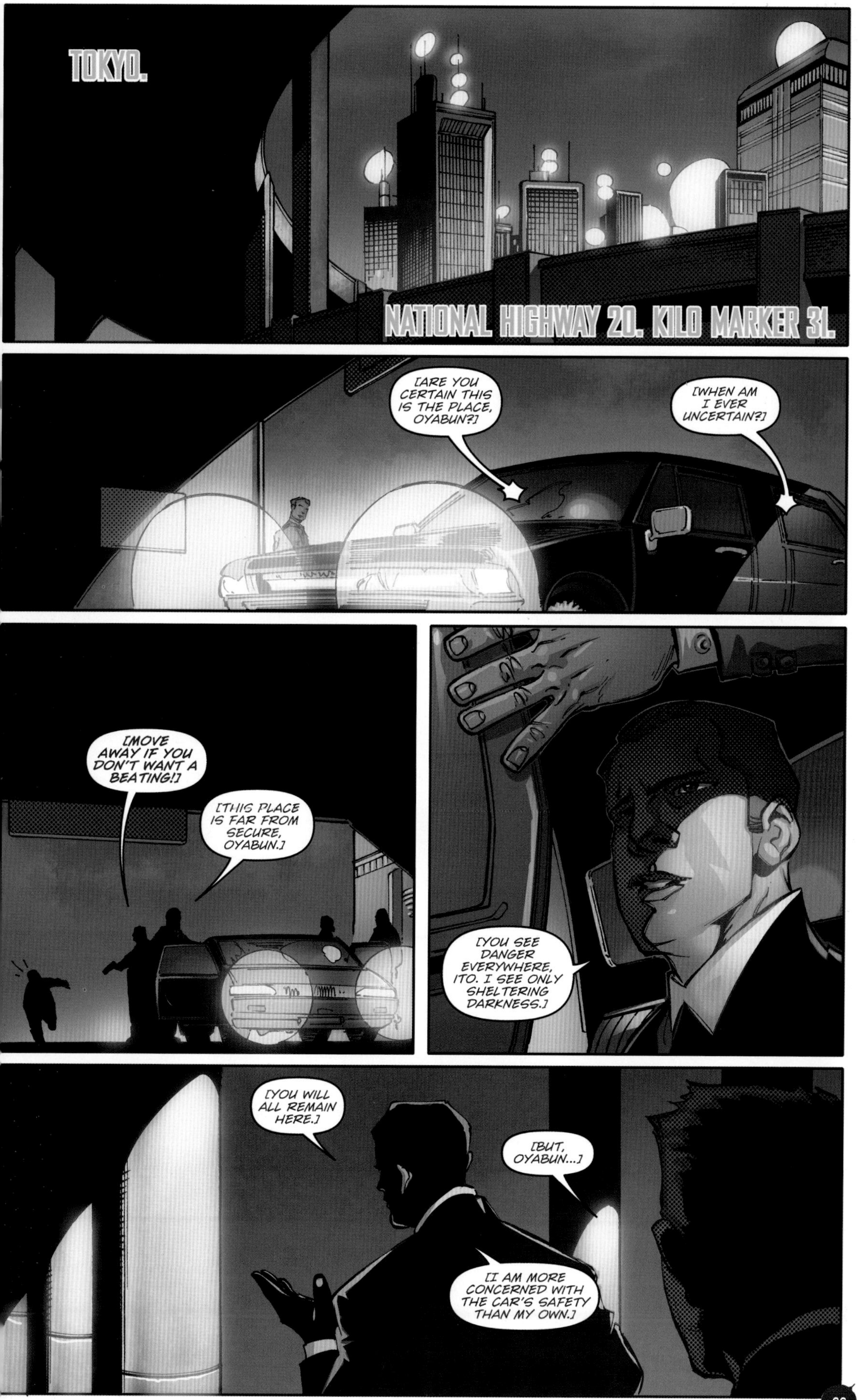
TOKYO.
NATIONAL HIGHWAY 20. KILO MARKER 31.
[ARE YOU CERTAIN THIS IS THE PLACE, OYABUN?]
[WHEN AM I EVER UNCERTAIN?]
[MOVE AWAY IF YOU DON'T WANT A BEATING!]
[THIS PLACE IS FAR FROM SECURE, OYABUN.]
[YOU SEE DANGER EVERYWHERE, ITO. I SEE ONLY SHELTERING DARKNESS.]
[YOU WILL ALL REMAIN HERE.]
[BUT, OYABUN...]
[I AM MORE CONCERNED WITH THE CAR'S SAFETY THAN MY OWN.]

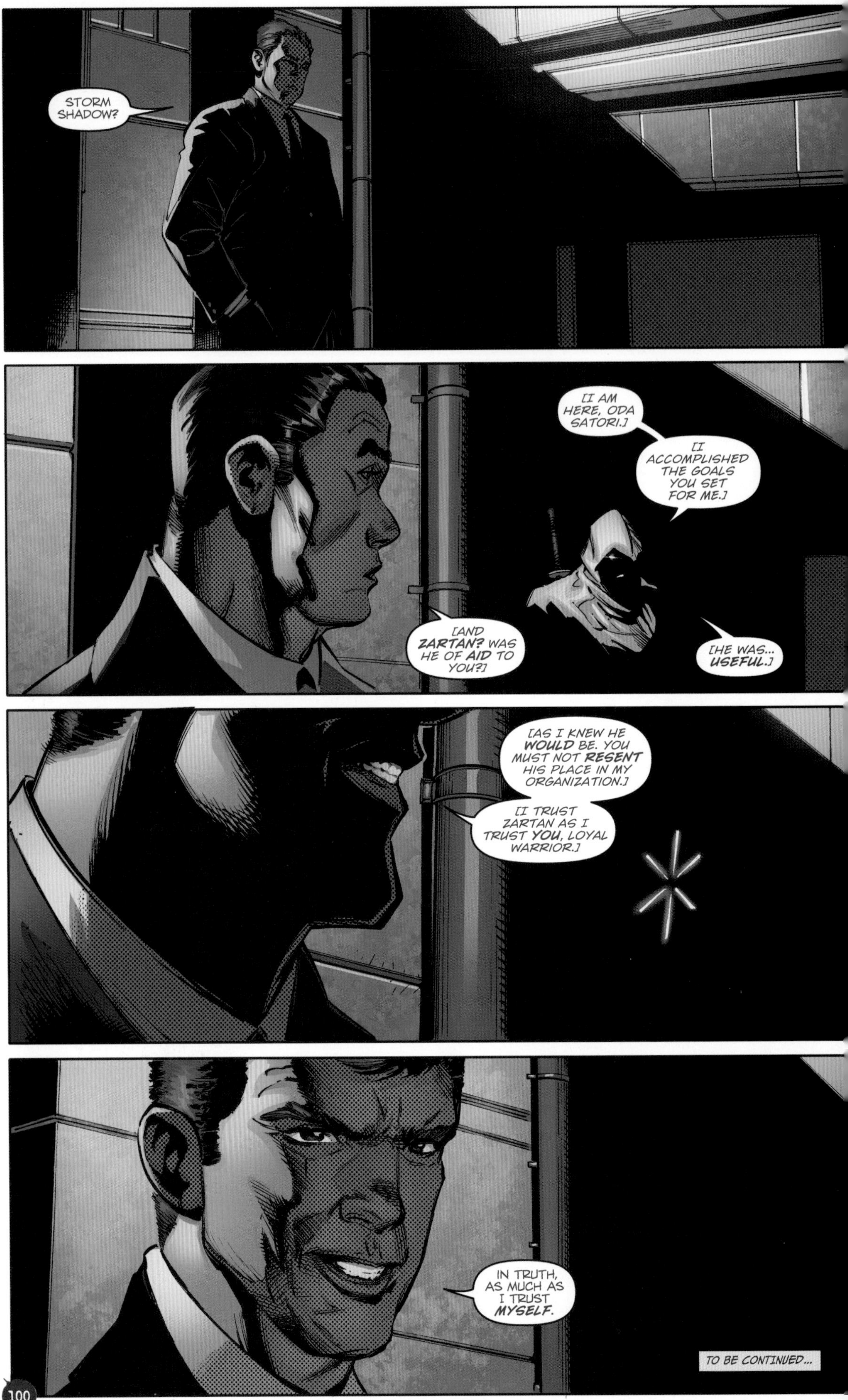
STORM SHADOW?
[I AM HERE, ODA SATORI.]
[I ACCOMPLISHED THE GOALS YOU SET FOR ME.]
[AND ZARTAN? WAS HE OF AID TO YOU?]
[HE WAS... USEFUL.]
[AS I KNEW HE WOULD BE. YOU MUST NOT RESENT HIS PLACE IN MY ORGANIZATION.]
[I TRUST ZARTAN AS I TRUST YOU, LOYAL WARRIOR.]
IN TRUTH, AS MUCH AS I TRUST MYSELF.
TO BE CONTINUED...

ART GALLERY

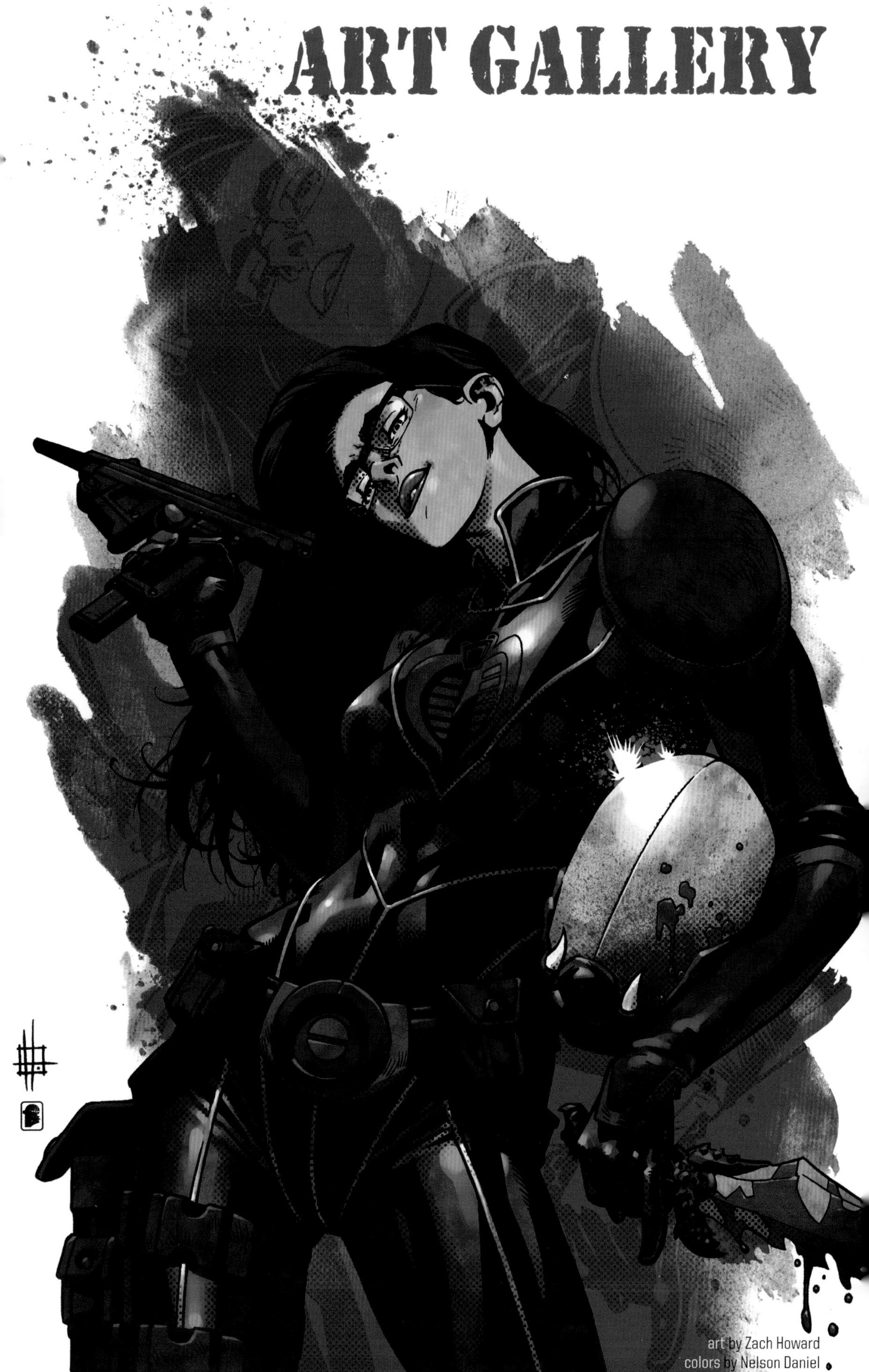

art by Zach Howard
colors by Nelson Daniel

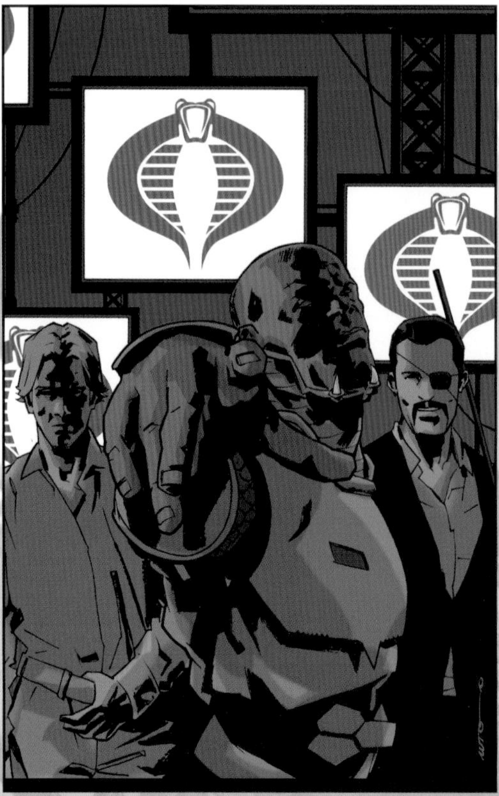

art by Antonio Fuso

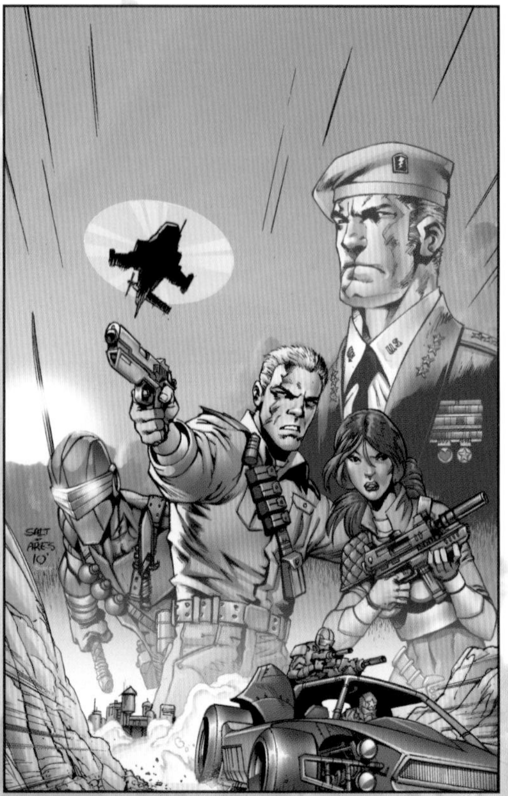
SALT
ARES
10'

art by Javier Saltares

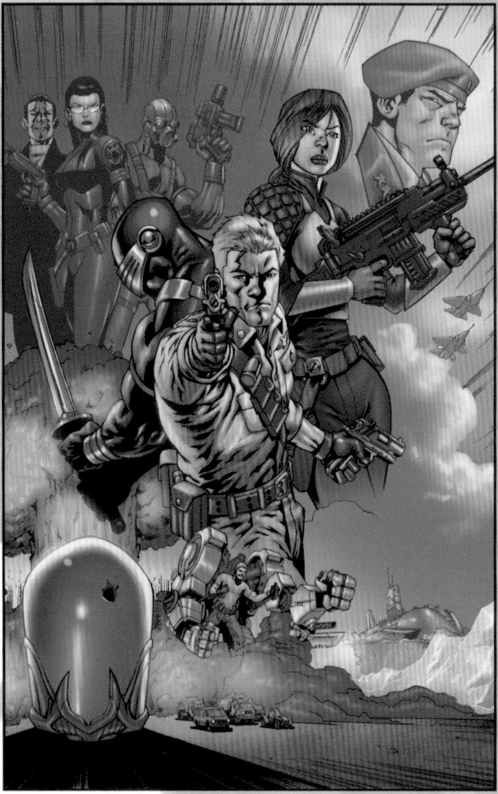

art by Javier Saltares

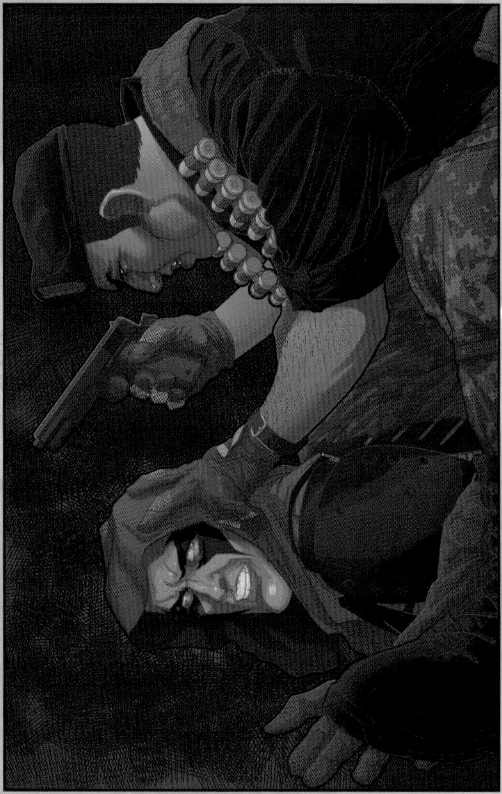

art by Tom Feister

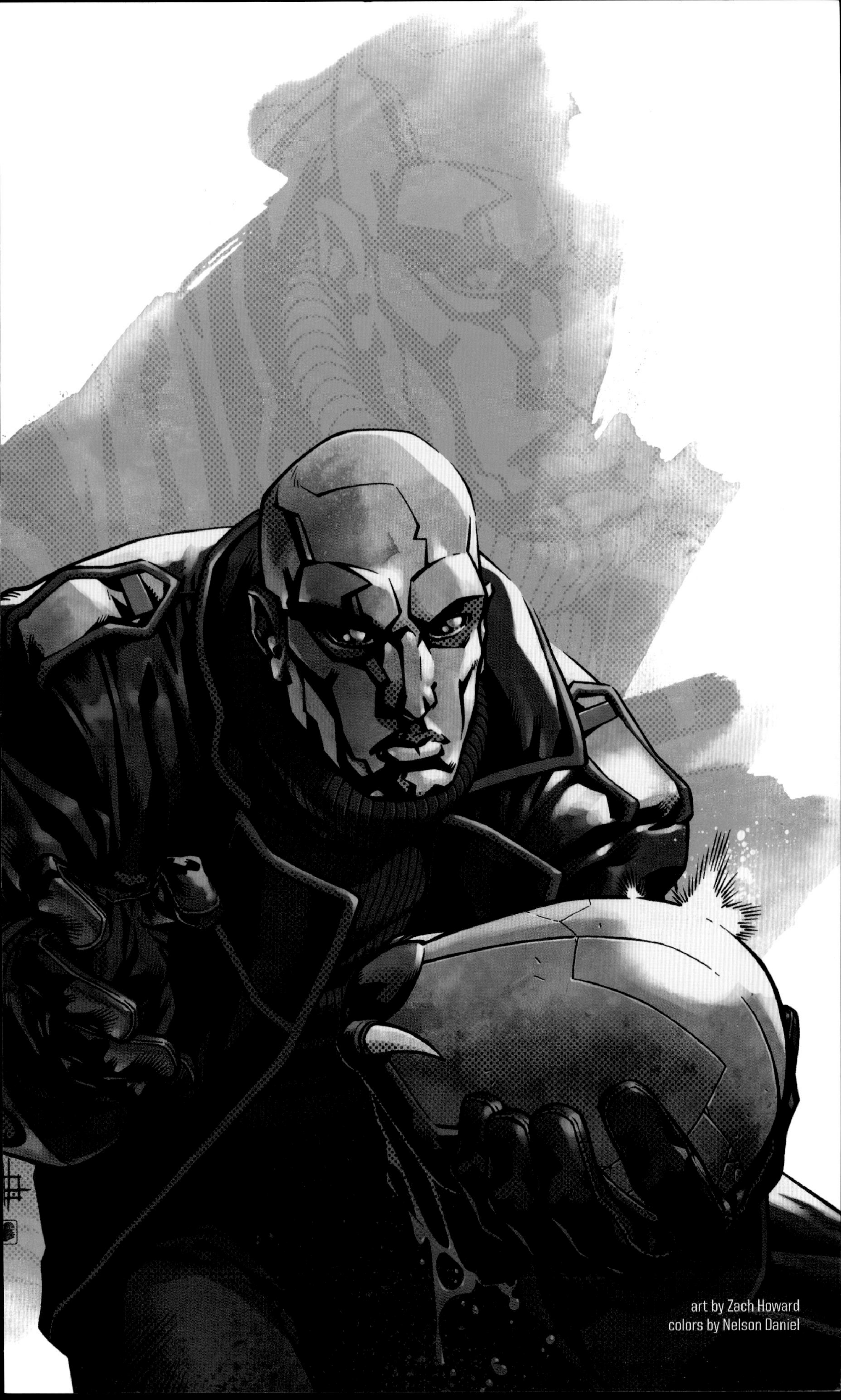

art by Zach Howard
colors by Nelson Daniel

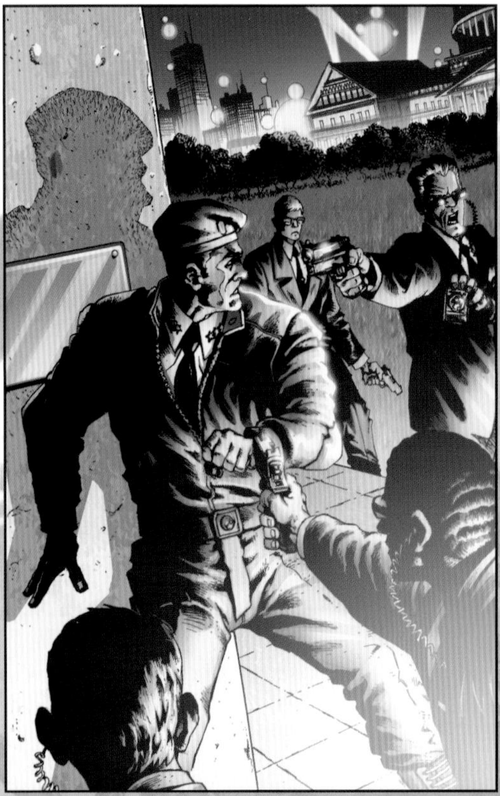

art by Javier Saltares
colors by Andrew Crossley

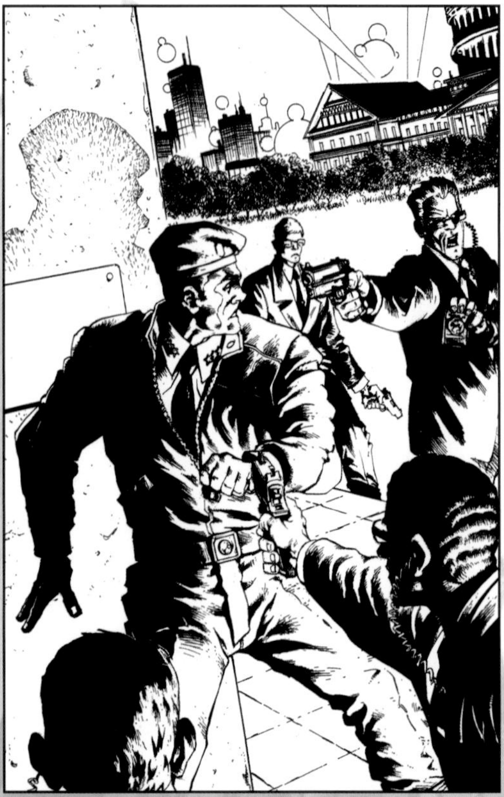

art by Javier Saltares

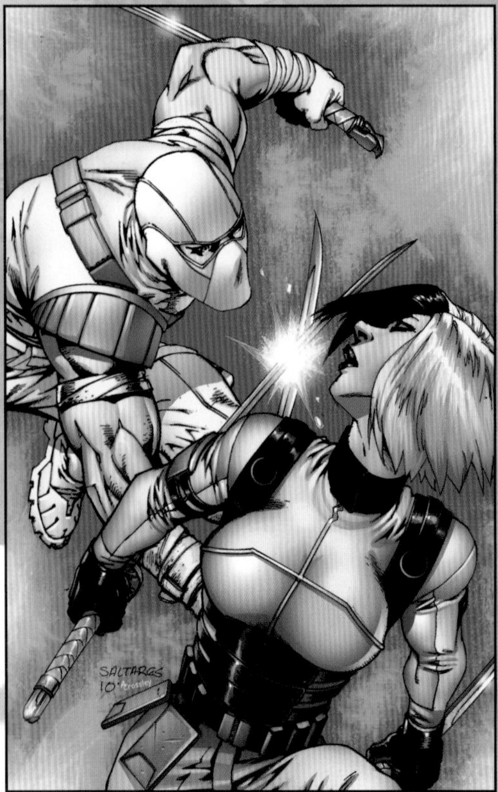
SALTARES
10'

art by Javier Saltares
colors by Andrew Crossley

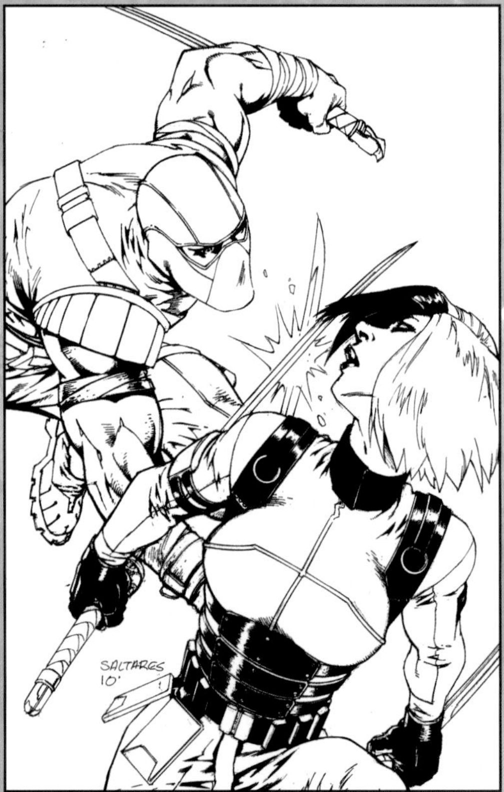
SALTARES
10'

art by Javier Saltares

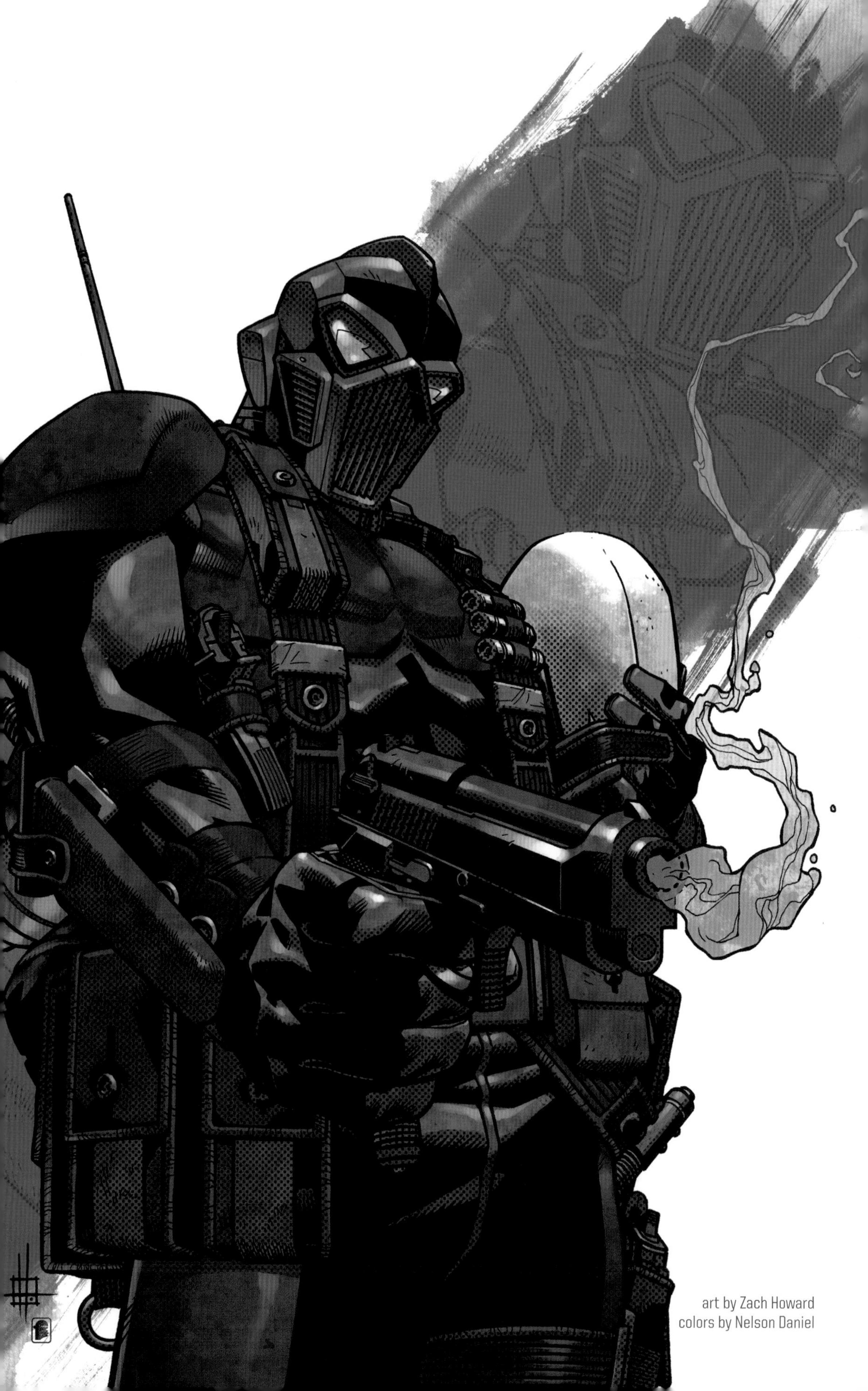

art by Zach Howard
colors by Nelson Daniel

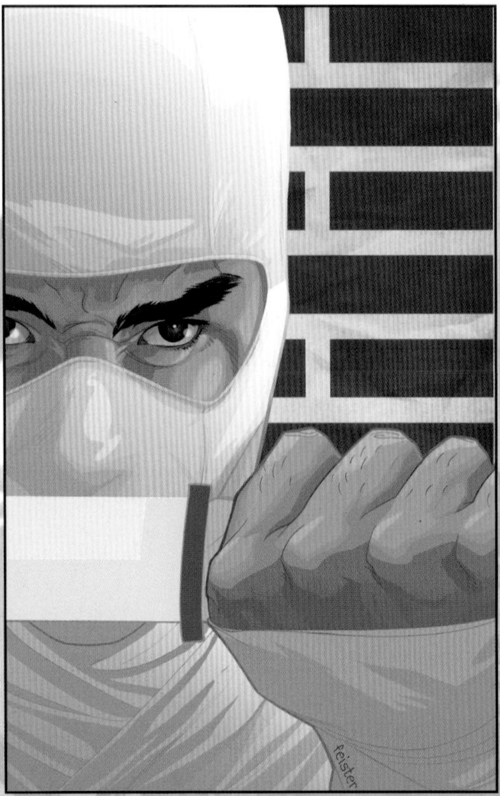

art by Tom Feister

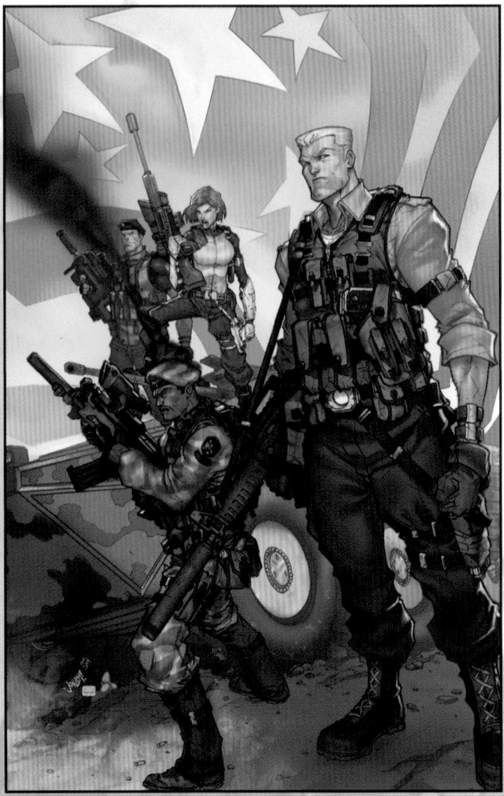

art by JonBoy Meyers
colors by Chuck Pires

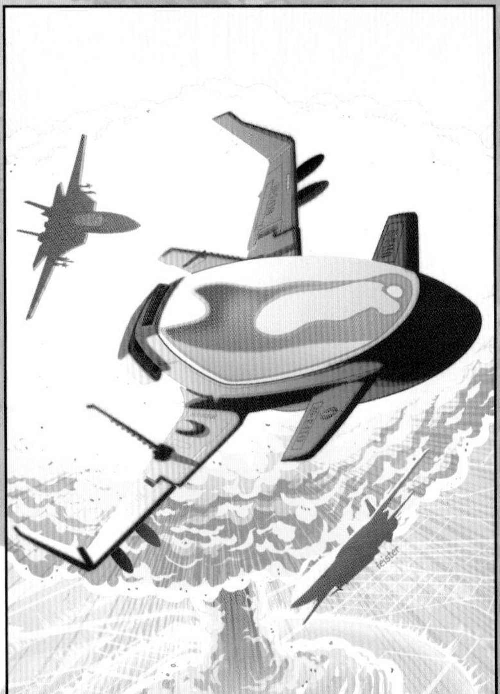

art by Tom Feister

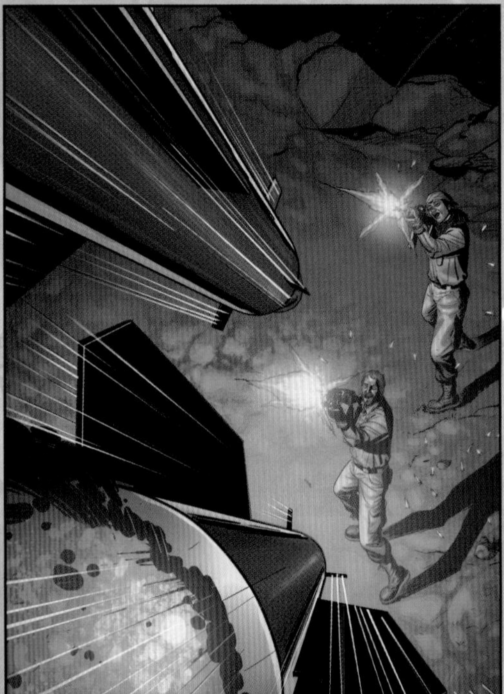

art by Javier Saltares
colors by Andrew Crossley

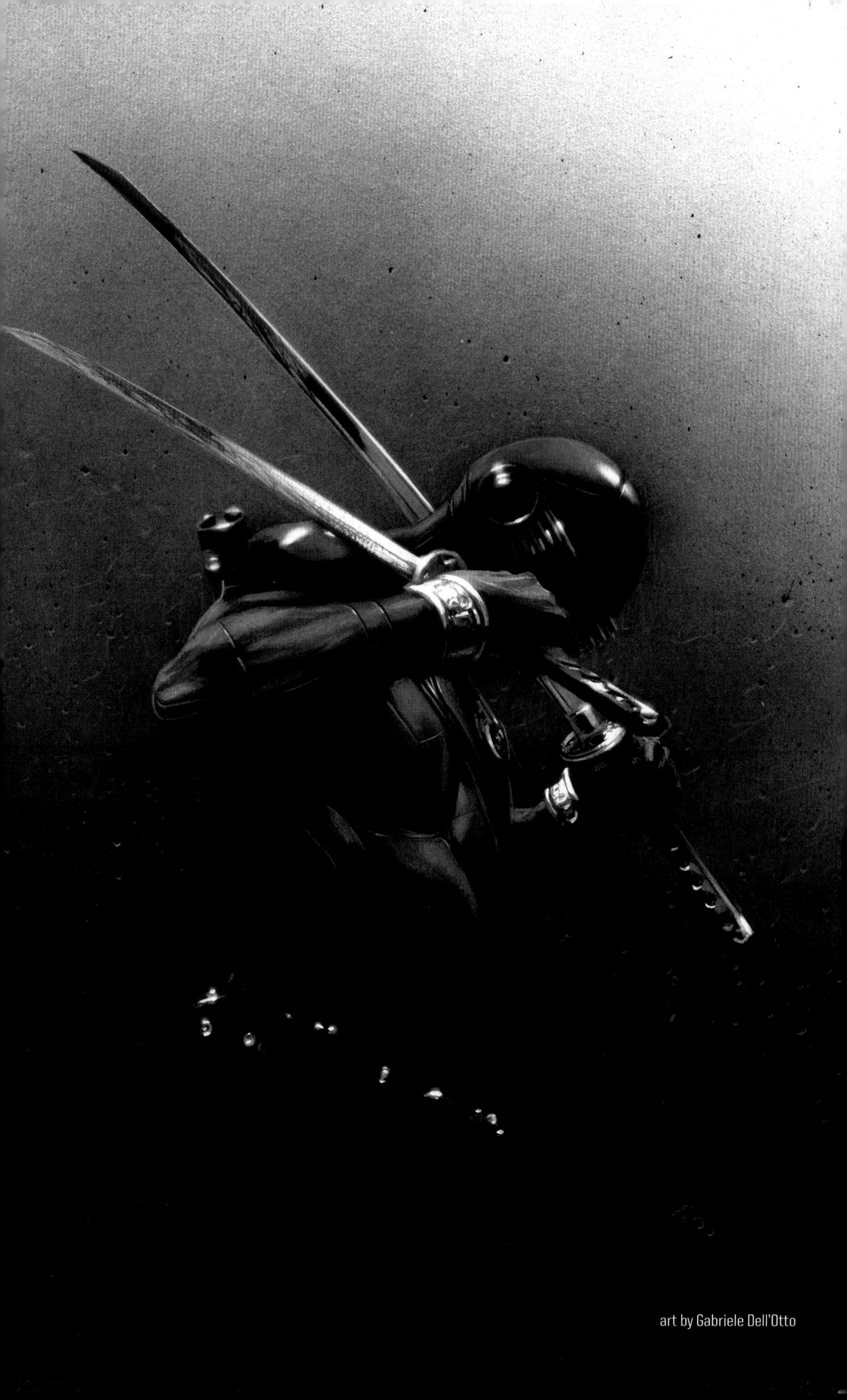

art by Gabriele Dell'Otto

COBRA CIVIL WAR
G.I.JOE

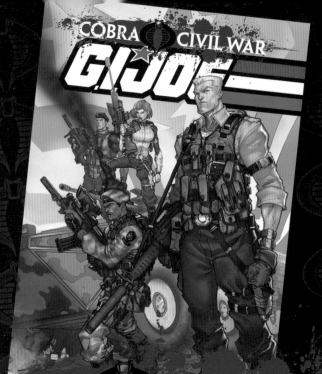

COBRA CIVIL WAR

THE STORIES CONTINUE IN THESE UPCOMING GRAPHIC NOVELS:

NOVEMBER 2011

G.I.JOE
COBRA CIVIL WAR

Snake Eyes: Cobra Civil War, Vol. 1

DECEMBER 2011

G.I.JOE
COBRA CIVIL WAR
COBRA

Cobra: Cobra Civil War, Vol. 1

FEBRUARY 2012

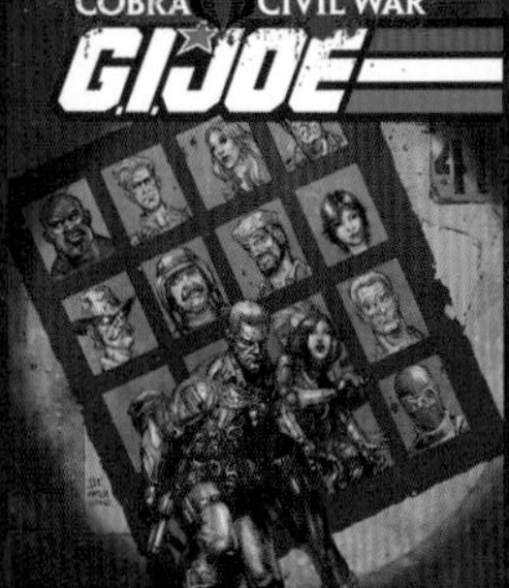

COBRA CIVIL WAR
G.I.JOE
VOLUME 2

G.I. Joe: Cobra Civil War, Vol. 2

MARCH 2012

G.I.JOE
COBRA CIVIL WAR
SNAKE EYES
VOLUME 2

Snake Eyes: Cobra Civil War, Vol. 2

APRIL 2012

G.I.JOE
COBRA CIVIL WAR
COBRA
VOLUME 2

Cobra: Cobra Civil War, Vol. 2